CSS Cookbook™

Other resources from O'Reilly

Related titles

Cascading Style Sheets:
  The Definitive Guide
HTML and XHTML:
  The Definitive Guide
JavaScript:
  The Definitive Guide

JavaScript and DHTML
  Cookbook
Web Design in a Nutshell
Dynamic HTML:
  The Definitive Reference
CSS Pocket Reference

oreilly.com

oreilly.com is more than a complete catalog of O'Reilly books. You'll also find links to news, events, articles, weblogs, sample chapters, and code examples.

oreillynet.com is the essential portal for developers interested in open and emerging technologies, including new platforms, programming languages, and operating systems.

Conferences

O'Reilly brings diverse innovators together to nurture the ideas that spark revolutionary industries. We specialize in documenting the latest tools and systems, translating the innovator's knowledge into useful skills for those in the trenches. Visit *conferences.oreilly.com* for our upcoming events.

Safari Bookshelf (*safari.oreilly.com*) is the premier online reference library for programmers and IT professionals. Conduct searches across more than 1,000 books. Subscribers can zero in on answers to time-critical questions in a matter of seconds. Read the books on your Bookshelf from cover to cover or simply flip to the page you need. Try it today with a free trial.

CSS Cookbook™

Christopher Schmitt

O'REILLY®

Beijing · Cambridge · Farnham · Köln · Paris · Sebastopol · Taipei · Tokyo

CSS Cookbook™
by Christopher Schmitt

Copyright © 2004 O'Reilly Media, Inc. All rights reserved.
Printed in the United States of America.

Published by O'Reilly Media, Inc., 1005 Gravenstein Highway North, Sebastopol, CA 95472.

O'Reilly books may be purchased for educational, business, or sales promotional use. Online editions are also available for most titles (*safari.oreilly.com*). For more information, contact our corporate/institutional sales department: (800) 998-9938 or *corporate@oreilly.com*.

Editors:	Nathan Torkington and Tatiana Apandi Diaz
Production Editor:	Mary Anne Weeks Mayo
Cover Designer:	Ellie Volckhausen
Interior Designer:	David Futato

Printing History:

August 2004:	First Edition.

 This book uses RepKover™, a durable and flexible lay-flat binding.

ISBN: 0-596-00576-8
[M]

Table of Contents

Foreword

Any great chef will tell you that the key to creating good food is using quality ingredients. Author Christopher Schmitt has just gone shopping for you. By compiling hundreds of CSS recipes into this single book, he's giving you a one-stop shop to create stylish, flexible web pages.

When I was first learning the wonders of CSS, trial and error prevailed as my primary means for discovering its creative powers. "Hmm, I'd like to turn this list into a horizontal navigation bar," or "I need to stylize the components of a form using CSS for a client." Several hours (or days) would go by after plugging in various CSS rules, removing some, and experimenting with endless combinations. This hit-or-miss approach worked (at times), and while a curious person like myself may even consider it "fun," it sure ate up a lot of time in the process.

I wish I'd had this book. Instead of stumbling upon the solution for styling every element of the page, I could have just thumbed through the *CSS Cookbook*, grabbed the recipe and started baking. The guesswork would've been eliminated, and I could have, instead, spend my time doing what I love to do best: creating.

The modular nature of this book makes it an indispensable reference for designers and developers of any caliber. Posed with problems from how best to handle typography, links and navigation to even entire page layouts, Christopher clearly explains not only the styles necessary to complete the task, but the caveats that may be attached for certain browsers. By additionally explaining the helpful workarounds to everyday CSS problems, he's arming you with the critical knowledge needed to be a successful CSS designer.

For example, a recent article told of a common usability problem: when posed with a Submit button at the end of a form, some users just can't shake their double-clicking habits. The button may get clicked twice, with the results of the form getting duplicated. What to do? A solution wasn't offered in the aforementioned article. However, unsurprisingly, there's a recipe in this very book that'll solve this little problem using CSS and a dash of JavaScript.

And that's the heart of this book's purpose: real problems and the goods that will deliver real results. You've heard about how CSS will simplify your life, making pages lighter and easier to maintain. Now it's time to start *using* it, and with this book, you'll have one less excuse not to.

So, my advice is to clear off a space on your desk because the *CSS Cookbook* will take up permanent residency in the corner. Hopefully for you, a spot that is easily within arm's reach.

—Dan Cederholm
Founder, SimpleBits
http://www.simplebits.com
Salem, Massachusetts

Preface

Cascading Style Sheets (CSS) is a simple standardized system that gives designers extensive control over the presentation of their web pages. CSS is an essential component of web design today. Compared to 90's-era workarounds, web builders have greater control over a web site's design and spend less time editing and maintaining that design. CSS also extends beyond the traditional web design to design and control the look of a web page when it's printed.

This book is a collection of CSS-based solutions to common web design problems. The solutions range from the simple to the complex, but hopefully everyone will learn something from this book.

CSS is easy to use: it doesn't demand any special hardware or software. The basic requirements are a computer, a modern browser like Mozilla or Internet Explorer for Windows (to name a few), and your favorite web page editor. A web page editor could be anything from a simple text editor like Window's Notepad or Macintosh's Simple-Text to a full-fledged WYSIWYG tool like Macromedia Dreamweaver in code view.

Audience

This book is for web designers and developers struggling with the problems of designing with CSS. With this book, web builders can solve common problems associated with CSS-enabled web page designs.

This book is good for people who have wanted to use CSS for web projects, but have shied away from learning a new technology. If you are this type of reader, use the solutions in the book one or a few at a time. Use it as a guidebook and come back to it when you are ready or need to learn another technique or trick.

If you consider yourself an expert with CSS but not an expert in basic design knowledge, this book is useful to have by the side of your computer. It covers elements of design from web typography to page layouts, and a motivational chapter called "Designing with CSS" is included.

Assumptions This Book Makes

This book assumes that the reader is at least a part-time web designer or developer wanting a book that provides fast answers to common CSS problems. You should also have a working knowledge of JavaScript for a few of the recipes in order to properly place the code into a page. Most recipes, however, do not use JavaScript.

Web designers familiar with traditional, HTML table-based methods are going to find CSS challenging. This frustration is a natural part of the learning process. Learning how to design with CSS should be approached with patience and a good sense of humor. The "browser hell" often associated with cross-browser development still exists in CSS, as it does with HTML tables, font tags, and single-pixel GIFs. CSS is a different, better way of constructing those web page designs, not a cure-all.

What this book is neither an introduction to CSS, nor is it a book that goes into great detail on how CSS should work in browsers. If you need a book that delves into such topics about the CSS specification, you should look into *Cascading Style Sheets: The Definitive Guide* (O'Reilly Media, Inc.).

While some of the solutions in the *CSS Cookbook* touch on JavaScript along with CSS, the book is geared toward finding solutions rooted in CSS. If you are looking for a solution-focused book that deals with CSS in tandem with the Document Object Model (DOM) and JavaScript, that book would be *JavaScript and DHTML Cookbook* (O'Reilly).

If you use programs like Macromedia Dreamweaver only in its WYSIWG or "design" mode and rarely touch the markup in "code" view, you might have trouble getting the most out of this book right away. To get an introduction to coding HTML directly, look into *Learning Web Design* (O'Reilly).

While WYSWIYG tools allow for CSS-enabled designs, some of the tools have not caught up with some of the unorthodox approaches recommended in this book and might cause some trouble if you attempt to implement them by editing solely in WYSIWG mode. To benefit from this book, you must be able to edit HTML and CSS by hand. Some of the code in this book can be recreated using dialog-box–driven web page building applications, but you may run into some problems along the way.

The solutions in this book are geared for modern browsers with version numbers of 5 or greater. Whenever possible, there is mention of when a technique might cause problems in Version 5 or higher browsers. While there is a chapter on hacks and workarounds to hide style sheets from browsers with poor implementations of the complete CSS specification, this book makes no assurances that the reader is going create pixel-perfect designs in every browser. Even with traditional web design methods from the 90s, this has never been the case. Unfortunately, that's the nature of cross-platform, cross-browser web design.

Contents of This Book

The most common way I use a book like this is to crack it open from time to time when trying to solve a particular problem. To that end, this book will serve well on a web builder's desk—always within reach to resolve a problem with CSS. However, you are still free to read the book from the first page to the last.

The following paragraphs review the contents of each chapter:

Chapter 1, *Web Typography*, discusses how to use CSS to specify fonts in web pages, headings, pull quotes, and indents within paragraphs, as well as other solutions.

Chapter 2, *Page Elements*, covers a loose collection of items that don't necessarily fit in every chapter, but that all carry a theme of affecting the design of the overall page. Solutions in this chapter include centering elements, setting a background image, placing a border on a page, and other techniques.

Chapter 3, *Links and Navigation*, shows how to use CSS to control the presentation of a link and sets of links. Solutions range from the basic, like removing the underlining from links, to the more complex, such as creating a dynamic visual menu.

Chapter 4, *Lists*, describes how to style the basic list items in various ways. Solutions include cross-browser indentation, making hanging indents, inserting custom images for list markers, and more.

Chapter 5, *Forms*, discusses ways to work around the basic ways browsers render forms. Solutions reviewed in this chapter include setting styles to specific form elements, setting a submit once-only button, and styling a login form.

Chapter 6, *Tables*, shows how to style HTML tables. While CSS can help eliminate HTML table-based designs, sometimes need to style tabular data such as calendars and statistical data. This chapter includes solutions for things such as setting cell padding, removing gaps in table cells with images, and styling a calendar.

Chapter 7, *Page Layouts*, talks about how CSS can be used to engineer layouts. The solutions in this chapter include methods for hybrid (HTML tables and CSS) layouts, and one-column to multicolumn layouts.

Chapter 8, *Print*, provides information on how to set styles that are used when printing web pages. Solutions discussed in this chapter include adding a separate print style sheet to a web page, setting styles for web forms, and inserting URLs after links.

Chapter 9, *Hacks and Workarounds*, covers solutions on how to hide style sheets that cannot be handled by certain browsers. Recipes include hiding style sheets for browsers like Netscape Navigator 4 and Internet Explorer for Windows 5. Also included are tips on how to stop the CSS-related flicker effect in Internet Explorer for Windows 5 and how to keep background images fixed in Internet Explorer for Windows 6.

Chapter 10, *Designing with CSS*, is an inspirational chapter. Focusing on the notion that CSS is merely a tool that implements design, this chapter covers things like playing with enlarging type sizes, working with contrast, and building a panoramic presentation.

The appendix, *Resources*, is a collection of links and web sites covering items related to learning more about CSS.

Conventions Used in This Book

The following typographical conventions are used in this book:

Plain text
> Indicates menu titles, menu options, menu buttons, and keyboard accelerators (such as Alt and Ctrl).

Italic
> Indicates new terms, URLs, email addresses, filenames, and file extensions.

Constant width
> Indicates commands, options, attributes, functions, types, classes, methods, properties, values, events, event handlers, XML tags, and HTML tags.

> This icon signifies a tip, suggestion, or general note.

> This icon indicates a warning or caution.

Using Code Examples

This book is here to help you get your job done. In general, you may use the code in this book in your programs and documentation. You don't need to contact us for permission unless you're reproducing a significant portion of the code. For example, writing a program that uses several chunks of code from this book *does not* require permission. Selling or distributing a CD-ROM of examples from O'Reilly books *does* require permission. Answering a question by citing this book and quoting example code *does not* require permission. Incorporating a significant amount of example code from this book into your product's documentation *does* require permission.

We appreciate, but do not require, attribution. An attribution usually includes the title, author, publisher, and ISBN. For example: "*CSS Cookbook,* by Christopher Schmitt. Copyright 2004 O'Reilly Media, Inc., 0-596-00576-8."

If you feel your use of code examples falls outside fair use or the permission given above, feel free to contact us at *permissions@oreilly.com*.

Comments and Questions

Please address comments and questions concerning this book to the publisher:

> O'Reilly Media, Inc.
> 1005 Gravenstein Highway North
> Sebastopol, CA 95472
> (800) 998-9938 (in the United States or Canada)
> (707) 829-0515 (international or local)
> (707) 829-0104 (fax)

We have a web page for this book, where we list errata, examples, and any additional information. You can access this page at:

> *http://www.oreilly.com/catalog/cssckbk*

To comment or ask technical questions about this book, send email to:

> *bookquestions@oreilly.com*

For more information about our books, conferences, Resource Centers, and the O'Reilly Network, see our web site at:

> *http://www.oreilly.com*

Acknowledgments

First, thanks to David Siegel and Lynda Weinman for their inspiration and support from the beginning of web design.

I wouldn't be writing any books for an industry I love so very much without the support and friendship of Molly Holzschlag.

A lot of appreciation and respect to fellow web builders for pushing CSS-enabled web designs forward: Douglas Bowman, Tantek Çelik, Dan Cenderhlem, Mike Davidson, Ethan Marcotte, Eric A. Meyer, Mark Newhouse, Dave Shea, and Jeffrey Zeldman.

Special thanks go to the technical editors, Erik J. Barzeski, Liza Daly, and Porter Glendinning, as well as copy editor Audrey Doyle for their time, expertise, and patience.

To my friend, Porter Glendinning, who seems to have a knack for not only being able to read W3C specifications and see their implications two or three steps ahead of most web developers, but also to articulate those thoughts in such a way to make me believe my grandmother could even understand what he's talking about. Your translation services and thoughts are a truly appreciated.

I want to say thanks to Paula Ferguson. While she left O'Reilly before the project got underway, she did accept my proposal for the book you have in your hands. While not the most time-intensive contribution to the project, it's probably the most important.

To fill Paula's shoes, Tatiana Diaz and Nathan Torkington did a great job of making sure my questions were answered and guiding me throughout the life of the project. This writing process has been my most challenging but most rewarding experience to date. And, frankly, I wouldn't have wanted it any other way with any other publisher.

Thanks to my friends who know me as the web geek I truly am: Judy Crawford, Dee Lalley, Richard Grillotti, Katrina Ferguson, Gail Rubini, Linda Sierra, Miles Tilmann, and Andrew Watson.

Thanks to my family for the love and appreciation. Your support through good times and bad has been a rock. As always, I'm looking forward to our next reunion.

And, Dad, this book is dedicated to you.

CHAPTER 1

Web Typography

1.0   Introduction

Before Cascading Style Sheets (CSS) came along, web developers used font tags to set the color, size, and style of text on different parts of a web page:

```
<font face="Verdana, Arial" size="+1" color="blue">Hello,
World!</font>
```

Although this method is effective for changing the appearance of type, using it to manipulate an entire web site containing multiple font tags results in time-consuming updates, adds to the overall file size of the web document, and increases the likelihood that errors will occur in the markup.

CSS helps to eliminate these design and maintenance problems. We can solve this problem in many ways, such as placing the content in a p element:

```
<p>Hello, World!</p>
```

Then use CSS to dictate the style of the document by placing this CSS block in the head of the document:

```
<style type="text/css" media="all">
p {
  color: blue;
  font-size: small;
  font-family: Verdana, Arial, sans-serif;
}
</style>
```

Now the document's structure and its visual presentation are separated. Because they are in separate areas, the process of editing and maintaining a web site's design including typography is simplified immensely.

It is important to be able to read the contents of a web page online, and CSS enables you to accomplish myriad tasks for controlling web page typography. In addition to setting the color, style, and size of fonts, this chapter also covers techniques for setting initial caps, creating visually compelling pullquotes, modifying leading, and more.

1.1   Specifying Fonts and Inheritance

Problem

You want to set the typeface of text on a web page.

Solution

Use the `font-family` property:

```
p {
  font-family: Georgia, Times, "Times New Roman", serif;
}
```

Discussion

You can specify the fonts you want the browser to render on a web page by writing a comma-delimited list for the value of the `font-family` property. If the browser can't find the first font on the list, it tries to find the next font, and so on, until it finds a font.

If the font name contains spaces, enclose the name with single or double quotation marks. You can enclose all font names in quotes, regardless of whether they contain spaces, but if you do, browsers with poor CSS implementations might not render the fonts accurately.

At the end of the list of font choices, you should insert a generic font family. CSS offers five font family values to choose from, as shown in Table 1-1.

Table 1-1. Generic font family values and examples

Generic font family values	Font examples
serif	Georgia, Times, Times New Roman, Garamond, and Century Schoolbook
sans-serif	Verdana, Arial, Helvetica, Trebuchet, and Tahoma
monospace	Courier, MS Courier New, and Prestige
cursive	Lucida Handwriting and Zapf-Chancery
fantasy	Comic Sans, Whimsey, Critter, and Cottonwood

All web browsers contain a list of fonts that fall into the five families shown in Table 1-1. If a font is neither chosen via a CSS rule nor available on the user's computer, the browser uses a font from one of these font families.

The most problematic generic font value is `fantasy` because this value is a catchall for any font that doesn't fall into the other four categories. Designers rarely use this font because they can't know what symbols will be displayed! Another problematic generic value is cursive because some systems can't display a cursive font. If a browser can't use a cursive font, it uses another default font in its place. Because text marked as cursive may not actually be displayed in a cursive font, designers often avoid this generic font value as well.

If you want to use an unusual font that might not be installed on most peoples' machines, the rule of thumb is to set the last value for the font-family property to either serif, sans-serif, or monospace. This will maintain at least some legibility for the user viewing the web document.

You don't have to set the same properties for every tag you use. A child element *inherits*, or has the same property values of, its parent element if the CSS specification that defines a given property can be inherited. For example, if you set the font-family property to show a serif font in a paragraph that contains an em element as a child, that text in the em element is also set in a serif font:

```
<p style="font-family: serif; ">The water fountain
with the broken sign on it is <em>indeed</em>  broken.</p>
```

Inheritance doesn't occur under two circumstances. One is built into the CSS specification and concerns elements that can generate a box. Elements such as h2 and p are referred to as *block-level elements* and can have other properties such as margins, borders, padding, and backgrounds, as shown in Figure 1-1.

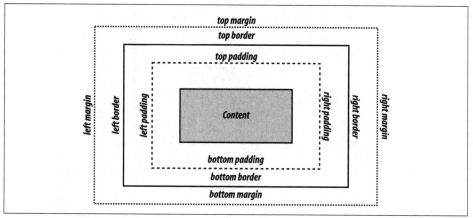

Figure 1-1. The box model for a block-level element

Because these properties aren't passed to child block-level elements, you don't have to write additional rules to counter the visual effects that would occur if they were passed. For example, if you applied a margin of 15% to a body element, that rule would be applied to every h2 and p element that is a child of that body element. If these properties were inherited, the page would look like that shown in Figure 1-2.

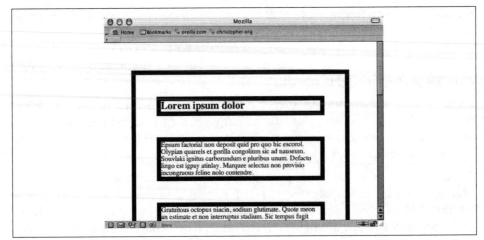

Figure 1-2. Hypothetical mock-up of margins and border properties being inherited

Because certain properties are defined to be inheritable and others aren't, the page actually looks like that shown in Figure 1-3 in a modern CSS-compliant browser.

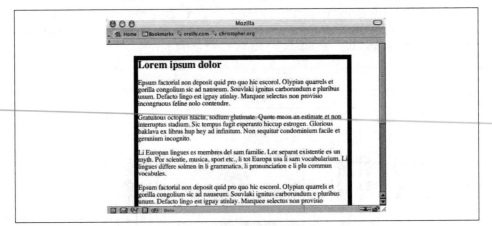

Figure 1-3. How the page looks when block-level elements don't inherit certain properties

The other circumstance under which inheritance doesn't work is, of course, if your browser doesn't follow the CSS specification. For example, in Netscape Navigator 4, child elements may not inherit the font-family and color values set in a body type selector. To work around this problem, implicitly set the font-family and color values for block-level elements:

```
body {
  font-family: Georgia, Times, "Times New Roman", serif;
  color: #030;
}
h1, h2, h3, h4, h5, h6, p, td, ul, ol, li, dl, dt, dd, {
```

```
    font-family: Georgia, Times, "Times New Roman", serif;
    color: #030;
}
```

See Also

The CSS 2.1 specification for inheritance at *http://www.w3.org/TR/CSS21/cascade.html#inheritance*; the CSS 2.1 specification for font-family values at *http://www.w3.org/TR/CSS21/fonts.html#propdef-font-family*; more about CSS and Netscape 4 issues at *http://www.mako4css.com/cssfont.htm*.

1.2   Specifying Font Measurements and Sizes

Problem

You want to set the size of type used on a web page.

Solution

Set the values of fonts using the font-size property:

```
P {
  font-size: 0.9em;
}
```

Discussion

Setting the size of the font with percentages causes the browser to calculate the size of the font based on the size of the parent element. For example, if the font size for the body is set to 12 pixels and the font size for p element is set to 125%, the font size for the text in paragraphs is 15 pixels.

You can use percentages, length units, and font-size keywords to set type size. Length units fall into two categories: absolute and relative. Absolute length units include the following:

- Inches (in)
- Centimeters (cm)
- Millimeters (mm)
- Points (pt)
- Picas (pc)

A point, in terms of the CSS specification, is equal to 1/72nd of an inch and a pica is equal to 12 points.

Because browser displays vary due to different operating systems and video settings, setting type in a *fixed* (or *absolute*) value doesn't make much sense. In fact, it's best to avoid absolute measurements for web documents, unless you're styling documents for fixed output. For example, when you create a style sheet to print a web document, absolute length units are preferred. For more on creating style sheets for printing, see Chapter 9.

The CSS specification doesn't dictate how browser vendors should treat text when the font-size property is set to a value of zero. Therefore different browsers interpret the value unpredictably. For example, such text isn't visible in the Mozilla browser. In Internet Explorer for Macintosh and Safari, the text isn't hidden, but, rather, is displayed at the default value of the font size. The Opera browser displays the text at a smaller, but still legible, size. And Internet Explorer for Windows sets the type size to a small, illegible, but still visible line of text that appears to be equal to the size of 0.1em, as shown in Figure 1-4. If you want to make text invisible, use the CSS properties visibility or display instead of setting the size of fonts to zero.

```
p {visibility: none}
```

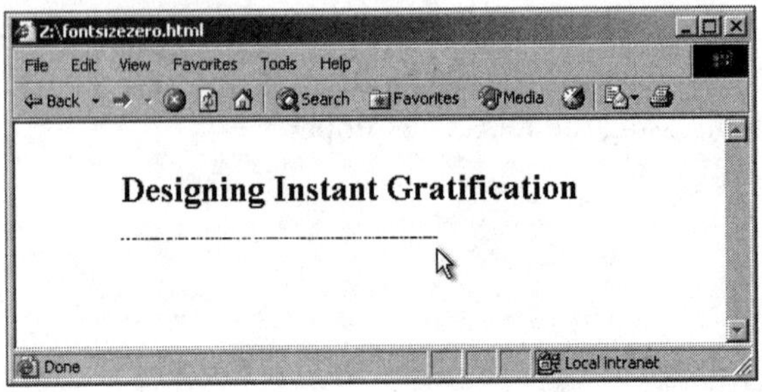

Figure 1-4. Internet Explorer for Windows showing illegible type when the font size is set to zero

A negative length value, such as –25cm, for the font-size property isn't allowed.

Relative units set the length of a property based on the value of another length property. Relative length units include the following:

- Em
- X-height (ex)
- Pixels (px)

Em units refer to the default font size set in the preference of the user's browser, while *x-height* refers to the height of the lowercase letter x in the font.

Pixels consistently control the size of typography in a web document across most platforms and browsers. However, it's not a good idea to use pixels when designing for the following browsers:

- Netscape Navigator 4.7*x*, which doesn't display pixel size values correctly
- Opera 5 for the Macintosh, which displays pixel lengths smaller than the size set in the style sheet

If most visitors to your site use browsers other than Netscape Navigator 4.7x and Opera 5 for the Mac, you can safely use pixels to set the size of your type.

The main issue in regard to setting type size in pixels isn't one of accurate sizing, but of accessibility. People with poor vision might want to resize the type to better read the document. However, if you use pixels to set the type on your web page, people using Internet Explorer for Windows will be unable to resize the type. Because Internet Explorer for Windows is the most popular browser on the planet, the use of pixels to set type size becomes a problem for most users who need to resize the type in their browsers.

If you do require an absolute size measurement, pixels should be used rather than points, even though print designers are more accustomed to point measurements. The reason is that Macintosh and Windows operating systems render point sizes differently, but pixel size stays the same.

If accessibility is a concern, switch to em units. In the Solution, we set the text in a paragraph to 0.9em units. This value is equivalent to setting the font size to 90% of the default font size set in the browser's preference.

However, the use of em units raises another concern. This time the problem pertains to usability. Although you might be able to resize the type in a web page, if you set a font to a size that is smaller than the default text size of the browser (for example, to 0.7em), Internet Explorer for Windows will display small, almost illegible lines of text, as shown in Figure 1-5. So, the lesson here is: be careful with relative sizes, as it is easy to make text illegible.

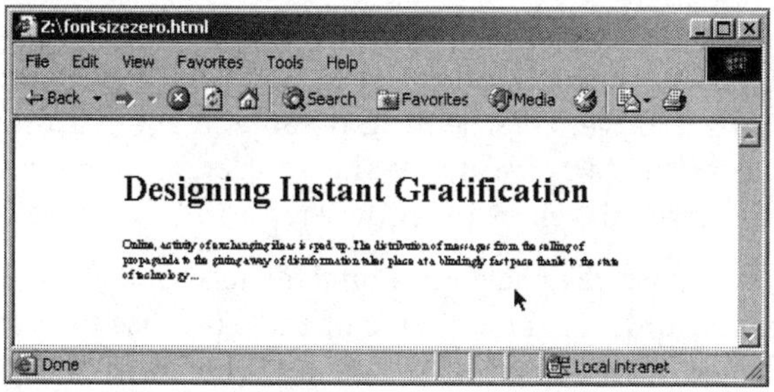

Figure 1-5. Almost illegible type set with em units

This brings up the possibility of another solution: the use of font-size keywords. The CSS 2.1 specification has seven font keywords for absolute sizes that you can use to set type size (see Figure 1-6): xx-small, x-small, small, medium, large, x-large, xx-large.

There are two other font-size keywords for relative measurements: larger and smaller. If a child element is set to larger, the browser can interpret the value of the

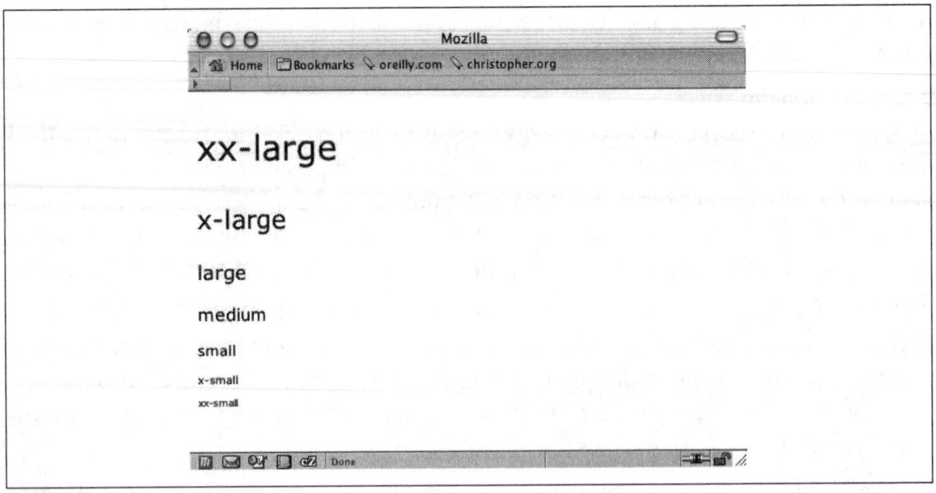

Figure 1-6. The font-size keywords on display

parent's font-size value of small and increase the text inside the child element to medium.

Font-size keywords provide two benefits: they make it easy to enlarge or reduce the size of the text in most browsers, and the font sizes in browsers never go smaller than nine pixels, ensuring that the text is legible. If you do set text to a small size, use a sans-serif font such as Verdana to increase the chances for legibility.

The main drawback with font-size keywords is that Internet Explorer 4–5.5 sets the small value as the default setting instead of the recommended medium setting. Because of this decision, Internet Explorer actually maps all the font-size keywords to one level lower than other browsers. In other words, the value for xx-large in IE 4–5.5 is every other browser's x-large, x-large in IE is large in another browser, and so on. Another drawback is that in Netscape 4, the smaller sizes are sometimes illegible because they aren't rendered well by the browser.

The workaround for these drawbacks is to first create a separate style sheet that contains the font-size keywords for the web document. Then use the @import method for associating a style sheet, as explained in Recipe 9.1 and as shown here (this step keeps Navigator 4 from rendering illegible type):

```
<link href="/_assets/basic.css" media="all"
rel="style sheet" />
<style type="text/css" media="screen">
 @import url(/_assets/fontsize.css);
</style>
```

To keep Internet Explorer 5 and 5.5 for Windows from displaying the wrong sizes for the font-size keywords, use the voice-family workaround for delivering alternative values in Internet Explorer, as explained in Recipe 9.2 and as shown here:

```
#content {
 /*
  font-size workaround for WinIE 5:
  1) WinIE 5/5.5 value first:
 */
 font-size: x-small;
 voice-family: "\"}\"";
 voice-family: inherit;
 /*
  2) Then the correct value next 2 times:
 */
 font-size: small;
}
html>#content
 font-size: small;
}
```

See Also

The article "CSS Design: Size Matters," written by Todd Fahrner (an invited member to the W3C CSS Working Group) available at *http://www.alistapart.com/articles/sizematters/*; Recipe 10.1 for enlarging text to gain attention; the CSS 2.1 specification at *http://www.w3.org/TR/CSS21/cascade.html#q1* for more on how a browser determines values; the CSS 2 specification for length units at *http://www.w3.org/TR/REC-CSS2/syndata.html#length-units*; the section "Font Size" in Chapter 5 of *Cascading Style Sheets: The Definitive Guide* (O'Reilly).

1.3   Enforcing Font Sizes

Problem

You want to override control over font sizes.

Solution

Use the !important rule to override a user's style sheet rules:

```
P {
 font-size: 12px !important;
}
```

Discussion

The !important rule consists of an exclamation mark (!) followed immediately by the word *important*.

In some browsers, a user can have a style sheet set up for browsing the Web that enables him to set font sizes (and other CSS properties) to his liking. However, as a designer of a web document, you might want to make sure your designs render in the manner you planned. The !important rule gives you a little insurance that your designs remain intact. (However, the nature of the medium means that designs are never precise or "pixel-perfect" from one display to another.)

Although you as the designer write the !important CSS rules, the user also can write these rules in his own style sheet. And in the CSS 2 specification, !important rules the user writes override any !important rules the designer writes.

See Also

The CSS 2.1 specification on !important rules at *http://www.w3.org/TR/CSS21/cascade.html#important-rules.*

1.4   Setting a Simple Initial Cap

Problem

You want a paragraph to begin with an initial cap.

Solution

Mark up the paragraph of content with a p element:

```
<p>Online, activity of exchanging ideas is sped up. The
distribution of messages from the sellin of propaganda to the
giving away of disinformation takes place at a blindingly fast
pace thanks to the state of technology...</p>
```

Use the pseudo-element :first-letter to stylize the first letter of the paragraph, as shown in Figure 1-7:

```
p:first-letter {
  font-size: 1.2em;
  background-color: black;
  color: white;
}
```

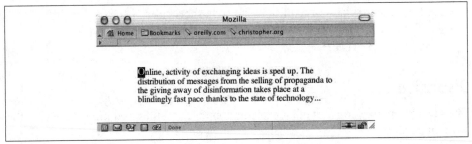

Figure 1-7. A simple initial cap

Discussion

The CSS specification offers an easy way to stylize the first letter in a paragraph as a traditional initial or drop cap: use the :first-letter pseudo-element (:first-letter isn't supported in most browsers, including Internet Explorer 4 and 5 for Windows, Netscape Navigator 4, and Internet Explorer 4.5 for Macintosh).

Wrap a span element with a class attribute around the first letter of the first sentence of the first paragraph:

```
<p><span class="initcap">O</span>nline, activity of exchanging ideas is sped
up. The distribution of messages from the selling of propaganda
to the giving away of disinformation takes place at a blindingly
fast pace thanks to the state of technology...</p>
```

Then set the style for the initial cap:

```
p .initcap {
  font-size: 1.2em;
  background-color: black;
  color: white;
}
```

Initial caps, also known as *versals*, traditionally are enlarged in print to anything from a few points to three lines of text.

See Also

The CSS 2.1 specification for the :first-letter pseudo-element at *http://www.w3.org/TR/CSS21/selector.html#x52*; for more information on initial caps in general, see *http://fonts.lordkyl.net/fonts.php?category=vers*.

1.5   Setting a Larger, Centered Initial Cap

Problem

You want to place a large initial cap in the center of a paragraph.

Solution

Wrap a span element with a class attribute around the first letter of the first sentence of the first paragraph:

```
<p><span class="initcap">O</span>nline, activity of exchanging ideas is sped
up. The distribution of messages from the selling of propaganda
to the giving away of disinformation takes place at a blindingly
fast pace thanks to the state of technology...</p>
```

In conjunction with styling the initial letter through the span tag with a class selector, create the decoration that sets the text indent for the paragraph (see Figure 1-8):

```
p {
  text-indent: 37%;
```

```
    line-height: 1em;
}
p .initcap {
  font-size: 6em;
  line-height: 0.6em;
  font-weight: bold;
}
```

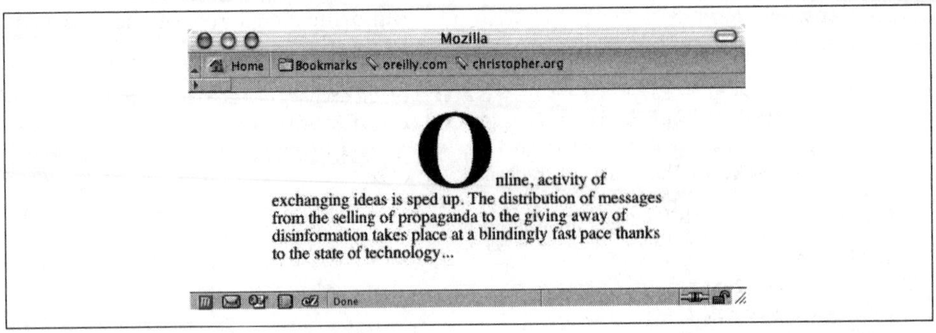

Figure 1-8. A larger, centered initial cap

Discussion

This Solution works due to the interaction of three CSS properties. The first is the text-indent property, which moves the first line toward the middle of the paragraph. The value is set to 37%, which is a little bit more than one-third the distance from the left side of the paragraph, as shown in Figure 1-9, but not enough to "center" the initial cap.

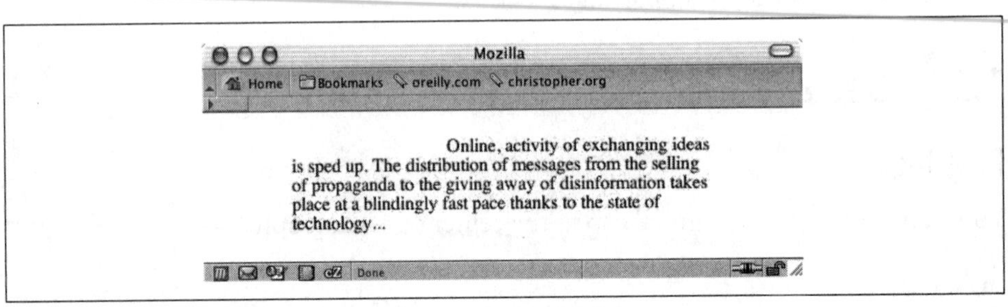

Figure 1-9. The indented text

The next property that helps is the font-size property. Setting the size to 6em makes the font six times (or 600%) larger than the default size set for fonts in the browser, as shown in Figure 1-10.

Because the font size is six times as large as the rest of the type, the leading on the first line is now deeper than it is on the remaining lines. To help adjust that, set the line height for the span element to 0.6em.

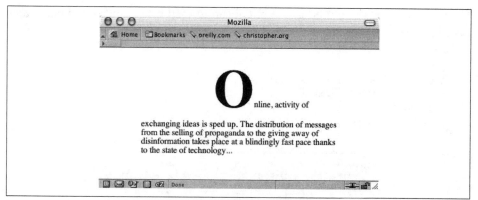

Figure 1-10. The initial cap enlarged six times its normal height

Note that this recipe centering the initial cap works, technically, when the character's width is equal to 26% of the paragraph's width. In other words, if the letter for the initial cap or the width of the paragraph is different for your own work, adjustments to the values in the CSS rules are necessary to move the initial cap to the center.

See Also

Recipe 1.19 for adjusting leading with line height; the CSS 2.1 specification for text-indent at *http://www.w3.org/TR/CSS21/text.html#propdef-text-indent*.

1.6 Setting an Initial Cap with Decoration (Imagery)

Problem

You want to use an image for an initial cap.

Solution

Wrap a span element around the first letter of the first sentence of the first paragraph:

```
<p><span class="initcap">O</span>nline, activity of exchanging
ideas is sped up. The distribution of messages from the selling of
propaganda to the giving away of disinformation takes place at a
blindingly fast pace thanks to the state of technology...</p>
```

Set the contents inside the span to be hidden:

```
p.initcap {
  display: none;
}
```

Then set an image to be used as the initial cap in the background of the paragraph (see Figure 1-11):

```
p {
  line-height: 1em;
  background-image: url(initcap-o.gif);
  background-repeat: no-repeat;
  text-indent: 35px;
  padding-top: 45px;
}
```

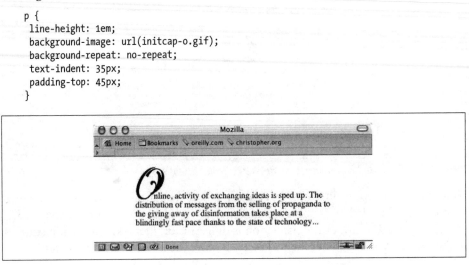

Figure 1-11. An image used as an initial cap

Discussion

The first step of this Solution is to create an image for use as the initial cap. Once you have created the image, make a note of its width and height. In this example, the image of the letter measures 55 by 58 pixels (see Figure 1-12).

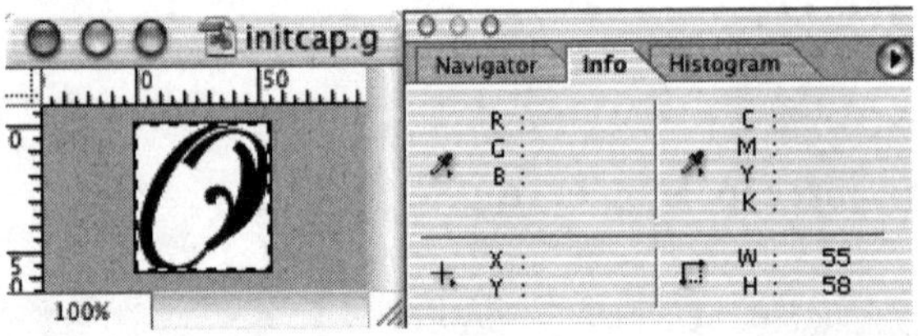

Figure 1-12. The image of the initial cap

Next, hide the first letter of the HTML text by setting the display property to none. Then put the image in the background of the paragraph, making sure that the image doesn't repeat by setting the value of background-repeat to no-repeat:

```
background-image: url(initcap-o.gif);
background-repeat: no-repeat;
```

With the measurements already known, set the width of the image as the value for text-indent and the height of the image as the padding for the top of the paragraph (see Figure 1-13):

```
text-indent: 55px;
padding-top: 58px;
```

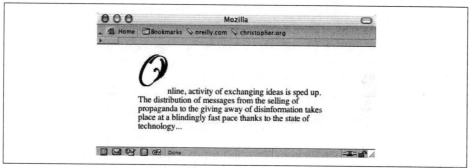

Figure 1-13. Adjusting the space for the initial cap

Then change the text-indent and padding-top values so that the initial cap appears to rest on the baseline, as was shown in Figure 1-11.

Note that users with images turned off aren't able to see the initial cap, especially since the solution doesn't allow for an alt attribute for the image. If you want to use an image but still have an alt attribute show when a user turns off images, use an image to replace the HTML character:

```
<p><img src="initcap-o.gif" alt="O" >nline, activity of exchanging
ideas is sped up. The distribution of messages from the selling
of propaganda to the giving away of disinformation takes place at
a blindingly fast pace thanks to the state of technology...</p>
```

Note that while the alt attribute is displayed in this solution, the ability to kern the space between the initial cap and the HTML text is lost. The HTML text begins exactly at the right side of the image and can't be moved closer to the letter being displayed in the graphic itself.

See Also

Recipe 1.4 for setting a simple initial cap.

1.7   Creating a Heading with Stylized Text

Problem

You want to use CSS properties to design a heading that is different from the default. For example, you want to put the heading in Figure 1-14 into italics, as shown in Figure 1-15.

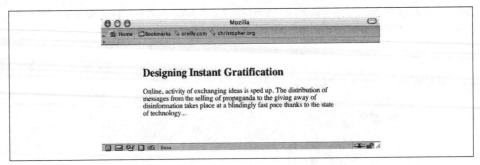

Figure 1-14. *The default rendering of a heading*

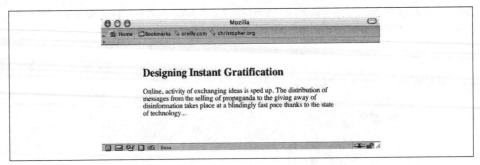

Figure 1-15. *The stylized text of a heading*

Solution

First, properly mark up the heading:

```
<h2>Designing Instant Gratification</h2>
<p>Online, activity of exchanging ideas is sped up. The
distribution of messages from the selling of propaganda to the
 giving away of disinformation takes place at a blindingly fast
pace thanks to the state of technology...</p>
```

Then, use the font shorthand property to easily change the style of the heading:

```
h2 {
 font: bold italic 2em  Georgia, Times, "Times New Roman", serif;
 margin: 0;
 padding: 0;
}
p {
 margin: 0;
 padding: 0;
}
```

Discussion

A *shorthand property* combines several properties into one. The font property is just one of these timesavers. One font property can represent the following values:

- `font-style`
- `font-variant`
- `font-weight`
- `font-size/line-height`
- `font-family`

The first three values can be placed in any order, while the others need to be in the order shown.

When you want to include the `line-height` value, put a forward slash between the `font-size` value and the `line-height` value:

```
p {
  font: 1em/1.5em Verdana, Arial, sans-serif;
}
```

When setting the style headings, remember that browsers have their own default values for padding and margins of paragraphs and heading tags. These default values are generally based on mathematics, not aesthetics, so don't hesitate to adjust them to further enhance the look of your web document.

See Also

50+ CSS heading styles at *http://www.cssbook.com/resources/css/headings/*; the CSS 2.1 specification for the font shorthand property at *http://www.w3.org/TR/CSS21/fonts.html#propdef-font*.

1.8 Creating a Heading with Stylized Text and Borders

Problem

You want to stylize the borders on the top and bottom of a heading, as shown in Figure 1-16.

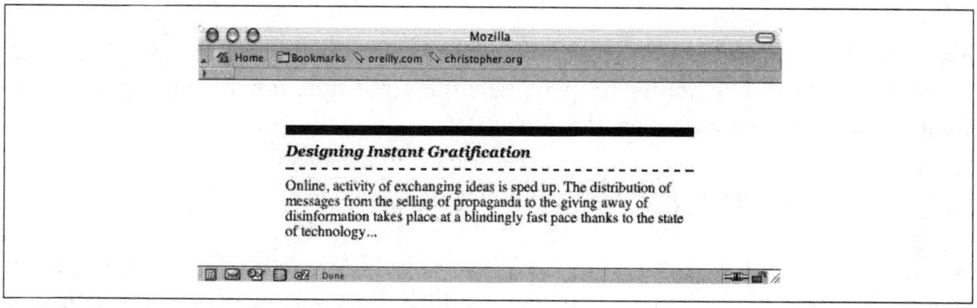

Figure 1-16. A heading stylized with borders

Solution

Use the border-top and border-bottom properties when setting the style for the heading:

```
h2 {
    font: bold italic 2em Georgia, Times, "Times New Roman", serif;
    border-bottom: 2px dashed black;
    border-top: 10px solid black;
    margin: 0;
    padding: 0.5em 0 0.5em 0;
    font-size: 1em;
}
p {
    margin: 0;
    padding: 10px 0 0 0;
}
```

Discussion

In addition to top and bottom borders, a block-level element also can have a border on the left and right sides via the border-left and border-right properties, respectively. The border-top, border-bottom, border-left, and border-right properties are shorthand properties that enable developers to set the width, style, and color of each side of a border.

Without the two shorthand border declarations in the Solution, the CSS rule for the heading would be expanded by four extra declarations:

```
h2 {
    font: bold italic 2em Georgia, Times, "Times New Roman", serif;
    border-bottom-width: 2px ;
    border-bottom-style: dashed;
    border-bottom-color: black;
    border-top-width: 10px;
    border-top-style: solid;
    border-top-color: black;
    margin: 0;
    padding: 0.5em 0 0.5em 0;
    font-size: 1em;
}
```

Also available is a shorthand property for the top, bottom, left, and right shorthand properties: border. The border property sets the same style for the width, style, and color of the border on each side of an element:

```
h2 {
    border: 3px dotted #33333;
}
```

When setting the borders, make sure to adjust the padding to put enough whitespace between the borders and the text of the heading. This aids in readability. Without enough whitespace on a heading element, the text of the heading can appear cramped.

See Also

Recipe 2.8 for more information on styles of borders and the shorthand border property.

1.9 Stylizing a Heading with Text and an Image

Problem

You want to place a repeating image at the bottom of a heading, like the grass in Figure 1-17.

Figure 1-17. A background image used with a heading

Solution

Use the background-image, background-repeat, and background-position properties:

```
h2 {
  font: bold italic 2em Georgia, Times, "Times New Roman", serif;
  background-image: url(tall_grass.jpg);
  background-repeat: repeat-x;
  background-position: bottom;
  border-bottom: 10px solid #666;
  margin: 10px 0 0 0;
  padding: 0.5em 0 60px 0;
}
```

Discussion

Make a note of the height of the image used for the background. In this example, the height of the image is 100 pixels (see Figure 1-18).

Figure 1-18. An image of tall grass

Set the background-repeat property to a value of repeat-x, which will cause the image to repeat horizontally:

```
background-image: url(tall_grass.jpg);
background-repeat: repeat-x;
```

Next, set the background-position property to bottom:

```
background-position: bottom;
```

The background-position can take up to two values corresponding to the horizontal and vertical axes. Values for background-position can be a length unit (such as pixels), a percentage, or a keyword. To position an element on the x axis, use the keyword values left, center, or right. For the y axis, use the keyword values top, center, or bottom.

When the location of the other axis isn't present, the image is placed in the center of that axis, as shown in Figure 1-19.

```
background-position: bottom;
```

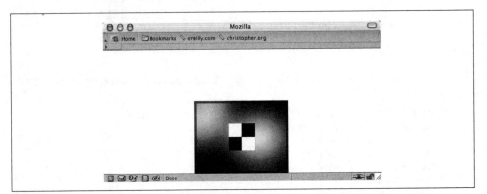

Figure 1-19. The image aligned on the bottom of the y axis and in the middle of the x axis

So, in this Solution, the image is placed at the bottom of the y axis but is centered along the x axis.

See Also

Recipe 2.4 for setting a background image in an entire web page.

1.10   Creating a Pull Quote with HTML Text

Problem

You want to stylize the text for a pull quote so that it is different from the default. Undifferentiated quotes aren't obviously from another writer (see Figure 1-20), whereas stylized quotes are (see Figure 1-21).

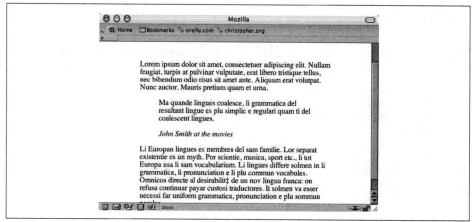

Figure 1-20. The default rendering of the text for a pull quote

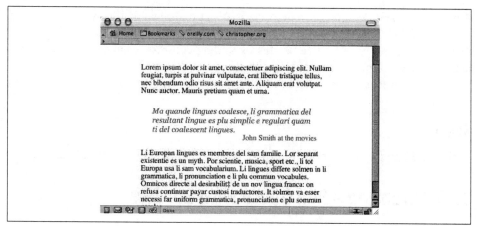

Figure 1-21. The stylized pull quote

Solution

Use the blockquote element to indicate the pull quote semantically in the markup:

```
<blockquote>
  <p>Ma quande lingues coalesce, li grammatica del resultant
  lingue es plu simplic e regulari quam ti del coalescent
lingues.</p>
  <div class="source">John Smith at the movies</div>
</blockquote>
```

With CSS, apply the margin, padding, and color values to the blockquote element:

```
blockquote {
  margin: 0;
  padding: 0;
  color: #555;
}
```

Next, set the style for the p and div elements nested in the blockquote element:

```
blockquote p {
  font: italic 1em Georgia, Times, "Times New Roman", serif;
  font-size: 1em;
  margin: 1.5em 2em 0 1.5em;
  padding: 0;
}
blockquote .source {
  text-align: right;
  font-style: normal;
  margin-right: 2em;
}
```

Discussion

A pull quote is used in design to grab a reader's attention so that he will stick around and read more. One easy way to create a pull quote is to change the color of a portion of the main text. Improve on this by adding contrast: change the generic font family of the pull quote so that it is different from that of the main text. For example, if the main text of a web document is set in sans-serif, set the pull quote text to a serif font.

See Also

Recipes 1.11 and 1.12 for more information on designing pullquotes with CSS.

1.11 Creating a Pull Quote with Borders

Problem

You want to stylize a pull quote with borders on the top and bottom, as in Figure 1-22.

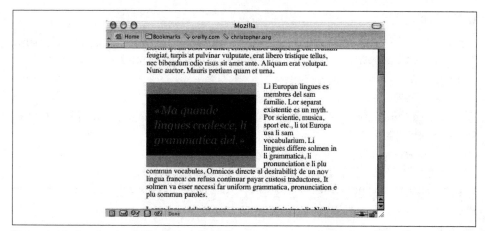

Figure 1-22. A stylized pull quote using borders

To put borders on the left and right, instead of the top and bottom, use the border-left and border-right properties:

```
border-left: 1em solid #999;
border-right: 1em solid #999;
```

Solution

Use the blockquote element to mark up the pull quote content:

```
<blockquote>
<p>&laquo;Ma quande lingues coalesce, li
grammatica del.&raquo;</p>
</blockquote>
```

Next, set the CSS rules for the border and text within the pull quote:

```
blockquote {
 float: left;
 width: 200px;
 margin: 0 0.7em 0 0;
 padding: 0.7em;
 color: #666;
 background-color: black;
 font-family: Georgia, Times, "Times New Roman", serif;
 font-size: 1.5em;
 font-style: italic;
 border-top: 1em solid #999;
 border-bottom: 1em solid #999;
}
blockquote p {
 margin: 0;
 padding: 0;
 text-align: left;
 line-height: 1.3em;
}
```

Discussion

Set the float property as well as the width property for the blockquote element. These two CSS properties allow the main content to wrap around the pull quote:

```
float: left;
width: 200px;
```

Contrast the pull quote with the surrounding text by changing the quote's foreground and background colors:

```
color: #666;
background-color: black;
```

Use the border-top and border-bottom properties to match the color of the text in the pull quote:

```
border-top: 1em solid #999;
border-bottom: 1em solid #999;
```

See Also

Chapter 7 for several page-layout techniques that take advantage of the float property; Recipe 1.8 for styling headings with borders; Recipes 10.3 and 10.4 for more on designing with contrast.

1.12   Creating a Pull Quote with Images

Problem

You want to stylize a pull quote with images on either side, such as the curly braces in Figure 1-23.

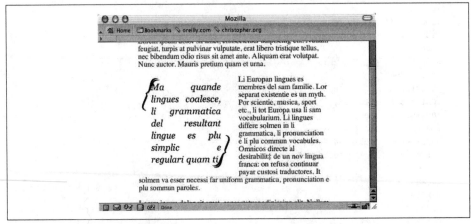

Figure 1-23. A Pull quote with images

Solution

Use the blockquote element to mark up the pull quote content:

```
<blockquote>
<p>Ma quande lingues coalesce, li grammatica del resultant
lingue es plu simplic e regulari quam ti.</p>
</blockquote>
```

Then set the style for the pull quote, placing one image in the background of the blockquote element and another in the background of the p:

```
blockquote {
  background-image: url(bracket_left.gif);
  background-repeat: no-repeat;
  float: left;
  width: 175px;
  margin: 0 0.7em 0 0;
  padding: 10px 0 0 27px;
  font-family: Georgia, Times, "Times New Roman", serif;
  font-size: 1.2em;
  font-style: italic;
  color: black;
}
blockquote p {
  margin: 0;
  padding: 0 22px 10px 0;
  width:150px;
  text-align: justify;
  line-height: 1.3em;
  background-image: url(bracket_right.gif);
  background-repeat: no-repeat;
  background-position: bottom right;
}
```

Discussion

For this Solution, the bracket images for the pull quote come in a pair, with one at the upper left corner and the other at the bottom right corner. Through CSS, you can assign only one background image per block-level element.

The workaround is to give these images the proper placement; put one image in the background of the blockquote element and the other in the p element that is a child of the blockquote element:

```
blockquote {
  background-image: url(bracket_left.gif);
  background-repeat: no-repeat;
  float: left;
  width: 175px;
}
blockquote p {
  background-image: url(bracket_right.gif);
```

```
  background-repeat: no-repeat;
  background-position: bottom right;
}
```

Then adjust the padding, margin, and width of the blockquote and p elements so that you have an unobstructed view of the images:

```
blockquote {
  background-image: url(bracket_left.gif);
  background-repeat: no-repeat;
  float: left;
  width: 175px;
  margin: 0 0.7em 0 0;
  padding: 10px 0 0 27px;
}
blockquote p {
  margin: 0;
  padding: 0 22px 10px 0;
  width:150px;
  background-image: url(bracket_right.gif);
  background-repeat: no-repeat;
  background-position: bottom right;
}
```

A benefit of this Solution is that if the text is resized, as shown in Figure 1-24, the images (brackets) stretch like rubber bands.

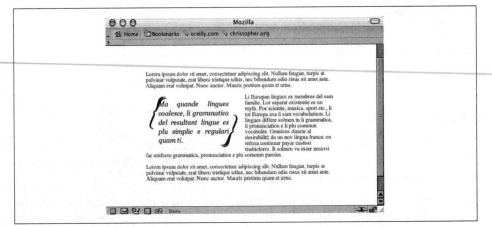

Figure 1-24. The background images staying in the corners as the text is resized

See Also

Recipe 3.11 for another example of the rubber-band technique.

1.13 Setting the Indent in the First Line of a Paragraph

Problem

You want to place an indent in the first line of each paragraph, turning the paragraphs shown in Figure 1-25 to the paragraphs shown in Figure 1-26.

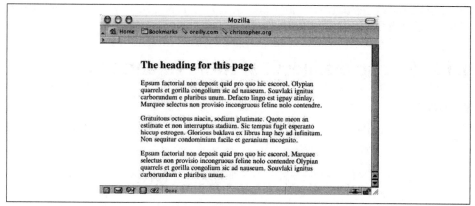

Figure 1-25. The default rendering of the paragraphs

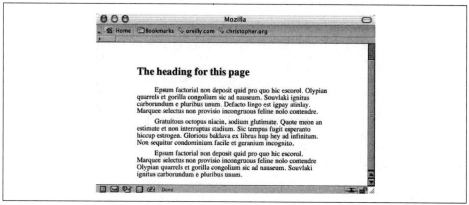

Figure 1-26. The paragraphs with first lines indented

Solution

Use the text-indent property to create the indent:

```
p {
  text-indent: 2.5em;
  margin: 0 0 0.5em 0;
  padding: 0;
}
```

Discussion

The text-indent property can take absolute and relative length units as well as percentages. If you use percentages, the percentage refers to the element's width and not the total width of the page. In other words, if the indent is set to 35% of a paragraph that is set to a width of 200 pixels, the width of the indent is 70 pixels.

See Also

The CSS 2.1 specification for more on the text-indent property at *http://www.w3. org/TR/CSS21/text.html#propdef-text-indent*.

1.14   Setting the Indent of Entire Paragraphs

Problem

You want to indent entire paragraphs, turning Figure 1-27 into Figure 1-28.

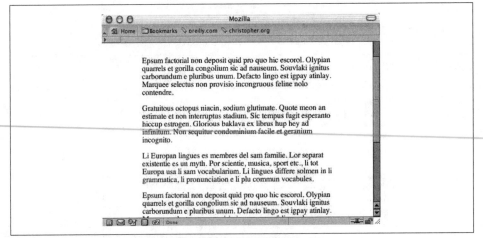

Figure 1-27. The paragraphs as the browser usually renders them

Solution

To achieve the desired effect, use class selectors:

```
p.normal {
 padding: 0;
 margin-left: 0;
 margin-right: 0;
}
p.large {
 margin-left: 33%;
 margin-right: 5%;
}
```

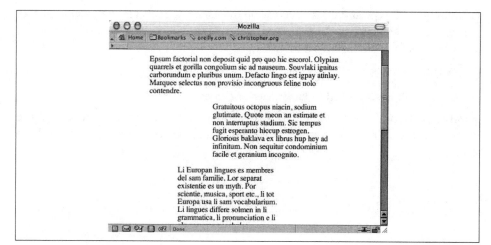

Epsum factorial non deposit quid pro quo hic escorol. Olypian quarrels et gorilla congolium sic ad nauseum. Souvlaki ignitus carborundum e pluribus unum. Defacto lingo est igpay atinlay. Marquee selectus non provisio incongruous feline nolo contendre.

Gratuitous octopus niacin, sodium glutimate. Quote meon an estimate et non interruptus stadium. Sic tempus fugit esperanto hiccup estrogen. Glorious baklava ex librus hup hey ad infinitum. Non sequitur condominium facile et geranium incognito.

Li Europan lingues es membres del sam familie. Lor separat existentie es un myth. Por scientie, musica, sport etc., li tot Europa usa li sam vocabularium. Li lingues differe solmen in li grammatica, li pronunciation e li

Figure 1-28. Indented paragraphs

```
p.medium {
 margin-left: 15%;
 margin-right: 33%;
}
```

Then place the appropriate attribute in the markup:

```
<p class="normal">Lorem ipsum dolor sit amet, consectetuer
adipiscing elit,  sed diam nonummy nibh euismod tincidunt ut
laoreet dolore magna al iquam erat volutpat.</p>
<p class="large">Epsum factorial non deposit quid pro quo hic
escorol. Olypian quarrels et gorilla congolium sic ad nauseum.
Souvlaki ignitus carborundum e pluribus unum.</p>
<p class="medium ">Li Europan lingues es membres del sam
familie. Lor separat existentie es un myth. Por scientie, musica,
sport etc., li tot Europa usa li sam vocabularium</p>
```

Discussion

Class selectors pick any HTML element that uses the class attribute. The difference between class and type selectors is that selectors pick out every instance of the HTML element. In the following two CSS rules, the first selector is a type selector that signifies all content marked as h2 be displayed as red while the following CSS rule, a class selector, sets the padding of an element to 33%:

```
h2 {
   color: red;
}
.largeIndent {
   padding-left: 33%;
}
```

Combining both type and class selectors on one element gains greater specificity over the styling of elements. In the following markup, the third element is set to red and also has a padding on the left set to 33%:

```
<h2>This is red.</h2>
<h3 class="largeIndent">This has a rather large indent.</h3>
<h2 class="largeIndent">This is both red and indented.</h2>
```

Another solution that could be used instead of class selectors is to apply the indent using margins and then use adjacent sibling selectors to apply the style to the paragraphs:

```
p, p+p+p+p {
  padding: 0;
  margin-left: 0;
  margin-right: 0;
}
p+p, p+p+p+p+p {
  margin-left: 33%;
  margin-right: 5%;
}
p+p+p, p+p+p+p+p+p {
  margin-left: 15%;
  margin-right: 33%;
}
```

This method takes advantage of the adjacent sibling selectors, which are represented by two or more regular selectors separated by plus sign(s). For example, the h2+p selector stylizes the paragraph *immediately following* an h2 element.

For this Recipe we want to stylize certain paragraphs in the order in which they appear on-screen. For example, p+p selects the paragraph element that follows another paragraph. However, when there are more than two paragraphs, the third paragraph (as well as others after the third paragraph) is rendered in the same style as the second paragraph. This occurs because the third paragraph is immediately followed by a paragraph.

To separate the styles from the second and third paragraphs, set up another CSS rule for the third paragraph that selects three paragraphs that follow each other:

```
p+p+p {
  margin-left: 15%;
  margin-right: 33%;
}
```

Then, build off of these CSS rules by *grouping* the selectors. Instead of writing two CSS rules to stylize the third and sixth paragraphs, separate the selectors by a comma and a space:

```
p+p+p, p+p+p+p+p+p {
  margin-left: 15%;
  margin-right: 33%;
}
```

The main problem with adjacent sibling selectors is that they aren't supported by all versions of Internet Explorer for Windows. Therefore, these users will not see the paragraphs indented. Adjacent sibling selectors are supported in Internet Explorer for Macintosh 5, Netscape Navigator 6+, and Operat 5+.

See Also

The CSS 2.1 specification about class selectors at *http://www.w3.org/TR/CSS21/ selector.html#class-html*; the CSS 2.1 specification about adjacent sibling selectors at *http://www.w3.org/TR/CSS21/selector.html#adjacent-selectors*.

1.15 Setting Text to Be Justified

Problem

You want to align text to be justified on both the left and right sides, as in Figure 1-29.

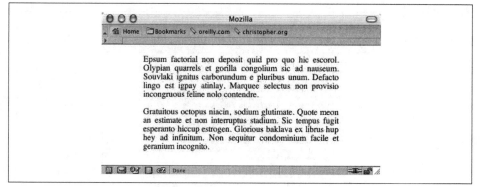

Figure 1-29. The paragraph justified on both sides

Solution

Use the text-align property:

```
P {
  width: 600px;
  text-align: justify;
}
```

Discussion

How well does text justification work? According to the CSS 2.1 specification, it depends on the algorithms developed by the engineers who made the browser being used to view the web page. Because there isn't an agreed-upon algorithm for justifying text, the look of the text varies from browser to browser, even though the browser vendor technically supports justification.

Browser support for the property is good in Internet Explorer 4+ for Windows, Internet Explorer 5 for Macintosh, Safari, and Opera 3+. In those browsers, justified text looks pleasing to the eye. In other browsers, justified text may look bad; for example, it might have large whitespace between words.

See Also

The CSS 2.1 specification about the `text-align` property at *http://www.w3.org/TR/REC-CSS2/text.html#alignment-prop.*

1.16 Styling the First Line of a Paragraph

Problem

You want to set the first line of a paragraph in boldface, as in Figure 1-30.

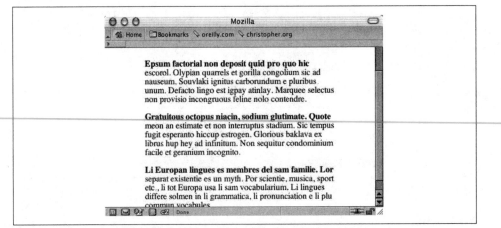

Figure 1-30. The first line set to bold

Solution

Use the `:first-line` pseudo-element to set the style of the first line:

```
p:first-line {
  font-weight: bold;
}
```

Discussion

Just like a class selector, a *pseudo-element* enables you to manipulate the style of parts of a web document. Unlike a class selector, however, resizing a browser window or changing the size of the font can change the area marked by a pseudo-element. In this Solution, the amount of text in the first line can change if the browser is resized, as shown in Figure 1-31.

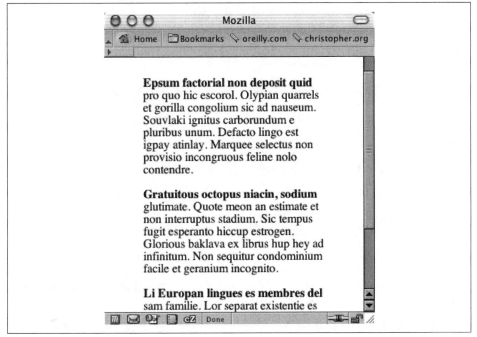

Figure 1-31. The amount of text changing when the browser is resized

See Also

The CSS 2.1 specification for the :first-line pseudo-element at *http://www.w3.org/ TR/CSS21/selector.html#first-line-pseudo*.

1.17 Styling the First Line of a Paragraph with an Image

Problem

You want to stylize the first line of a paragraph and include an image; for example, see Figure 1-32.

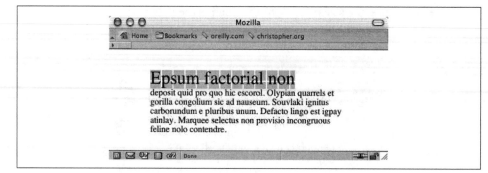

Figure 1-32. The first line with a background image

Solution

Use the background-image property within the :first-line pseudo-element:

```
p:first-line {
  font-size: 2em;
  background-image: url(background.gif);
}
```

Discussion

Through the :first-line selectors styles can only be applied to the first line of text of an element and not the width of the element itself.

In addition to the background-image property, the :first-line pseudo-element also supports the following properties allowing for greater design control:

```
font
color
background
word-spacing
letter-spacing
text-decoration
vertical-align
text-transform
text-shadow
line-height
clear
```

See Also

The CSS 2.1 specification for the :first-line pseudo-element at *http://www.w3.org/TR/CSS21/selector.html#first-line-pseudo*.

1.18 Creating a Highlighted Text Effect

Problem

You want to highlight a portion of the text in a paragraph, as in Figure 1-33.

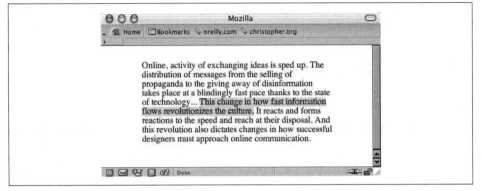

Figure 1-33. Highlighted text

Solution

Use the strong element to mark up the portions of text you want to highlight:

```
<p>The distribution of messages from the selling of propaganda
to the giving away of disinformation takes place at a blindingly
fast pace thanks to the state of technology... <strong>This
change in how fast information flows revolutionizes the
culture.</strong></p>
```

Then set the CSS rule to set the highlighted:

```
strong {
 font-weight: normal;
 background-color: yellow;
}
```

Discussion

Although the strong element is used in this Solution, you also can use the em element instead of the strong element to mark highlighted text. The HTML 4.01 specification states that em should be used for marking *emphasized* text, while strong "indicates stronger emphasis."

Once the text has been marked, set the highlighter color with the background-color property. Because some browsers apply a bold weight to text marked as strong, set the font-weight to normal. When using the em element, be sure to set the font-style to normal as this keeps browsers from setting the type in italic, as shown in the next code listing.

```
em {
  font-style: normal;
  background-color: #ff00ff;
}
```

See Also

The HTML specification for strong and em at *http://www.w3.org/TR/html401/struct/text.html#edef-STRONG*.

1.19   Changing Line Spacing

Problem

You want to leave more or less space between lines. Figure 1-34 shows the browser default, and Figure 1-35 shows paragraphs with half as much space again.

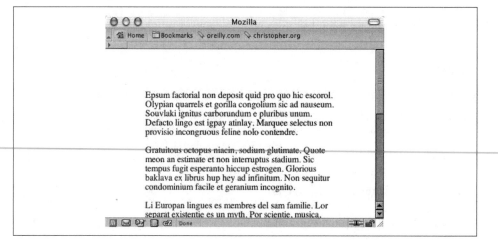

Figure 1-34. The default leading of a paragraph

Solution

Use the line-height:

```
P {
  line-height: 1.5em;
}
```

Discussion

As the line-height value increases, the distance between the lines of text grows. As the value decreases, the distance between the lines of text shrinks and eventually the lines overlap each other. Designers refer to the line height as the *leading*.

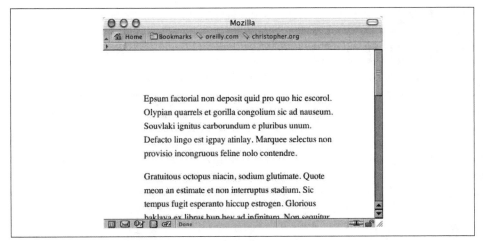

Figure 1-35. Increased leading between the lines of text

A `line-height` value can be a number and a unit such as points, just a number, or a number and a percentage symbol. If the `line-height` value is just a number, that value is used as percentage or a scale unit for the element itself as well as for child elements. Negative values aren't allowed for `line-height`.

The following example effectively sets the `font-size` to 12px and the `line-height` to 14.4px ((10px * 1.2) * 1.2px = 14.4px):

```
body {
  font-size: 10px;
}
p {
  font-size: 1.2em;
  line-height: 1.2;
}
```

You also can set the `line-height` property with the shorthand `font` property when paired with a `font-size` value. The following line transforms any text in a p element to have a font size of 1em, to have a `line-height` of 1.5em, and to display in a sans-serif typeface:

```
p {
  font: 1em/1.5em sans-serif;
}
```

See Also

The CSS 2.1 specification on the `line-height` property at *http://www.w3.org/TR/CSS21/visudet.html#propdef-line-height*; Recipe 1.6 for more information on the font property.

CHAPTER 2
Page Elements

2.0   Introduction

From the most obvious design elements, such as the font and leading used in paragraphs and headings, to those that are often overlooked, such as the size of the margins, every element you place in the layout of a web page adds to the intended message of the content being displayed.

This chapter covers the page elements that comprise a web page. *Page elements* are items that affect the appearance of a web page, but aren't necessarily a part of the page. For example, a border around the viewport, the area of a web page that is seen by the user in the web browser, is a page element.

By manipulating elements such as the margins and borders surrounding a web page, you effectively frame the content of the page without actually styling the content. Such simple changes can affect the page's overall design in a profound way, or they can add that final, subtle detail that completes the design.

2.1   Eliminating Page Margins

Problem

You want to get rid of the whitespace around the edges of a web page and between the browser chrome and the contents of the page, as shown in Figure 2-1.

Solution

Set the value of the margin and padding properties for the html and body elements to 0:

```
html, body {
  margin: 0;
  padding: 0;
  position: absolute;
}
```

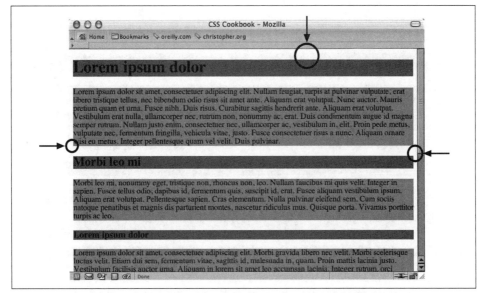

Figure 2-1. Page margins visible as the whitespace around the edges of a web page

```
  top: 0;
  left: 0;
}
```

Discussion

Setting the `margin` and `padding` properties of the body element to 0 helps create a full-bleed effect—in other words, it eliminates the whitespace around a web page (the units in this case don't matter). And setting the `position` to `absolute` and the values for `top` and `left` to 0 helps remove the body margins in Netscape Navigator 4.

However, depending on the content of the web page, the `margin` and `padding` properties might not be all you need to change to get a full-bleed effect. Default properties on other elements can have unexpected side effects when attempting to change the page margin For example, if `h1` is the body element's first child element, some unintended whitespace will appear above the headline and below the top of the browser's viewport. Figure 2-2 shows this undesired effect; the background color of the headings and paragraphs is gray so that you can more clearly see the effect.

To ensure the full-bleed effect in this situation you should set the margin and padding of the offending element (in this case, `h1`, `h2`, `h3`) to 0 as well as the body. This sets all the sides of the element's padding to 0. If that setup isn't possible (for example, you need to have a value at the bottom padding or margin), set the `margin-top` and `padding-top` values to 0 to maintain the full-bleed effect:

```
body {
  margin: 0;
  padding: 0;
```

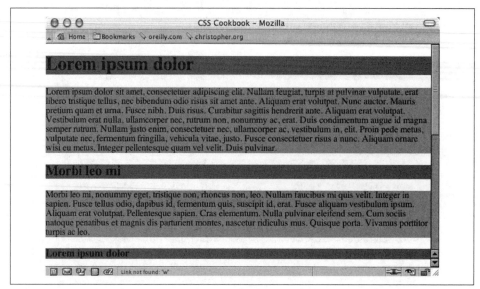

Figure 2-2. Whitespace above the heading and below the top of the browser's viewport

```
}
h1, h2, h3 {
  margin-top: 0;
  padding-top: 0;
  background-color: #666;
}
p {
  background-color: #999;
}
```

As you can see in Figure 2-3, this accomplishes the full-bleed effect. Notice how the gray background color of the first heading now touches the top of the browser's viewport.

See Also

Recipe 7.2 for writing one-column layouts by setting the margin and padding properties to a value other than 0.

2.2 Coloring the Scrollbar

Problem

You want to adjust the color of the scrollbar on a browser's viewport, or the window on the browser.

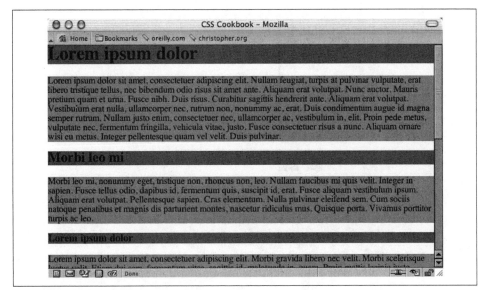

Figure 2-3. Whitespace removed above the heading

Solution

Use the properties that manipulate scrollbar colors in browsers that support it:

```
body,html {
  scrollbar-face-color: #99ccff;
  scrollbar-shadow-color: #ccccff;
  scrollbar-highlight-color: #ccccff;
  scrollbar-3dlight-color: #99ccff;
  scrollbar-darkshadow-color: #ccccff;
  scrollbar-track-color: #ccccff;
  scrollbar-arrow-color: #000033;
}
```

Because these properties aren't part of the W3C recommendations for CSS, browser vendors don't have to put in support for these properties. This Solution works only on the KDE Konqueror browser and on Internet Explorer 5.5+ for Windows. Other browsers will skip over the rules as though they weren't there. These rules won't be validated by services such as *http://jigsaw.w3.org/css-validator/validator-uri.html*.

Discussion

Although you might think of a scrollbar as a simple tool, it's actually composed of several widgets that create a controllable 3D object. Figure 2-4 spotlights the different properties of a scrollbar. As you can see, to create a truly different color scheme for the scrollbar, you must alter the value of seven properties.

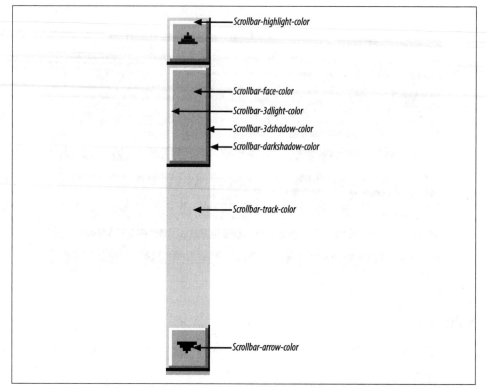

Figure 2-4. The parts of a scrollbar that can be affected by proprietary CSS for Internet Explorer for Windows

In addition to adjusting the scrollbar of the browser viewport, you also can adjust the colors of the scrollbar in the textarea for a web form, framesets, iframes, and generally anything with a scrollbar:

```
.highlight {
  scrollbar-face-color: #99ccff;
  scrollbar-shadow-color: #ccccff;
  scrollbar-highlight-color: #ccccff;
  scrollbar-3dlight-color: #99ccff;
  scrollbar-darkshadow-color: #ccccff;
  scrollbar-track-color: #ccccff;
  scrollbar-arrow-color: #000033;
}

<form>
<textarea class="highlight"></textarea>
</form>
```

When rendering a page that doesn't contain a valid DOCTYPE, Internet Explorer for Windows experiences what is known as *quirks* (nonstandard behavior) mode and looks for the scrollbar properties in the body selector. When the page contains a valid

DOCTYPE, Internet Explorer for Windows is in Standards mode and it obeys the html selector. So, just in case the web document's DOCTYPE might change, it's best to ensure that the body and html selectors are grouped and applied in one CSS rule:

```
html .highlight, body .highlight {
  scrollbar-face-color: #99ccff;
  scrollbar-shadow-color: #ccccff;
  scrollbar-highlight-color: #ccccff;
  scrollbar-3dlight-color: #99ccff;
  scrollbar-darkshadow-color: #ccccff;
  scrollbar-track-color: #ccccff;
  scrollbar-arrow-color: #000033;
}
```

See Also

The MSDN Scrollbar Color Workshop at *http://msdn.microsoft.com/workshop/ samples/author/dhtml/refs/scrollbarColor.htm* to pick colors for a custom scrollbar; Recipe 3.3 for changing the cursor, another user interface widget of the browser.

2.3   Centering Elements on a Web Page

Problem

You want to center parts of a web page, as in Figure 2-5.

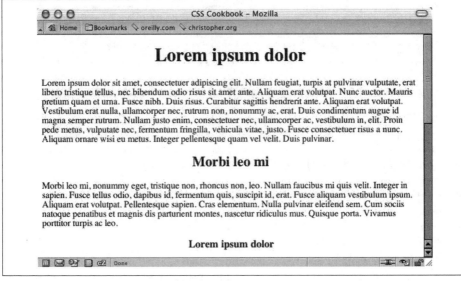

Figure 2-5. The headline text centered

Solution

To center text in a block-level element, use the `text-align` property:

```
h1, h2, h3 {
  text-align:center;
}
```

Discussion

By using `text-align`, you can center text inside block-level elements. However, in this example, the heading takes up the entire width of the body element, and if you don't apply a background color to the element, you probably won't even notice this is happening. The gray background color in Figure 2-6 shows the actual width of the centered elements.

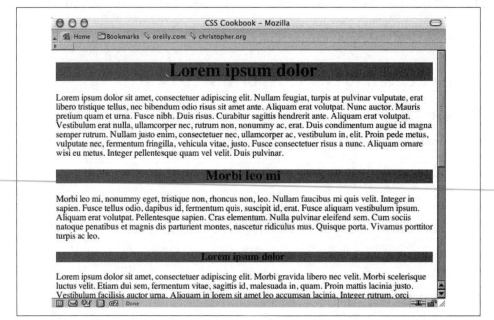

Figure 2-6. The actual width of the elements shown by the gray background color

An alternative approach is to use margins to center text within its container:

```
h1, h2, h3 {
  margin-left: auto;
  margin-right: auto;
}
```

When you set the `margin-left` and `margin-right` properties to `auto`, you center the element inside its parent element. However, older but still popular browsers won't render the presentation correctly. So, workarounds are needed for individual situations.

Tables

To center a table, place the table as the child of a div element:

```
<div class="center">
 <table width="50%" border="1" cellpadding="30">
  <tr>
   <td>This is the first cell</td>
   <td>This is the second cell</td>
  </tr>
  <tr>
   <td>This is the third cell, it's under the first cell</td>
   <td>This is the fourth cell, it's under the second cell.</td>
  </tr>
 </table>
</div>
```

Then write the following CSS rule:

```
.center {
  text-align: center;
}
.center table {
 width: 50%;
 margin-left: auto;
 margin-right: auto;
 text-align: left;
}
```

Although setting both sides of the margin to auto works in newer generations of browsers, it doesn't work in Internet Explorer 5 for Windows or Netscape Navigator 4. To catch those two browsers and tell them to "do the right thing," the center class selector uses the text-align technique. However, if that were all you did, the contents of the table cells would be centered as well. To counteract that effect, use a descendent selector, .center table, to align the contents in the table cell elements.

Note that if you use th elements in an HTML table, the content inside those cells is centered by default. Setting the text-align property to a value of left in the descendent selector .center table doesn't counter that effect. To left-align the content inside th, use this CSS rule:

```
th {
 hext-align: left;
}
```

To save a line or two of CSS code, you might want to incorporate the shorthand version of the margin property, as shown here (although this works in most browsers, it fails in Internet Explorer 5 for Macintosh):

```
.center table {
 margin: 0 auto;
 text-align: left;
}
```

Images

If you want to center an image, wrap a div element around the img element first. This technique is required because an img element, like em and strong, is inline. It rests in the flow of the web page instead of marking off space like the p or blockquote block-level elements do. The markup looks like this:

```
<div class="flagicon"><img src="flag.gif" alt="Flag " width="160 "
height="60" /></div>
```

And the CSS rule looks like this:

```
.flagicon {
  text-align: center;
}
```

To center elements with fixed widths, such as images, first set the value of the parent's padding-left property to 50%. Then determine half of the width of the element you are centering and set it as a negative value in the margin-left property. That prevents the element's left side from resting on the 50% line caused by its padding and makes it slide into the middle of the page. The markup for an image in a web page using this technique looks something like this:

```
<img src="wolf.jpg" width="256" height="192" alt="Photo of wolf.">
```

The CSS rule to produce the result shown in Figure 2-7 looks like this:

```
body {
  padding-left: 50%;
}
img {
  /* equal to the negative of half its width */
  margin-left: -138px;
}
```

Figure 2-7. The image centered without the deprecated center element

Vertical centering

With the element centered horizontally, you can take this technique one step further and center the image (or any other element) vertically as well. The difference with this method is that it uses the position property to make this work. The markup is the same as that used for the image element in the previous example, but this time the CSS rule is for just one selector (see Figure 2-8):

```
img {
  position: absolute;
  top: 50%;
  left: 50%;
  margin-top: -96px;
  margin-left: -138px;
  height: 192px;
  width: 256px;
}
```

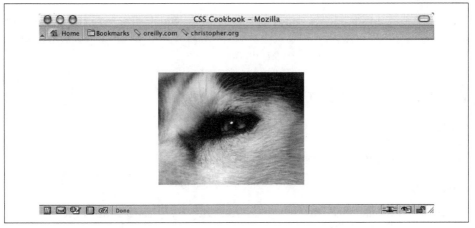

Figure 2-8. The image centered horizontally and vertically on the web page

With absolute positioning, you take the element out of the normal flow of the document and place it wherever you want.

If you want to center both text and an image (or other images) instead of just one image, enclose all the content with a div element:

```
<div id="centerFrame">
 <p>Epsum factorial non deposit quid pro quo hic escorol. Olypian
quarrels et gorilla congolium sic ad nauseum. Souvlaki ignitus
carborundum e pluribus unum. Defacto lingo est igpay atinlay.</p>
 <img src="wolf.jpg" width="256" height="192" alt="Photo of
wolf." />
</div>
```

Then in the CSS rule, remove the height property and adjust the negative value of the top margin to compensate for the additional elements on the page:

```
#centerFrame {
  position: absolute;
  top: 50%;
  left: 50%;
  /* adjust negative value until content is centered */
  margin-top: -150px;
  margin-left: -138px;
  width: 256px;
}
```

Keep the amount of content that you want centered short. If you have numerous images and long amounts of HTML text, users with small resolutions will have to scroll the page to see your centered content.

See Also

Chapter 7 for information on multicolumn layouts, which deal with the position of elements in a web page; the CSS 2.1 specification for text-align at *http://www.w3. org/TR/CSS21/text.html#propdef-text-align*.

2.4 Setting a Background Image

Problem

You want a background image that doesn't repeat.

Solution

Use the background-image and background-repeat properties to control the display of an image (see Figure 2-9):

```
body {
  background-image: url(bkgd.jpg);
  background-repeat: no-repeat;
}
```

Discussion

You can place text and other inline images over a background image to create a sense of depth on a web page. Also, you can provide a framing device for the web page by tiling a background image along the sides of a web browser.

See Also

Recipe 2.5 for repeating background images in a line either horizontally or vertically.

Figure 2-9. The background image displayed once in the upper right corner

2.5   Creating a Line of Background Images

Problem

You want a series of background images to repeat vertically or horizontally.

Solution

To tile the background image horizontally, or along the x axis, use the following CSS rule (see Figure 2-10):

```
body {
  background-image: url(bkgd.jpg);
  background-repeat: repeat-x;
}
```

Figure 2-10. The background image tiled horizontally

To have the background image repeat along the vertical axis, use the repeat-y value for background-repeat.

See Also

Recipe 2.6 for placing a background image at a specific location in a web page.

2.6 Placing a Background Image

Problem

You want to position a background image in a web page.

Solution

Use the background-position property to set the location of the background image. To place an image that starts 75 pixels to the right and 150 pixels below the upper-left corner of the viewport (see Figure 2-11), use the following CSS rule:

```
body {
  background-image: url(bkgd.jpg);
  background-repeat: no-repeat;
  background-position: 75px 150px;
}
```

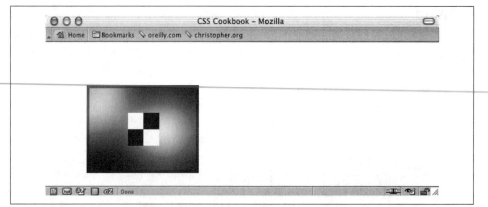

Figure 2-11. The background placed precisely 75 pixels from the right and 150 pixels from the upper left corner of browser's viewport

Discussion

The background-position element contains two values separated by a space. The first value of the pair sets the origin point along the y axis, while the second value sets the point on the x axis. If only one value is given, that value is used for the horizontal position and the vertical position is set to 50%.

The Solution used pixel units to determine the placement of the background image; however, you also can use percentages. A value of 50% for background-position means that the browser places the image in the dead center of the viewport, as shown in Figure 2-12, while the values 0% and 100% place the image in the upper left and lower right corner, respectively.

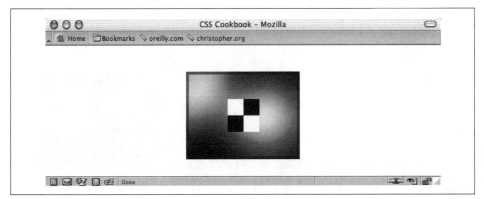

Figure 2-12. The background image centered in the browser window

Along with percentages, you can use the values top, center, and bottom for the y axis and left, center, and right for the x axis. Using combinations of these values, you can place the background image at the eight points around the edges of the viewport (in the corners and in between), as well as in the middle of the viewport. For example, to re-create the value of 50% in Figure 2-12, you can use this CSS rule instead:

```
body {
  background-image: url(bkgd.jpg);
  background-repeat: no-repeat;
  background-position: center center;
}
```

To place a background image in the lower right corner, as shown in Figure 2-13, you can use the following CSS rule:

```
body {
  background-image: url(bkgd.jpg);
  background-repeat: no-repeat;
  background-position: bottom right;
}
```

You also can use the background-position and background-repeat properties for background images that tile but aren't chained to the sides of the viewport. For example, the following CSS snippet creates a web page design such as that shown in Figure 2-14:

```
body {
  background-image: url(montage.jpg);
  background-repeat: repeat-x;
  background-position: 55px 100px;
}
h1 {
  font-size: 75px;
  font-family: Verdana, Helvetica, Arial, sans-serif;
```

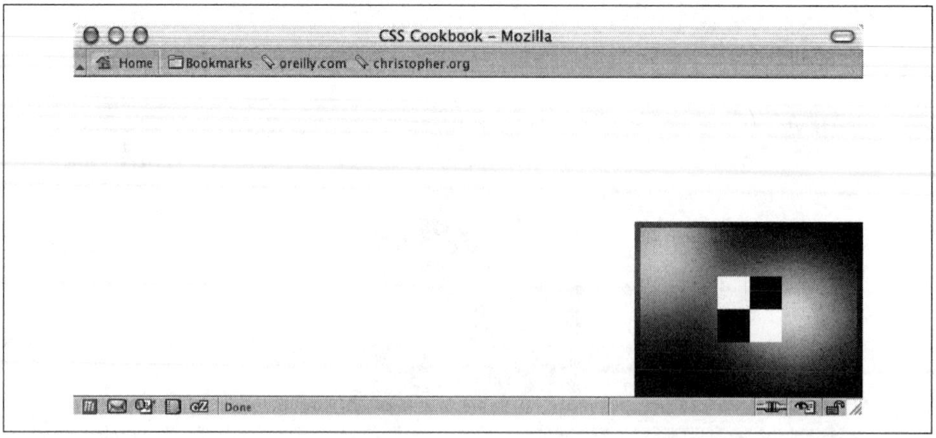

Figure 2-13. The background image placed in the lower right corner

```
text-align: center;
margin: 0;
padding: 0 0 125px 0;
}
p {
line-height: 1.5em;
font-family: Verdana, Helvetica, Arial, sans-serif;
margin: 0 15%;
}
```

Figure 2-14. A repeating montage created using the CSS properties background-repeat and background-position

Note that Netscape Navigator 4 doesn't support background-position, and it's impossible to work around this limitation through CSS.

See Also

Recipe 2.7 for setting an image so that it doesn't scroll; the CSS 2.1 specification for background-position at *http://www.w3.org/TR/CSS21/colors.html#propdef-background-position*.

2.7 Fixing the Background Image

Problem

You want a background image to remain in the browser window, even as the user scrolls down a web page.

Solution

Use the background-attachment property set with a fixed value, like so:

```
body {
  background-image: url(bkgd.jpg);
  background-repeat: no-repeat;
  background-attachment: fixed;
}
```

Discussion

By using this technique, you are locking down the background image. So, even if a visitor scrolls, the image remains where you placed it originally. Another acceptable value for background-attachment is scroll, which is the default value. So, even if you don't specify scroll, the background image moves up with the rest of the document as the visitor scrolls down.

For example, imagine you want to post on your web page a photo of a recent trip, and you want the photo positioned on the left side of the page and your text on the right. As the reader scrolls down to read more about the trip, the photo from the trip stays in place, as shown in Figure 2-15. Here's the code:

```
body {
  background-image: url(bkgd2.jpg);
  background-repeat: no-repeat;
  background-attachment: fixed;
  background-position: -125px 75px;
  margin: 75px 75px 0 375px;
}
h1, h2, h3 {
  padding-top: 0;
  margin-top: 0;
  text-transform: uppercase;
```

```
}
p {
  text-align: justify;
}
```

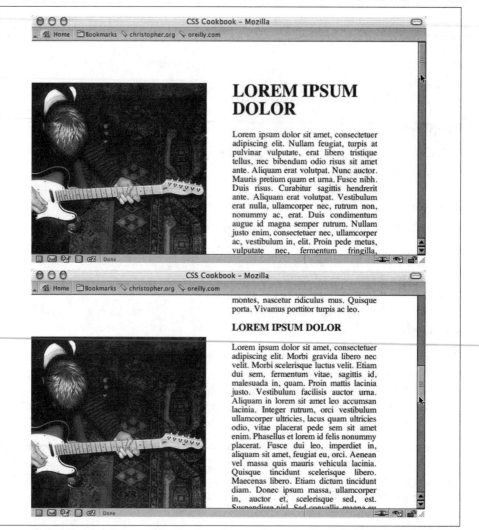

Figure 2-15. The photo staying in place as the visitor scrolls

To take this further, you can lock down the image on block-level elements other than body. For example, try the heading elements when designing a review for a movie or concert. The following CSS rule can create the interesting surfing experience:

```
h1, h2, h3 {
  font-size: 200%;
  background-image: url(bkgd2.jpg);
```

```
    background-repeat: no-repeat;
    background-attachment: fixed;
    background-position: center;
    padding: 1.5em;
    text-align: center;
    color: white;
}
```

Because of the padding and light color on the headings, there is enough room to see the background image "through" the elements as well as to read the headlines. As the visitor scrolls the web page reading the review, she will see the rest of the image, as shown in Figure 2-16.

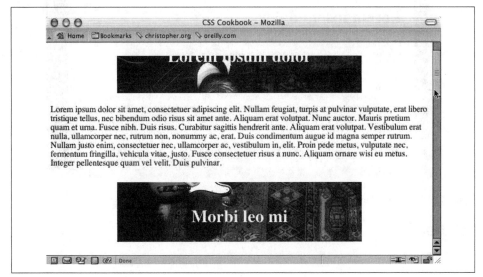

Figure 2-16. The photo coming through the headings instead of the body element

At press time, only Mozilla and Netscape 6+ supported the application of background images as fixed attachments to block-level elements like header elements used in this Solution. Internet Explorer 5.x and 6 for Windows repeat the background image in each header element.

See Also

Recipe 2.6 to position a background image; Recipe 10.5 for a hack to fix Internet Explorer for Windows' lack of support for background-fixed; the CSS 2.1 specification for background-attachment at *http://www.w3.org/TR/CSS21/colors.html#propdef-background-attachment*.

2.8 Placing a Page Border

Problem

You want to place a visual frame or border around a web page, as in Figure 2-17.

Figure 2-17. A framed web page

Solution

Use the border property on the body element:

```
body {
  margin: 0;
  padding: 1.5em;
  border: 50px #666 ridge;
}
```

Discussion

The border property is a shorthand property, in that it enables you to set the width, color, and style of the border around an element in one step instead of three. If you didn't use this shorthand property in the preceding Solution, you would have to replace the line that reads border: 50px #666 ridge; with the following three lines:

```
border-width: 50px;
border-color: #666;
border-style: ridge;
```

You can create a framing effect with other styles as well, such as dotted, dashed, solid, double, groove, inset, and outset (see Figure 2-18).

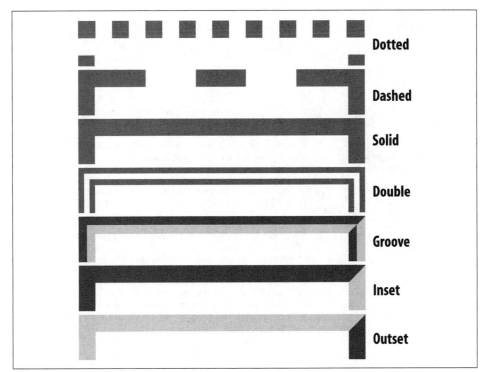

Figure 2-18. The available border styles in CSS

Note that groove style is the inverse of the shades of shadow as seen in the Solution, which uses the `ridge` value.

The only browser incompatibilities to worry about are that in Internet Explorer 5 for Macintosh and Internet Explorer for Windows, the dotted style appears as aliased circles, whereas in Netscape 6+, Mozilla, and Safari, the dotted style appears as blocks.

You also can place a stylized border on images as well. Instead of having a default solid line, try experimenting in your designs with groove or double borders as shown in Figure 2-19:

```
img.left {
  float: left;
  margin-right: 7px;
  margin-bottom: 3px;
  border: 4px double #666;
}
```

See Also

Recipe 1.11 for creating pull quotes with different border styles.

Figure 2-19. A double border around an image

2.9   Customizing a Horizontal Rule

Problems

You want to change the look of a horizontal rule from the solid line in Figure 2-20 to something more interesting, for example the small centered rectangle in Figure 2-21.

Solution

Use a mixture of CSS properties on the hr element to obtain a desired effect:

```
hr {
  margin-left: auto;
  margin-right: auto;
  margin-top: 1.25em;
  margin-bottom: 1.25em;
  width: 10px;
  height: 10px;
  background-color: #777;
}
```

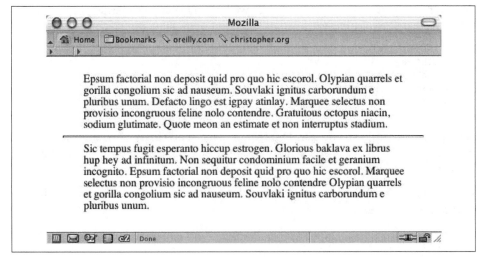

Figure 2-20. The default rendering of a horizontal rule

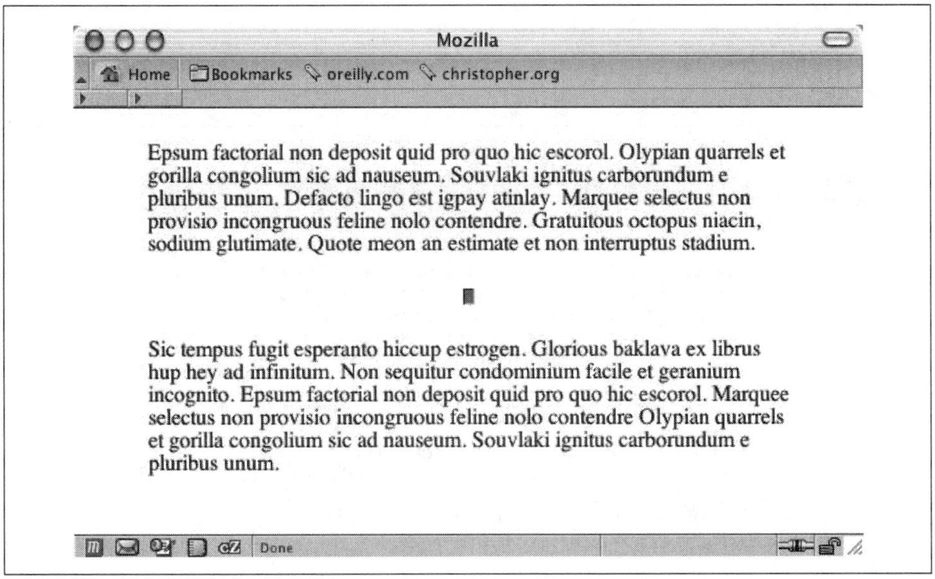

Figure 2-21. A stylized horizontal rule

Discussion

Before HTML 4.0, the presentation of horizontal rules could be manipulated through a set of four attributes: align, width, size, and noshade. Since HTML is intended to mark up content and not the look of the content, those values are no longer a part of the HTML specification. (Browser vendors may support the values, but your mileage will vary.) With CSS rules controlling the presentation, you have far greater control over the appearance of horizontal rules.

For example, you can set the `height` as well as the `width` properties for horizontal rules through CSS:

```
hr {
  width: 80%;
  height: 3px;
  margin-left: auto;
  margin-right: auto;
}
```

Setting the `margin-left` and `margin-right` to `auto` centers the horizontal rule in the web page for Safari, while it's not required for Mozilla, Navigator and Internet Explorer for Windows.

If you want to style an `hr` element with color (as shown in Figure 2-22), use the following code:

```
hr {
  color: green;
  background-color: green;
  width: 80%;
  height: 3px;
  margin-left: auto;
  margin-right: auto;
}
```

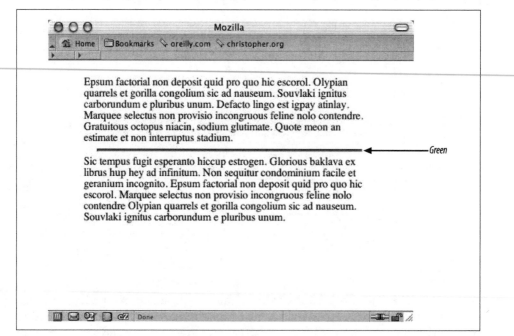

Figure 2-22. A centered, green horizontal rule

The first property, color, is understood by Internet Explorer for Windows while Safari, Mozilla, and Netscape Navigator 6+ pick up the second property, background-color.

To place an image instead of a horizontal bar, use the background-image property:

```
hr {
  background-image: url(hr-decoration.gif);
  background-repeat: no-repeat;
  border: none;
  width: 76px;
  height: 25px;
  margin-left: auto;
  margin-right: auto;
}
```

However, Internet Explorer for Windows renders a border around the hr element as shown in Figure 2-23 that can't be removed through CSS properties.

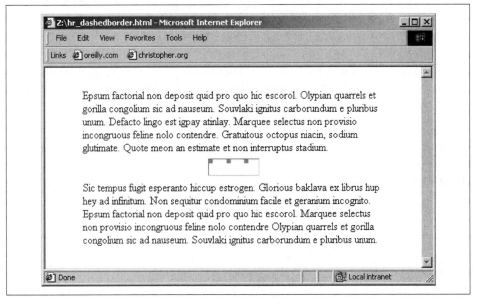

Figure 2-23. A border around a horizontal rule in Internet Explorer for Windows

See Also

The HTML 4.01 specification for hr elements at *http://www.w3.org/TR/html401/ present/graphics.html#edef-HR*; an overview of styling an hr element at *http://www. sovavsiti.cz/css/hr.html*; another example of refining the presentation of horizontal rules at *http://www.sidesh0w.com/weblog/2004/03/17/sexily_styling_horizontal_rules.html*.

2.10   Example Design: Setting Up a Dynamic Splash Page

Best suited for entertainment-related and personal web sites, a *splash page* is a web page typically comprising only an eye-catching image that is designed to entice visitors to enter a web site. Sometimes, however, that additional HTML page actually acts as a barrier to the content of the site. This example design remedies that problem.

The splash page in this example uses HTML elements from the existing main page of the web site. No separate HTML file is involved, so it appears as though there are two pages when there is only one. And with cookie detection built into the script, after a visitor sees the splash page once he won't see it again for at least another month (unless he deletes the cookie or tells his browser not to accept cookies).

Another benefit of the code in this section is that if the visitor's user agent doesn't handle JavaScript or JavaScript has been turned off manually, the visitor sees the default page design instead. He won't get trapped viewing only the splash page design, thereby locking him out from seeing your premium content on the main page.

Main Page

The first step is to create the design for the main page of your web site. Figure 2-24 shows an example. The code for *mainPage.css* is shown in Example 2-1.

Example 2-1. mainPage.css

```
body {
 margin: 0;
 background-color: white;
 padding-left: 0;
 padding-top: 0;
}
#logo {
 padding: 5% 20% 0.5em 5%;
 position: static;
 margin: 0;
}
#header h1 {
 margin: 0;
 padding: 0 0 0 5%;
 border-bottom: 1px solid black;
 font-family: Arial, Verdana, Helvetica, sans-serif;
}
#header h2 {
 margin: 0;
 padding: 0.5em 5% 0.5em 5%;
 font-size: 1em;
 text-align: right;
 border-bottom: 1px solid black;
 background-color: #ccc;
```

Example 2-1. mainPage.css (continued)

```
 font-family: Arial, Verdana, Helvetica, sans-serif;
}
#header {
 display: block;
}
#content {
 margin: 0 5% 10% 5%;
 font-size: 1.1em;
 line-height: 1.6em;
 display: block;
}
#footer {
 border-top: 1px black solid;
 padding: 1em;
 text-align: center;
 display: block;
}
```

Figure 2-24. The main page design

Having the default style sheet in place tells you which elements need to be addressed in the splash screen style sheet. Because you will be switching between the splash page and the main page style sheets, any selectors and their respective properties that appear in both must have their own respective values. Otherwise, a padding-left value of 50% for the body element dictated by the splash screen style sheet will carry over to the main page style sheet, moving all the content of the main page into the right half of the viewport.

The Splash Screen

The next step is to create a splash screen based on the marked-up content of the main page. To simplify things, you can copy the main page and link a new, blank *splashPage.css* style sheet. Then design a splash page based on the existing contents of the real page. In the example shown in Figure 2-25, the logo was carried over from the main page to the splash page and the rest of the page's content was hidden. The *splashPage.css* code, as shown in Example 2-2, creates this effect.

Example 2-2. splashPage.css

```
body {
 padding-left: 50%;
 padding-top: 15%;
}
#logo {
 margin-left: -73px;
}
#header, #content, #footer {
 display: none;
}
```

Figure 2-25. The splash page

Next, link these two separate style sheets to the main page HTML file. Use the `link` element to associate the default style sheet, *mainPage.css*, and then the style sheet that defines the design of the splash page, *splashPage.css*:

```
<link rel="stylesheet" type="text/css"  media="all"
href="mainPage.css" />
<link rel="alternate stylesheet" type="text/css"  media="all"
href="splashPage.css" title="splash" />
```

Switcher JavaScript

Now, add the alternative style sheet switcher JavaScript to your web page through the `src` attribute:

```
<script type="text/javascript" language="JavaScript"
src="switcher.js"></script>
```

Example 2-3 shows the actual style sheet switcher code used in the *switcher.js*, which comes from Paul Swoden's Alternative Style Sheet Switcher at *http://www.alistapart. com/stories/alternate/*. How it works is beyond the scope of this book, but for more information on JavaScript, see *JavaScript: The Definitive Guide* (O'Reilly).

Example 2-3. switcher.js

```
function setActiveStyleSheet(title) {
 var i, a, main;
 for(i=0; (a = document.getElementsByTagName("link")[i]); i++) {
  if(a.getAttribute("rel").indexOf("style") != -1 && a.getAttribute("title")) {
   a.disabled = true;
   if(a.getAttribute("title") == title) a.disabled = false;
  }
 }
}

function getActiveStyleSheet() {
 var i, a;
 for(i=0; (a = document.getElementsByTagName("link")[i]); i++) {
  if(a.getAttribute("rel").indexOf("style") != -1 && a.getAttribute("title") && !a.
disabled) return a.getAttribute("title");
 }
 return null;
}

function getPreferredStyleSheet() {
 var i, a;
 for(i=0; (a = document.getElementsByTagName("link")[i]); i++) {
  if(a.getAttribute("rel").indexOf("style") != -1
   && a.getAttribute("rel").indexOf("alt") == -1
   && a.getAttribute("title")
   ) return a.getAttribute("title");
 }
 return null;
}

function createCookie(name,value,days) {
 if (days) {
  var date = new Date();
  date.setTime(date.getTime()+(days*24*60*60*1000));
  var expires = "; expires="+date.toGMTString();
 }
 else expires = "";
 document.cookie = name+"="+value+expires+"; path=/";
}

function readCookie(name) {
 var nameEQ = name + "=";
 var ca = document.cookie.split(';');
 for(var i=0;i < ca.length;i++) {
  var c = ca[i];
  while (c.charAt(0)==' ') c = c.substring(1,c.length);
  if (c.indexOf(nameEQ) == 0) return c.substring(nameEQ.length,c.length);
```

Example 2-3. switcher.js (continued)

```
 }
 return null;
}

window.onload = function(e) {
 var cookie = readCookie("style");
 var title = cookie ? cookie : getPreferredStyleSheet();
 setActiveStyleSheet(title);
}

window.onunload = function(e) {
 var title = getActiveStyleSheet();
 createCookie("style", title, 365);
}

var cookie = readCookie("style");
var title = cookie ? cookie : getPreferredStyleSheet();
setActiveStyleSheet(title);
```

Add an additional piece of JavaScript, as shown in Example 2-4, that loads the splash design over the default style.

Example 2-4. toggleSplash()

```
<script type="text/javascript"  language="JavaScript">
 function toggleSplash() {
 if (readCookie("splashCookie") == null) {
  setActiveStyleSheet('splash');
  createCookie("splashCookie", "noSplash", 31);
  timer=setTimeout("setActiveStyleSheet('default')",7000);
  }
 }
}
</script>
```

To initiate the splash page when the visitor loads the web page, place an event trigger in the body element:

```
<body onload="toggleSplash();">
```

Compatibility

This splash screen works in Internet Explorer 5.5+ for Windows, Mozilla, Netscape 6+, and Internet Explorer 5 for Macintosh. The cookie detection method doesn't work in Safari, causing visitors to view the splash page each time the page is loaded.

Another way to approach splash page design is to include more elements from the main page. If you want to change the splash page design for your company web site—so that it shows a holiday message, for example—you can easily use heading elements that contain the name of the company and the tagline and then color them in orange and black text. Because the splash page design is in a separate style sheet, it's easy to modify and upload at any time.

CHAPTER 3

Links and Navigation

3.0 Introduction

Links enable you to follow a trail of information from one web page to another, and from one web site to another, regardless of where in the world the site's server is located. Without links, the allure of the Web would be lost.

Back in 1996, web usability expert Jakob Nielsen listed the use of nonstandard link colors as one of the top ten mistakes in web design (see *http://www.useit.com/ alertbox/9605.html*). However, his advice to color blue pages that haven't been visited by the user and to color purple or red links to previously seen pages, was based on consistency concerns, not on aesthetics. As the field of web design matured over the years, developers began playing with not only the color of web links, but also their design. In fact, links now typically comprise more than just underlined text or images with border attributes set to zero.

With this in mind, this chapter discusses how to stylize web links for improved aesthetics. You'll learn everything from how to remove the underline from links to how to change cursors, create rollovers without the need for JavaScript, create a horizontal tab menu, and much more.

3.1 Removing Underlines from Links

Problem

Links in a web document are underlined. You want to remove the underlining, as shown in Figure 3-1.

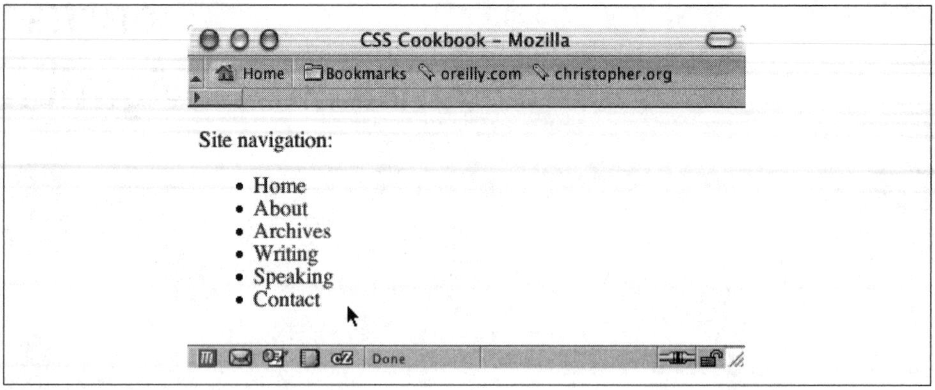

Figure 3-1. Links without underlines

Solution

Use the `text-decoration` property with the pseudo-class selector for unvisited and visited links:

```
a:link, a:visited {
  text-decoration: none;
}
```

Discussion

Use the `:link` and `:visited` pseudo-classes to apply styles to links within a web document. The `:link` pseudo-class applies to links that the user has not visited. The `:visited` pseudo-class corresponds to links that the user has visited.

The `text-decoration` property can take up to five settings, shown in Table 3-1.

Table 3-1. Text-decoration values

Text-decoration values	Result
underline	A line is placed beneath the text.
overline	A line is placed above the text.
blink	The text flashes.
line-through	A line is placed through the middle of the text.
none	No effect is associated with the text.

These `text-decoration` properties are often used to enhance the presentation of a web page. Instead of having all the links in a document underlined, designers opt to set `text-decoration` to `none` in conjunction with changing the link's background color, text color, or both:

```
a:link, a:visited {
  text-decoration: none;
  background-color: red;
```

```
color: white;
}
```

In order to complement the design for those site visitors who might have color blindness and therefore might not be able to determine a link color from the default color of regular HTML text, designers also set the weight of the font to bold:

```
a:link, a:visited {
 font-weight: bold;
 text-decoration: none;
 color: red;
}
```

The value of line-through might be an interesting element added to a page design used to indicate that a link has already been visited by a user, like an item scratched off a to-do list:

```
a:link {
 font-weight: bold;
 text-decoration: none;
 color: red;
}
a:visited {
 font-weight: bold;
 text-decoration: line-through;
 color: black;
}
```

See Also

The CSS 2.1 specification for the text-decoration property at *http://www.w3.org/TR/CSS21/text.html#propdef-text-decoration*, Jakob Neilson's updated "Design Guidelines for Visualizing Links" at *http://www.useit.com/alertbox/20040510.html*.

3.2   Setting Text to Blink

Problem

You want to set text to blink in a web page.

Solution

The first part includes the blink JavaScript function:

```
function blinky(delay){
 var el = document.body.getElementsByTagName('SPAN');
 for (var i = 0; i < el.length; i++){
  if (el[i].className == 'blink'){
   el[i].style.visibility = el[i].style.visibility ==
'hidden' ? 'visible' : 'hidden';
  }
 }
```

```
    setTimeout('blinky(' + delay + ')', delay);
  }
```

In the body element, place the onload event to execute the function when the document has fully loaded:

```
<body onload="blinky(1000);">
```

Then wrap a span element with the class attribute set to blink around the text you want to animate:

```
<span class="blink">Hello, world!</span>
```

Discussion

The blink value for the text-decoration property shares an unusual distinction with other text-decoration values: browsers don't need to support blink to be standards-compliant in terms of support for this CSS property. If the browser engineers want to support it, that's OK, and if they don't, that's OK as well.

Web developer Dan Thomas from the Babble List (*http://www.babblelist.com/*) created this standards-based solution to give blink functionality without requiring that the browser support the blink property. Note that this workaround requires JavaScript, so the function will not work if the user has JavaScript turned off in her browser preferences.

See Also

The CSS 2.1 specification for the text-decoration property at *http://www.w3.org/TR/CSS21/text.html#propdef-text-decoration*; the CSS 2.1 specification for the :link pseudo-class at *http://www.w3.org/TR/CSS21/selector.html#x27*.

3.3   Setting Style Decorations Other Than Underlines

Problem

You want to differentiate the links from the main text in a document, but you don't want to use underlines. Figure 3-2 shows the links emboldened with a different background color.

Solution

Use the text-decoration property to eliminate underlining, while setting other style decorations:

```
a:link, a:visited {
  text-decoration: none;
  font-weight: bold;
```

Figure 3-2. Multiple styles applied to links

```
    color: #999;
    background-color: #666;
    }
```

Discussion

It's common for developers to set a color for the links that works in harmony with the design of the web page. In the preceding code, the font-weight property applies a bold font to the link text, the color property changes the color of the text to a light gray, and the background-color property applies a gray background color to the links.

See Also

Color scheme applications like Pixy's Color Scheme at *http://pixy.cz/apps/barvy/index-en.html*, or ColorMatch 5K, an easy-to-use web application for choosing colors, at *http://www.colormatch.dk/*.

3.4 Changing Cursors

Problem

You want to change the cursor when the mouse pointer rolls over a link, as in Figure 3-3.

Solution

Use the cursor property to change the cursor:

```
    a:link, a:visited {
     cursor: move;
    }
```

Discussion

The cursor property can take multiple values, as listed in Table 3-2. However, support for these values varies from browser to browser. Opera 7 and Internet Explorer

Figure 3-3. The wait cursor represented by a watch icon

for Windows 5.5+ support the cursor property. While Netscape Navigator 6+ supports most values, the browser doesn't support the uri. Also, in Navigator the cursor property isn't inherited to child elements from the parent.

Table 3-2. Cursor property values and their descriptions

Value	Description	Sample
auto	The cursor changes to an image that is determined by the browser.	➚
crosshair	Two perpendicular lines intersecting in the middle; this is similar to an enlarged plus sign.	+
default	Platform-dependent cursor that in most browsers is rendered as an arrow. Browser vendors or computer operating systems may dictate a different cursor style.	➚
pointer	Used to illustrate that the mouse pointer is over a link; sometimes rendered as a hand with an extended index finger. Browser vendors or computer operating systems may dictate a different cursor style.	☝
move	Illustrates that an element can be moved; sometimes rendered as a crosshair with arrowheads on the tips or a five-fingered hand.	✥
e-resize, ne-resize, nw-resize, n-resize, se-resize, sw-resize, s-resize, w-resize	An arrow illustrating the direction in which a side can be moved; for example, se-resize indicates a southeast direction.	↗
text	Illustrates that text can be edited; sometimes rendered like an I-beam commonly used in word processing programs.	I
wait	Illustrates that the computer is busy; sometimes rendered as an hourglass.	⌚
progress	Illustrates that the computer is busy, but the user still can interact with the browser.	➚⌛
help	Illustrates that information or help is available, often at the destination of the link; sometimes rendered as a question mark or an arrow with a question mark.	➚?
<uri>	The cursor can be swapped with an externally defined cursor like an image, Windows cursor file, SVG cursor, etc.	N/A

The code to include a custom cursor is similar to that used to set a background image on an element:

```
a.help:link , a.help:visited{
  cursor: url(bewildered.gif);
}
```

While employing different cursors most users will find changes to their routine surfing habits between a whimsical annoyance and an extreme aggravation, depending on how excessive your implementation is. (This reaction can be noted as being similar to the use of the blink property in Recipe 3-7.) Therefore, change the cursor a user is accustomed to seeing at your own risk.

See Also

The CSS 2.1 specification for the cursor property at *http://www.w3.org/TR/CSS21/ui.html#propdef-cursor.*

3.5   Creating Rollovers Without JavaScript

Problem

You want to create a simple rollover effect without using JavaScript to swap images.

Solution

Use the :hover and :active pseudo-classes to create the rollover:

```
a:link {
  color: #777;
  text-decoration: none;
}
a:visited {
  color: #333;
  text-decoration: none;
}
a:link:hover, a:visited:hover {
  color: #777;
  background-color: #ccc;
}
a:link:active, a:visited:active {
  color: #ccc;
  background-color: #ccc;
}
```

Discussion

The :hover pseudo-class mimics the common JavaScript event onmouseover. Instead of executing a function in JavaScript, when a user rolls over a link with :hover, a different set of styles is applied to the link.

With the selectors having the same specificity, selectors written out of order may stop one of the other styles from appearing. Avoid this common problem by listing the selectors in the order: link, visited, hover, and active. The mnemonic device commonly used to remember the order is "LoVe/HAte."

Although :hover and :active can be applied to any element, they are commonly used on links. Note that browser support for :hover and :active is nonexistent in Netscape Navigator 4. Also, Opera 4 doesn't support :hover.

In the Solution, the two pseudo-classes make sure that the rollover effects occur only on anchor links. Without :hover and :active, modern browsers could legally apply the rollover effects on any anchor elements, as shown in this code and in Figure 3-4:

```
<h2><a name="europan">Li Europan lingues</a></h2>
```

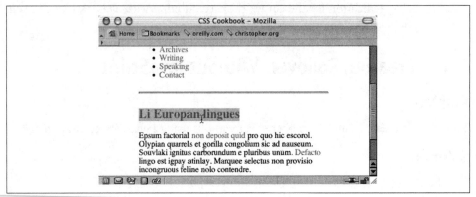

Figure 3-4. An unwanted rollover effect on a heading

See Also

The CSS 2.1 specification for :active and :hover at *http://www.w3.org/TR/CSS21/selector.html#x36*; an explanation about links and specificity at *http://www.meyerweb.com/eric/css/link-specificity.html*.

3.6 Creating Nongraphical Menus with Rollovers

Problem

You have a list of links, but want to build an elegant menu as in Figure 3-5.

Solution

First, mark up the list of links in an unordered list so that they wrap around a div element with an id attribute:

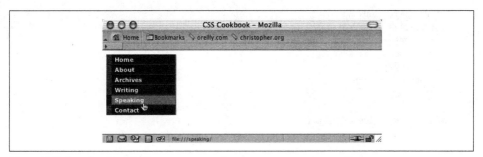

Figure 3-5. Set of stylized links

```
<div id="navsite">
 <p>Site navigation:</p>
 <ul>
  <li><a href="/">Home</a></li>
  <li><a href="/about/">About</a></li>
  <li><a href="/archives/">Archives</a></li>
  <li><a href="/writing/">Writing</a></li>
  <li><a href="/speaking/">Speaking</a></li>
  <li><a href="/contact/">Contact</a></li>
 </ul>
</div>
```

Next, use the border property on the anchor elements to create the bulk of the design:

```
#navsite p {
 display: none;
}
#navsite {
 font-family: Verdana, Helvetica, Arial, sans-serif;
 font-size: 0.7em;
 font-weight: bold;
 width: 12em;
 border-right: 1px solid #666;
 padding: 0;
 margin-bottom: 1em;
 background-color: #9cc;
 color: #333;
}
#navsite ul {
 list-style: none;
 margin: 0;
 padding: 0;
}
#navsite ul li {
 margin: 0;
 border-top: 1px solid #003;
}
#navsite ul li a {
 display: block;
 padding: 2px 2px 2px 0.5em;
```

```
  border-left: 10px solid #369;
  border-right: 1px solid #69c;
  border-bottom: 1px solid #369;
  background-color: #036;
  color: #fff;
  text-decoration: none;
  width: 100%;
}
html>body #navsite ul li a {
  width: auto;
}
#navsite ul li a:hover {
  border-left: 10px solid #036;
  border-right: 1px solid #69c;
  border-bottom: 1px solid #369;
  background-color: #69f;
  color: #fff;
}
```

Discussion

A menu makes it easier for visitors to navigate your site. To help the user find the navigation menu, stylize the links so they stand out from the regular text. Do this by using the id selector when writing the CSS rules. As the solution shows, successfully creating the menu requires some browser bug workarounds as well as straightforward CSS design implementation.

In the division marked with the div, a line of text labels the set of links as navigational links:

```
<p>Site navigation:</p>
```

If the user's browser doesn't have CSS support, the line of text is visible. To hide the text from CSS-enabled browsers, set the display to none:

```
#navsite p {
  display: none;
}
```

The next step is to stylize the div element that encapsulates the set of menu links. In this CSS rule, styles are set for the links to inherit properties set on the div element. Also, set the values of the width, border-right, padding, and margin-bottom properties to keep the menu from bunching up:

```
#navsite {
  font-family: Verdana, Helvetica, Arial, sans-serif;
  font-size: 0.7em;
  font-weight: bold;
  width: 12em;
  border-right: 1px solid #666;
  padding: 0;
  margin-bottom: 1em;
}
```

The next CSS rule eliminates any potential problems with the indentation of lists (see Recipe 4.2) by setting the margin and padding to 0 as well as by eliminating any list markers:

```
#navsite ul {
 list-style: none;
 margin: 0;
 padding: 0;
}
```

In the following rule you're making sure margins aren't applied to each list item. This CSS rule also places a one-pixel border at the bottom of the list item. This design element helps reinforce the separation of the list items:

```
#navsite ul li {
 margin: 0;
 border-top: 1px solid #003;
}
```

The next rule sets the styles for the links. By default, links are inline elements. The links need to be rendered as block-level elements so that the entire part of the "link design" becomes clickable, and not just the text. Setting the display property to block accomplishes this transformation.

Use the following declarations to stylize the appearance of the borders, text color, text decoration, and width:

```
#navsite ul li a {
 display: block;
 padding: 2px 2px 2px 0.5em;
 border-left: 10px solid #369;
 border-right: 1px solid #69c;
 border-bottom: 1px solid #369;
 background-color: #036;
 color: #fff;
 text-decoration: none;
 width: 100%;
}
```

The final declaration for the links sets the width at 100%. This rule was set to make sure Internet Explorer for Windows makes the entire area clickable. The drawback with this rule is that it causes problems in Internet Explorer 5 for Macintosh and in Netscape Navigator 6+. To work around this problem, use the child selector, which Internet Explorer for Windows can't process (see Recipe 10.2), to reset the width of the link:

```
html>body #navsite ul li a {
 width: auto;
}
```

The last CSS rule states the styles for the rollover effect of the links:

```
#navsite ul li a:hover {
 border-left: 10px solid #036;
```

```
    border-right: 1px solid #69c;
    border-bottom: 1px solid #369;
    background-color: #69f;
    color: #fff;
}
```

An unordered list is a perfect way to structure a menu of links in both theory and practical application. On the one hand, a set of links *is* a set of unordered items. And using unordered lists for navigation creates a solid structure for your web document based on both logic and semantically correct markup.

On the other hand, with the links set in an unordered list, it's easier to style the links into a menu presentation than it is to style a series of div elements:

```
<div id="navsite">
 <p>Site navigation:</p>
 <div><a href="/">Home</a></div>
 <div><a href="/about/">About</a></div>
 <div><a href="/archives/">Archives</a></div>
 <div><a href="/writing/">Writing</a></div>
 <div><a href="/speaking/">Speaking</a></div>
 <div><a href="/contact/">Contact</a></div>
</div>
```

See Also

The article "CSS Design: Taming Lists" by Mark Newhouse at *http://www.alistapart.com/articles/taminglists/*; the article/tutorial "Semantics, HTML, XHTML, and Structure" by Shirley E. Kaiser at *http://brainstormsandraves.com/articles/semantics/structure/*.

3.7 Creating Collapsible Menus

Problem

You want to hide a set of links and give the user a way to reveal those links when needed. For example, rather than two bullet lists of links, hide one (as shown in Figure 3-6) and let the user reveal it by clicking on a + sign as in Figure 3-7.

Solution

First, set up the HTML links to be collapsible with an id attribute in the ul element:

```
<h5>Interesting Links (+/-)</h5>
<ul id="menulink">
 <li><a href="http://www.ora.com/">O'Reilly</a></li>
 <li><a href="http://www.slashdot.org/">Slashdot</a></li>
 <li><a href="http://www.apple.com/">Apple</a></li>
 <li><a href="http://www.microsoft.com/">Microsoft</a></li>
 <li><a href="http://www.mozilla.org/">Mozilla</a></li>
</ul>
```

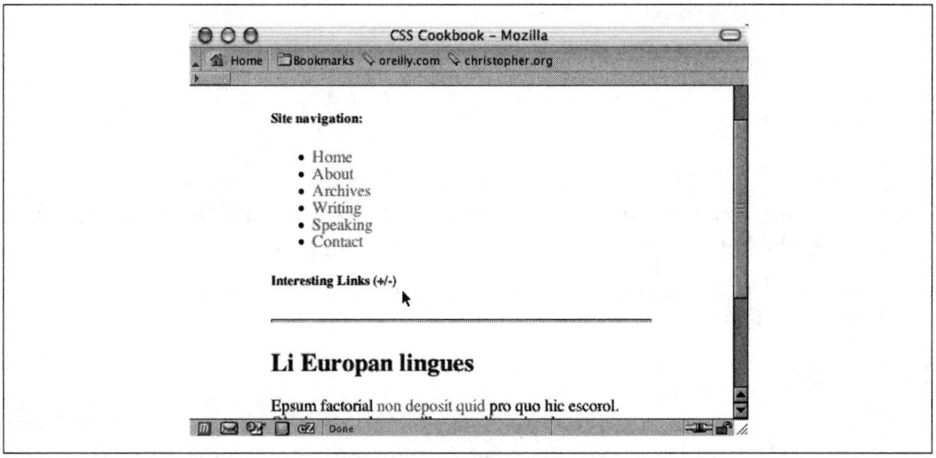

Figure 3-6. Preventing the second set of links from displaying

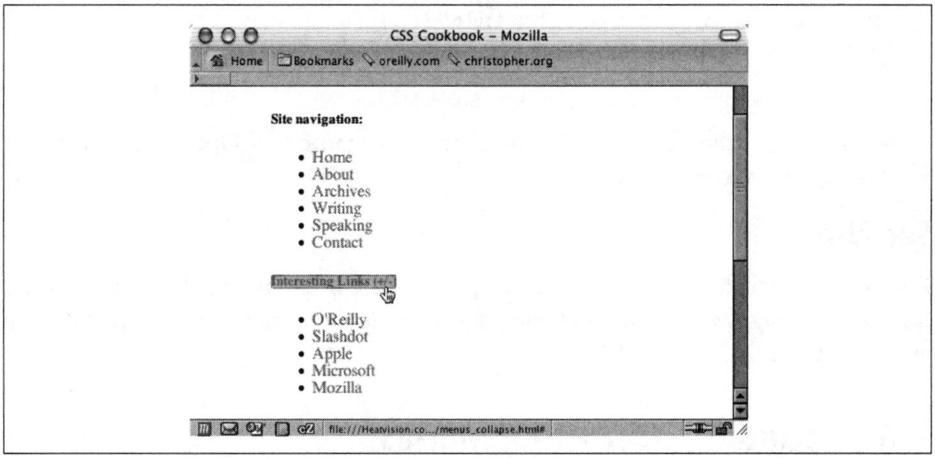

Figure 3-7. The links displayed when the link on the heading is clicked

Then create a CSS rule to prevent the second set of links from displaying when the page is first loaded:

```
#menulink {
 display: none;
}
```

Now add the following JavaScript function that toggles the list of links by swapping the value of display from block to none, or vice versa:

```
function kadabra(zap) {
 if (document.getElementById) {
  var abra = document.getElementById(zap).style;
  if (abra.display == "block") {
   abra.display = "none";
   } else {
```

```
    abra.display = "block";
  }
  return false;
  } else {
  return true;
  }
}
```

Insert an anchor element with a JavaScript onclick event around the heading. When a user clicks the link, the click triggers the JavaScript function:

```
<h5><a href="#" onclick="return kadabra('menulink');">
Interesting Links (+/-)</a></h5>
```

Discussion

The JavaScript in this function uses getElementbyId to toggle the display of the list of menu links. This technique can be scaled to show multiple menus or portions of a web document without adding additional lines of JavaScript:

```
<p>Are you sure you want to know the truth? If so,
follow <a href="#" onclick="return kadabra('spoiler'); ">this
link.</a></p>
<p id="spoiler">Darth Vadar was Luke's father!</p>
```

Note that this technique works in Netscape Navigator 6+, Opera 7.5+, Internet Explorer for Windows 5+, and Safari.

See Also

Recipe 2.10, which uses a similar concept to create a dynamic splash page; *http://www.mozilla.org/docs/dom/domref/dom_doc_ref48.html*, for more information on getElementbyId.

3.8 Building Horizontal Menus

Problem

You want to create a horizontal navigation menu out of an ordered set of links; Figure 3-8 shows the default, and Figure 3-9 shows what you want.

Solution

First create a properly constructed set of unordered links:

```
<div id="navsite">
<h5>Site navigation:</h5>
<ul>
 <li><a href="/">Home</a></li>
 <li><a href="/about/">About</a></li>
 <li><a href="/archives/">Archives</a></li>
 <li><a href="/writing/">Writing</a></li>
```

Figure 3-8. The default appearance of the links

Figure 3-9. The tab-based navigation

```
        <li><a href="/speaking/" id="current">Speaking</a></li>
        <li><a href="/contact/">Contact</a></li>
    </ul>
</div>
```

Then set the CSS rules for the navigation structure, making sure to set the display property of the list item to inline:

```
#navsite h5 {
  display: none;
}
#navsite ul {
  padding: 3px 0;
  margin-left: 0;
  border-bottom: 1px solid #778;
  font: bold 12px Verdana, sans-serif;
}
#navsite ul li {
  list-style: none;
```

```
  margin: 0;
  display: inline;
  }
#navsite ul li a {
  padding: 3px 0.5em;
  margin-left: 3px;
  border: 1px solid #778;
  border-bottom: none;
  background: #DDE;
  text-decoration: none;
  }
#navsite ul li a:link {
  color: #448;
  }
#navsite ul li a:visited {
  color: #667;
  }
#navsite ul li a:link:hover, #navsite ul li a:visited:hover {
  color: #000;
  background: #AAE;
  border-color: #227;
  }
#navsite ul li a#current {
  background: white;
  border-bottom: 1px solid white;
  }
```

Discussion

The first part of the Solution hides the heading. This is done because the visual representation of the tab navigation design is enough to inform users that these are navigation links:

```
#navsite h5 {
  display: none;
  }
```

The next rule defines the padding and margin for the box that is created by the unordered list element, ul. The line that stretches across the bottom of the folder tabs is drawn by the border-bottom property (see Figure 3-10):

```
#navsite ul {
  padding: 3px 0;
  margin-left: 0;
  border-bottom: 1px solid #669;
  font: bold 12px Verdana, Helvetica, Arial, sans-serif;
  }
```

The declaration that makes this horizontal navigation work with the unordered list is display: inline for the list item:

```
#navsite ul li {
  list-style: none;
  margin: 0;
  display: inline;
  }
```

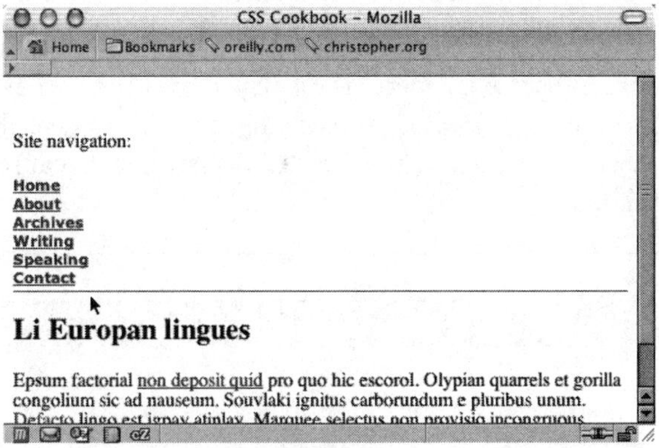

Figure 3-10. The line the navigation tabs rest upon

Instead of stacking the list items on top of each other by default, the browser now lays out the list items as it would text, images, and other inline elements (see Figure 3-11).

Figure 3-11. The list spread out horizontally

To create the look of the folder tab, use the `border` property in the following CSS rule:

```
#navsite ul li a {
  padding: 3px 0.5em;
  margin-left: 3px;
  border: 1px solid #669;
  border-bottom: none;
  background: #ccf;
  text-decoration: none;
}
```

The first border property is a shorthand property that dictates a solid, one-pixel border around the link. However, immediately following the border property is the border-bottom property, which tells the browser not to display a border beneath the link.

The value of the border-bottom property is displayed over the border shorthand property (as shown in Figure 3-12). This overwriting occurs because the border-bottom declaration overrides the values in the border declaration because of the order in which they are declared.

Figure 3-12. The tabs appear

After you've created the look of the border tab, set the color of the text links and rollover states:

```
#navsite ul li a:link {
  color: #339;
}
#navsite ul li a:visited {
  color: #666;
}
#navsite ul li a:link:hover, #navsite ul li a:visited:hover {
  color: #000;
  background: #aae;
  border-color: #336;
}
```

The final CSS rule defines how the "current" link appears. This style is applied to the link that represents the page being viewed by the user (see Figure 3-13):

```
#navsite ul li a#current {
  background: white;
  border-bottom: 1px solid white;
}
```

See Also

The original tab menu bar (as well as other navigation styles) at *http://css.maxdesign. com.au/listamatic/horizontal05.htm*.

Figure 3-13. The look of the current link

3.9   Creating Breadcrumb Navigation

Problem

You want to use a nesting listing as shown in Figure 3-14 to create a line of bread-crumb navigation, which is a set of links that lead back to the home page (see Figure 3-15).

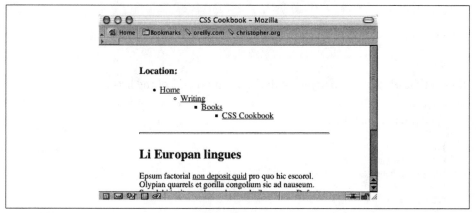

Figure 3-14. The default rendering of the nested listing

Solution

The first step is to create a properly constructed set of nested, unordered links that represent the page's location in the site:

```
<div id="crumbs">
 <h3>Location:</h3>
<ul>
 <li><a href="/">Home</a>
  <ul>
```

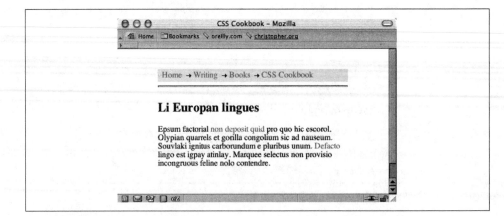

Figure 3-15. The breadcrumb trail

```
   <li><a href="/writing/">Writing</a>
    <ul>
     <li><a href="/writing/books/">Books</a>
      <ul>
       <li><a href="/writing/books/">CSS Cookbook</a></li>
      </ul>
     </li>
    </ul>
   </li>
  </ul>
 </li>
</ul>
</div>
```

Now set the display property of both the ul and the li of the lists:

```
#crumbs {
 background-color: #eee;
 padding: 4px;
}
#crumbs h3 {
 display: none;
}
#crumbs ul {
 display: inline;
 padding-left: 0;
 margin-left: 0;
}
#crumbs ul li {
 display: inline;
}
#crumbs ul li a:link {
 padding: .2em;
}
```

Within each nested list, place a small background image of an arrow to the left of the link:

```
crumbs ul ul li{
  background-image: url(arrow.gif);
  background-repeat: no-repeat;
  background-position: left;
  padding-left: 12px;
}
```

Discussion

Based on the fairy tale *Hansel and Gretel*, a *breadcrumb trail* is used to help people find their way home. On the Web, the breadcrumb trail illustrates a path to the page the user is viewing (as shown in Figure 3-16).

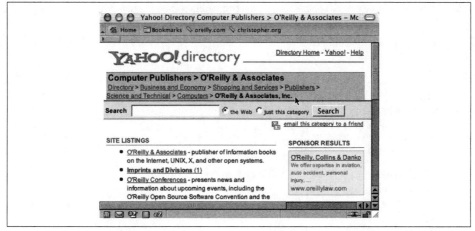

Figure 3-16. An example of a breadcrumb trail

The Solution could drop the background-image property if more browsers supported the :before pseudo-element. The solution would then incorporate another CSS rule (see Recipe 8.9), like so:

```
#crumbs ul ul li:before {
  content: url(arrow.gif);
}
```

As of this writing, only Netscape Navigator 6+ and Opera 5+ support the :before pseudo-element.

See Also

Recipes 1.9 and 2.4 for more information on setting a background image on an element; *http://www.surlalunefairytales.com/hanselgretel/index.html to* read an annotated version of *Hansel and Gretel*; a research paper into the effectiveness of breadcrumb navigation at *http://psychology.wichita.edu/surl/usabilitynews/52/breadcrumb.htm*.

3.10   Creating Image-Based Rollovers

Problem

You want image-based rollovers to replace text links.

Solution

First, wrap the text inside the anchor element in a span:

```
<a href="/" id="linkhome"><span>Homepage</span></a>
```

Next, instead of JavaScript, use the background-image property within the pseudo-class selectors :hover and :active to swap the images (see Figure 3-17):

```
a span {
 display: none;
}
a:link {
 display: block;
 width: 125px;
 height: 30px;
 background-image: url(btn.gif);
 background-repeat: no-repeat;
 background-position: top left;
}
a:link:hover {
 display: block;
 width: 125px;
 height: 30px;
 background-image: url(btn_roll.gif);
 background-repeat: no-repeat;
 background-position: top left;
}
a:link:active {
 display: block;
 width: 125px;
 height: 30px;
 background-image: url(btn_on.gif);
 background-repeat: no-repeat;
 background-position: top left;
}
```

Discussion

Replacing text with an image has five benefits. First, it separates the text from the presentation. The image that contains more elaborately formatted type is part of the presentation and therefore controlled by a style, while the content in the markup remains pure text. The second benefit is that an image heading can be modified across a whole site by one change of the style sheet. The third benefit is that this method works for alternative styles and style sheet switching.

Figure 3-17. The link with default, rollover, and active states

With a span element inside an element, it is possible to hide HTML text and let a design element, such as a rollover image, show as a background image. The fourth benefit of this Solution is that if a user doesn't have CSS enabled in his browser, the default HTML text will display instead, sparing the user from having to download unneeded images. The fifth benefit is that the solution is cleaner and simpler than one that involves JavaScript.

You also can use this technique for page elements that don't require a rollover—for example, inserting an image to replace heading text to ensure a specific font that isn't commonly found on people's computers is displayed as an image. To do so, first set up the markup (see Figure 3-18):

```
<h2 id="headworld"><span>Hello, World!</span></h2>
```

Then set the following CSS rules to insert the image (see Figure 3-19):

```
h2#headworld span {
  display: none;
}
h2#headworld {
```

Figure 3-18. Default rendering of heading

```
    width: 395px;
    height: 95px;
    background-image: url(heading.gif);
    background-repeat: no-repeat;
    background-position: top left;
}
```

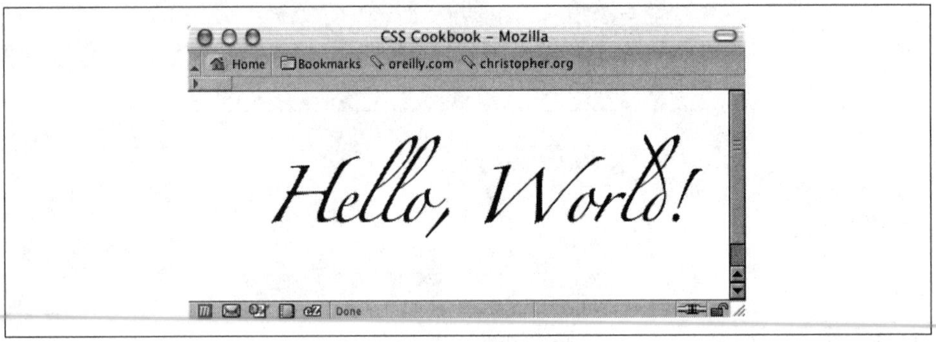

Figure 3-19. The HTML text heading replaced by an image

Many people refer to this method as the Fahrner Image Replacement (FIR) method, named after Todd Fahrner.

A drawback to this solution concerns *screen readers*, which are programs that make computers accessible to blind or severely visually impaired people. Certain screen readers won't read elements set to display: none. For more information, read "Facts and Opinion About Fahrner Image Replacement" at *http://www.alistapart.com/articles/fir/*.

An alternative to this solution is the Leahy-Langridge Image Replacement (LIR) method. Developed independently by Seamus Leahy and Stuart Langridge, the LIR method pushes the text out of view. A benefit for using this technique is that an extra span element isn't required in order to hide the text. For example, the HTML for a heading is basic:

```
    <h2 id="headworld">Hello, World!</h2>
```

The image for the heading comes through the background because the CSS rule sets the padding to the exact height of the image header. So, the height property is set to 0:

```
h2#headworld {
  /* The width of the image */
  width: 395px;
  /* The height of the image is the first padding value */
  padding: 95px 0 0 0;
  overflow: hidden;
  background-image: url("heading.gif");
  background-repeat: no-repeat;
  voice-family: "\"}\"";
  voice-family:inherit;
  height /**/: 95px;
  height: 0px !important;
}
```

The last four lines of the CSS rule are needed to work around Internet Explorer for Windows' poor box-model support, as explained in Recipe 10.2. Therefore, Internet Explorer for Windows gets a height value of 95 pixels, while the other browsers receive zero pixels.

Another method for creating an image-based rollover is performed by the background-position property. Known as the Pixy method, the technique involves attaching all three rollover states into one image and then moving the position of the image with the background-position property, as shown in Figure 3-20:

```
a span {
  display: none;
}
a:link, a:visited {
  display: block;
  width: 125px;
  height: 30px;
  background-image: url(btn_omni.gif);
  background-repeat: no-repeat;
  background-position: 0 0;
}
a:link:hover, a:visited:hover {
  display: block;
  width: 125px;
  height: 30px;
  background-image: url(btn_omni.gif);
  background-repeat: no-repeat;
  /* move the image 30 pixels up */
  background-position: 0 -30px;
}
a:link:active, a:visited:active  {
  display: block;
  width: 125px;
  height: 30px;
  background-image: url(btn_omni.gif);
  background-repeat: no-repeat;
  /* move the image 60 pixels up */
  background-position: 0 -60px;
}
```

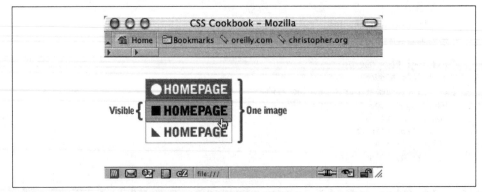

Figure 3-20. Showing a portion of the rollover image

 The drawback of almost all current image replacement techniques is that users see nothing if images are turned off, disabled, or simply don't load while the CSS is still supported. It is important to research and use the method that's best for your situation. Avoid replacing images in important titles.

See Also

Another demonstration of the LIR technique by Seamus P. H. Leahy at *http://www. moronicbajebus.com/playground/cssplay/image-replacement/*; an explanation on how to create faster CSS-enabled rollovers without having to preload images at *http:// www.pixy.cz/blogg/clanky/cssnopreloadrollovers/*; a rundown of the FIR technique at *http://www.stopdesign.com/also/articles/replace_text/*.

3.11   Designing a Dynamic Visual Menu

Problem

You want to build a curved tab navigation menu that works even when text is resized; Figure 3-21 shows the default.

Solution

First write the markup for the navigation menu:

```
<div id="header">
 <h2>Personal Site dot-com</h2>
 <h5>Site navigation:</h5>
 <ul>
  <li><a href="/">Home</a></li>
  <li><a href="/about/">About</a></li>
  <li><a href="/archives/">Archives</a></li>
  <li><a href="/writing/">Writing</a></li>
```

Figure 3-21. The dynamic folder tab navigation

```
<li id="current"><a href="/speaking/">Speaking</a></li>
<li><a href="/contact/">Contact</a></li>
</ul>
</div>
```

Then create two folder tab images: one tab for anchor links and another tab to represent the current page viewed by the user. Split the folder tab image into two images as shown in Figure 3-22.

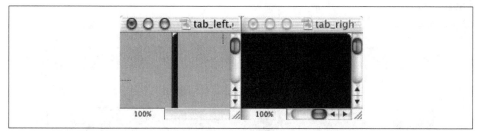

Figure 3-22. The folder tab image split in two; note the curves in the upper corners of the images

Then place the right side of the folder tab in the background of the list item:

```
#header li {
 float:left;
 background-image: url(tab_right.gif);
 background-repeat: no-repeat;
 background-position: right top;
 margin:0;
 padding: 0;
}
```

Place the left side of the folder tab in the background of the anchor element:

```
#header a {
  display: block;
  background-image: url("tab_left.gif");
  background-repeat: no-repeat;
  background-position: left top;
  padding: 5px 15px;
  color: #ccc;
  text-decoration: none;
  font-family: Georgia, Times, "Times New Roman", serif;
}
```

Assign a custom folder tab to represent the current web document being viewed:

```
#header #current {
  background-image:url("tab_right_current.gif");
}
#header #current a {
  background-image:url("tab_left_current.gif");
  color: black;
}
```

Place the image with a line measuring one-pixel high at the bottom of the grouping.

Discussion

Keeping the text in the navigation links aids in three areas of web development: accessibility, design, and maintenance. For example, users with poor eyesight can adjust the size of the text and that tabs without breaking the design, as shown in Figure 3-23.

Figure 3-23. The text resized

Because users can resize the text to very large settings, the background images that comprise the folder tabs need to be large as well; otherwise, the folder tabs will break, as shown in Figure 3-24. In this Solution, the folder tab images have a height of 450 pixels.

Figure 3-24. Note the breaking of the tab in the Archives link

Web developers prefer this method because it lets them easily maintain the list of links. To change a navigation label or correct a typo, developers can simply edit the HTML text without having to return to a digital imaging program to create folder tab images.

Another benefit of this method is that the folder tabs can be designed in a more aesthetically pleasing way. Recipe 3.8 demonstrates how to create a navigation setup with folder tabs using the border property. This look creates a boxy or squared edge to the folder tabs. With this current Recipe, however, web developers can curve the tabs and introduce color blending for improved aesthetics.

See Also

Recipe 1.12, which uses a similar rubber-band technique to create pull quotes with images; "Sliding Doors of CSS, Part II" at *http://www.alistapart.com/articles/slidingdoors2/,* which expands on this folder tab navigation concept.

3.12 Creating Contextual Menus

Problem

You have a navigation menu, created with Recipe 3.6. You want to highlight the current page's location on the menu, as in Figure 3-25.

Figure 3-25. The navigation set of links

Solution

Place an id attribute in the body element of the web document:

```
<body id="pagespk">
```

Also, place id attributes in the anchor elements for each link in the menu:

```
<div id="navsite">
  <h5>Site navigation:</h5>
  <ul>
  <li><a href="/" id="linkhom">Home</a></li>
  <li><a href="/about/" id="linkabt">About</a></li>
  <li><a href="/archives/" id="linkarh">Archives</a></li>
  <li><a href="/writing/" id="linkwri">Writing</a></li>
  <li><a href="/speaking/" id="linkspk">Speaking</a></li>
  <li><a href="/contact/" id="linkcnt">Contact</a></li>
  </ul>
</div>
```

With CSS, place two id selectors into one descendent selector to finish the menu (see Figure 3-26):

```
#pagespk a#linkspk {
  border-left: 10px solid #f33;
  border-right: 1px solid #f66;
  border-bottom: 1px solid #f33;
  background-color: #fcc;
  color: #333;
}
```

Discussion

If you have a small site, you can show a link in a set of navigation links representing the current page by stripping out the anchor link for that page:

Figure 3-26. The current link is different from the rest of the links

```
<div id="navsite">
 <h5>Site navigation:</h5>
 <ul>
  <li><a href="/"Home</a></li>
  <li><a href="/about/">About</a></li>
  <li><a href="/archives/">Archives</a></li>
  <li><a href="/writing/" >Writing</a></li>
  <li>Speaking</li>
  <li><a href="/contact/" >Contact</a></li>
 </ul>
</div>
```

For larger sites that might contain secondary menus, stripping out the link tags on each page increases production and maintenance time. By marking up the links appropriately, the links can be called from a server-side include, and then you can edit the CSS rules that control the style of the navigation links as needed.

To expand the one CSS to include all the links in the navigation menu, group the descendent selectors by a comma and at least one space:

```
#pagehom a#linkhom:link,
#pageabt a#linkabt:link,
#pagearh a#linkarh:link,
#pagewri a#linkwri:link,
#pagespk a#linkspk:link,
#pagecnt a#linkcnt:link  {
 border-left: 10px solid #f33;
 border-right: 1px solid #f66;
 border-bottom: 1px solid #f33;
 background-color: #fcc;
 color: #333;
}
```

In each web document, make sure to put the appropriate id attribute in the body element. For example, for the home or main page of the site, the body element is <body id="pagehom">.

See Also

The CSS 2.1 specification on descendent selectors at *http://www.w3.org/TR/CSS21/ selector.html#descendant-selectors*.

CHAPTER 4

Lists

4.0 Introduction

From a wife handing a husband a grocery list as he steps out the door to a music channel presenting their top 100 worst songs of all time, lists help people stay focused and organized. In web design, it's the same case. HTML lists facilitate the presentation to our site visitors with organized content.

HTML lists, which group key elements together, can be ordered or unordered. Both types of lists are appealing in part because of the way they appear on the page. List items typically are indented and are keyed off by a marker, usually a filled circle for an unordered list or numbers for an ordered list (see Figure 4-1). With a few lines of HTML, a web coder can create a bulleted list on a web page without opening an image editor. Through CSS, you can create even more visually compelling lists.

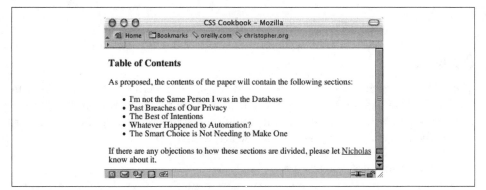

Figure 4-1. The default rendering of a list

With a little CSS magic, we can tailor the presentation of the list to complement the design of a web page instead of relying on the browsers' default styling. While Chapter 3 covered navigation lists, this chapter illustrates how to change the numbering of list items, use your own image for a list marker, create a hanging indent that doesn't use a list marker, and more.

4.1 Changing the Format of a List

Problem

You want to change the default list style, for example to change the bullet or numbering as in Figure 4-2.

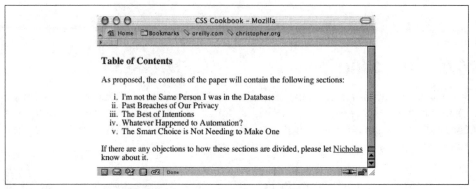

Figure 4-2. The list markers changed to lowercase Roman numerals

Solution

Use the list-style-type property to change the bullet or type of counter:

```
li {
  list-style-type: lower-roman;
}
```

Discussion

The CSS 2.1 specification offers several styles for numbering a list, as shown in Table 4-1. Browsers typically vary the bullet style from one level of nesting to the next. To stop lists from presenting this traditional system of setting the list marker, change the value of list-style-type for each child list.

Table 4-1. Styles available for list markers

Style/value	Description	Browser support
square	Usually a filled-in square, although the exact representation isn't defined.	All major browsers
disc	Usually a filled-in circle, although the exact representation isn't defined.	All major browsers

Table 4-1. Styles available for list markers (continued)

Style/value	Description	Browser support
circle	Usually an unfilled circle, although the exact representation isn't defined.	All major browsers
decimal	Starts with 1 and continues with 2, 3, 4, etc.	All major browsers
decimal-leading-zero	Starts with 01 and continues with 02, 03, 04, etc. The number of leading zeros may equal the number of digits used in a list. For example, 0001 might be used for a 5876-item list.	All major browsers, although leading zeros is optional
lower-roman	Starts with lowercase roman numbers.	All major browsers
upper-roman	Starts with uppercase roman numbers.	All major browsers
lower-alpha	Starts with lowercase ASCII letters.	All major browsers
upper-alpha	Starts with uppercase ASCII letters.	All major browsers
lower-latin	Starts with lowercase ASCII letters.	All major browsers
upper-latin	Starts with uppercase ASCII letters.	All major browsers
lower-greek	Starts with classical Greek letters, starting with alpha and then beta, gamma, etc.	Safari, Mozilla, Netscape 6+
hebrew	Starts counting with traditional Hebrew.	Safari, Mozilla, Netscape 6+
hiragana	Starts counting with the Japanese hiragana system.	Mozilla, Netscape 6+
katakana	Starts counting with the Japanese traditional katana system.	Mozilla, Netscape 6+
hiragana-iroha	Starts counting with the Japanese hiragana-iroha system.	Mozilla, Netscape 6+
katakana-iroha	Starts counting with the Japanese katakana-iroha system.	Mozilla, Netscape 6+
none	No marker is displayed.	All major browsers

See Also

Recipe 4.5 for using custom images for list markers; Chapter 12, "Lists and Generated Content" in *Cascading Style Sheets: The Definitive Guide* (O'Reilly).

4.2   Writing Cross-Browser Indentation in Lists

Problem

Different browsers use different methods to indent lists. You want to specify left margins for your list that will render on all browsers.

Solution

Set both the margin-left and padding-left properties for the ul element:

```
ul {
  margin-left: 40px;
  padding-left: 0px;
}
```

Discussion

Different browsers use different methods to pad or indent a list. Mozilla and Netscape 6+ browsers indent a list on the *padding*, while Internet Explorer and Opera pad a list through the *margin* of a list.

To gain cross-browser effectiveness, you need to set the values for *both* the left margins and the padding for the list. Keep the amount of the indentation in one of the properties. Splitting the amount into two different properties results in inconsistent presentation across the browsers.

If you set the margin and padding to zero while the list is contained by only the body element, the browser renders the markers outside the viewport, making them invisible to the user. To make sure the markers are visible, set the left margin or left padding of the ul to at least 1em.

See Also

Recipe 4.7 on creating hanging indents; CSS 2.1 specification for padding at *http://www.w3.org/TR/CSS21/box.html#propdef-padding*; CSS 2.1 specification for margin at *http://www.w3.org/TR/CSS21/box.html#propdef-margin*.

4.3   Creating Custom Text Markers for Lists

Problem

You want to use a custom text marker in a list.

Solution

Indent the first line of text and insert the custom text, along with the right-angle quotes acting as pointers, through auto-generated content (see Figure 4-3):

```
ul {
  list-style: none;
  margin: 0;
  padding: 0 0 0 1em;
  text-indent: -1em;
}
li {
  width: 33%;
  padding: 0;
  margin: 0 0 0.25em 0;
}
li:before {
  content: "\00BB \0020";
}
```

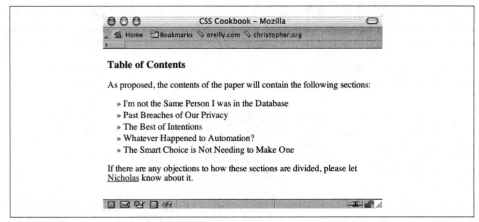

Figure 4-3. Text marker for a list

Discussion

Setting the list-style property to a value of none turns off the list marker usually associated with a list. Typically, a marker is appended to the left of each list item.

Instead of appending the marker to the list item, the custom text marker will be placed inline with the content of the item. Because the text marker is inside the list item, you need to push the marker out of the list item box. Indenting the first line of the marker with a negative value creates this push. The negative value for the text-indent property moves the first line to the left, whereas a positive value moves the indent to the right:

```
ul {
  list-style: none;
  margin: 0;
  padding: 0 0 0 1em;
  text-indent: -1em;
}
```

The :before pseudo-element generates the text marker. Because the marker used in this example falls outside of the American Standard Code for Information Interchange (ASCII) 256-character set, its numerical equivalent needs to be determined.

However, because the ASCII character will be used in the CSS property and not on an HTML page, you need to write out the character in its escaped hexadecimal equivalent. You escape values in CSS by inserting a backslash before each hexadecimal value:

```
li:before {
  content: "\00BB \0020";
}
```

At press time, this solution worked in Mozilla, Netscape 6+, Safari, and Opera browsers because they can handle the creation of auto-generated content. Unfortunately, this list omits Netscape 4 and Internet Explorer for Windows and Macintosh.

To create a cross-browser effect, don't use auto-generated content. Instead, insert the text marker manually before the list item:

```
<ul>
  <li>&#187; I'm not the Same Person I was in the Database</li>
  <li>&#187; Past Breaches of Our Privacy</li>
  <li>&#187; The Best of Intentions</li>
  <li>&#187; Whatever Happened to Automation?</li>
  <li>&#187; The Smart Choice is Not Needing to Make One</li>
</ul>
```

The main drawback with this approach is that you have two markers for every list item. Although this isn't a mission-critical problem, it adds an unneeded design element to the web page.

See Also

Recipe 8.9 on creating auto-generated content; the CSS 2.1 specification about escaping characters at *http://www.w3.org/TR/REC-CSS2/syndata.html#escaped-characters*; hexadecimal values for ASCII characters at *http://www.asciitable.com/*.

4.4   Creating Custom Image Markers for Lists

Problem

You want to use your own graphic for a list marker. For example, Figure 4-4 uses a diamond image.

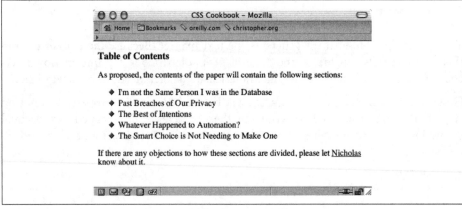

Figure 4-4. Custom-made image markers for a list

Solution

Use the `list-style-image` property to use a graphic for a bullet marker:

```
ul {
 list-style-type: disc;
 list-style-image: url(bullet.gif);
}
```

Discussion

Set the location of the image you want to use as a marker as the value of the `list-style-image` property. You can't control the size of the image used as a list marker through CSS, so the image you specify should already be at the correct size. Images that are too large might interfere with the legibility of the list item or the marker might not be displayed entirely in the viewport, as shown in Figure 4-5. When creating custom bullets, make sure they are of the appropriate size to compliment the design of your web page.

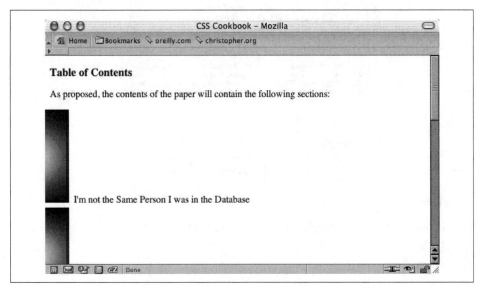

Figure 4-5. A large image used for a marker isn't fully displayed

The value for the image marker is *inherited*, meaning that nested lists pick up the image as the marker as does the parent. To stop this inheritance, the value of none needs to be set for the child lists.

```
ul {
 list-style-type: disc;
 list-style-image: url(bullet.gif);
}
ul ul {list-style-type: none:}
```

Always include the `list-style-type` property to provide a fallback should the image not be usable. In the Solution the list marker `disc` is used if the image, *bullet.gif*, can't be displayed.

See Also

Recipe 4.4 on creating custom text markers; the CSS 2.1 specification for list-image-type at *http://www.w3.org/TR/CSS21/generate.html#propdef-list-style-image*.

4.5   Creating Inline Lists

Problem

You want to list items to be displayed within a paragraph, as in Figure 4-6 in which the bold, comma-separated list was generated from an HTML `ul` list.

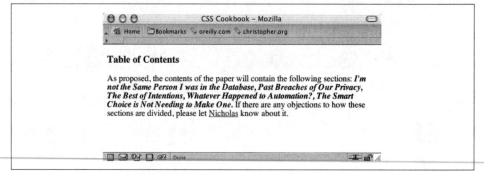

Figure 4-6. The list formatted to appear inside a paragraph

Solution

Set the paragraphs before (and, if needed, after) the list:

```
<h3>
 Table of Contents
</h3>
<p>
 As proposed, the contents of the paper will contain the
following sections:
</p>
<ul>
 <li>I'm not the Same Person I was in the Database</li>
 <li>Past Breaches of Our Privacy</li>
 <li>The Best of Intentions</li>
 <li>Whatever Happened to Automation?</li>
 <li class="last">The Smart Choice is Not Needing to Make One</li>
</ul>
<p>
 If there are any objections to how these sections are divided,
```

```
please let <a href="nick@heatvision.com">Nicholas</a> know about
it.
</p>
```

Through CSS, set the paragraph to display as inline elements and then use auto-generated content to show the commas between items and the period at the end of the list:

```
ul, li {
 display: inline;
 margin: 0;
 padding: 0;
 font-weight: bold;
 font-style: italic;
}
li:after {
 content: ", ";
}
li.last:after {
 content: ".";
}
p {
 display: inline;
}
```

Discussion

Through this method you retain the structure of lists and paragraphs, but you stretch CSS's capability to present the list inside a paragraph. However, you hide the obvious visual appearance of a list in favor of having the contents placed inside a paragraph.

See Also

The CSS 2.1 specification about the display property at *http://www.w3.org/TR/CSS21/visuren.html#propdef-display*.

4.6   Making Hanging Indents in a List

Problem

You want the first line of a list item to begin further to the left than the rest of the list, thereby creating a hanging indent as in Figure 4-7.

Solution

Use a negative value for the text-indent property:

```
ul {
 width: 30%;
 padding: 0 0 0.75em 0;
 margin: 0;
```

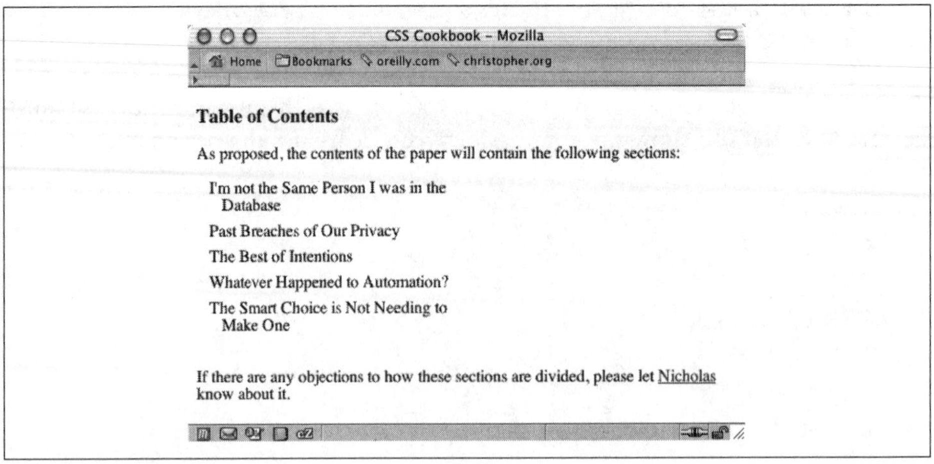

Figure 4-7. Hanging indents on a list

```
     list-style: none;
    }
    li {
      text-indent: -0.75em;
      margin: 0.33em 0.5em 0.5em 1.5em;
    }
```

Discussion

Although list markers (numeric, image, or text) help to call attention to the actual list, sometimes you might not want to add those kinds of design elements to a list. Instead of relying on markers to carry off the list design, use a hanging indent.

In this Solution, you indent the list by three-quarters of an em unit, creating a visible but almost subtle hanging indent effect. You can push this design technique from subtle to the foreground by reducing the negative value further, or by increasing the font size of the text in the list item.

See Also

Recipe 1.14 on setting indents in paragraphs; the CSS 2.1 specification for text-indent at *http://www.w3.org/TR/CSS21/text.html#propdef-text-indent*.

4.7 Moving the Marker Inside the List

Problem

You want the list marker to be pulled inside the border of the list items, as in Figure 4-8. This creates an effect in which the text wraps around the marker.

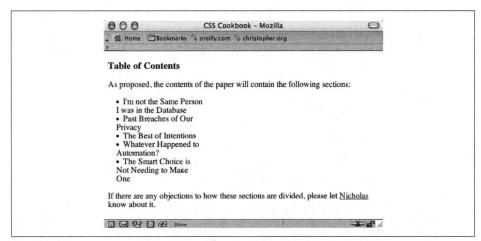

Figure 4-8. Moving the marker inside the list item

Solution

Use the `list-style-position` property and set the value to `inside`:

```
li {
  list-style-position: inside;
  width: 33%;
  padding: 0;
  margin: 0;
}
ul {
  margin: 0;
  padding: 0 0 0 1em;
}
```

Discussion

Normally the list marker stands outside the text and the result is a very distinctive list. Some designs, however, might require the marker to appear as part of the text. A designer might choose to keep the marker inside, for example, to eliminate the need to have enough whitespace on the left side. Also, replacing the list marker with your own custom marker can visually enhance this recipe. For example, Figure 4-9 shows arrows rather than the default bullet.

See Also

The CSS 2.1 specification for `list-style-position` at *http://www.w3.org/TR/CSS21/generate.html#propdef-list-style-position*.

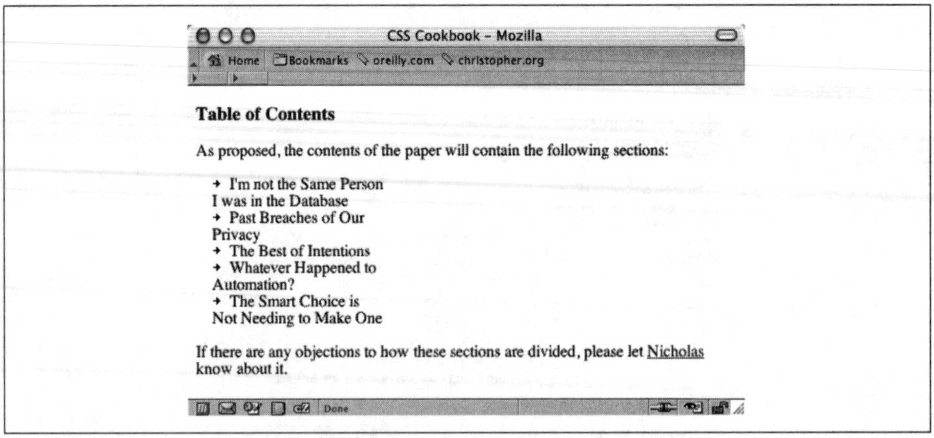

Figure 4-9. Custom marker inside the list item

CHAPTER 5

Forms

5.0   Introduction

Forms make the Web go 'round. Without forms we wouldn't be able to log in to web-based email accounts, order books with one click, or trade stocks online. The downside to forms, however, is the generic way in which browsers display them. In short, HTML forms usually look ugly and boring.

The default rendering of online forms usually includes beveled input and textarea fields, as well as boring-looking buttons. Such a look and feel might be acceptable if you are making a form for use on a small intranet or on a personal web page, but it is unacceptable if you want to project a professional image.

Fortunately, with a few CSS rules, you can create forms that stand out from the pack. If you are designing a company web site, for instance, you can create forms in the same color as the company's logo. What's more, you can implement rollover effects on Submit buttons without having to replace the buttons with an image.

CSS provides much control over the presentation of your forms and this chapter helps you get straight into the techniques. You will learn the settings for HTML user input elements such as buttons, text areas, and fields. Another technique covered is how to set up a submit-once-only button to keep site visitors from mistakenly sending several processes to the server. At the end of the chapter are two sample designs: a simple log-in form without tables and a long registration form with tables.

5.1   Setting Styles for Input Elements

Problem

You want to change the appearance of input elements' background color. Such effects can take you from Figure 5-1 to Figure 5-2.

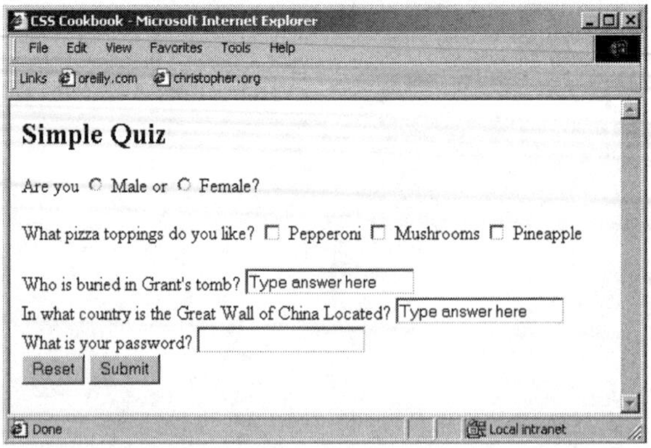

Figure 5-1. The form without styles

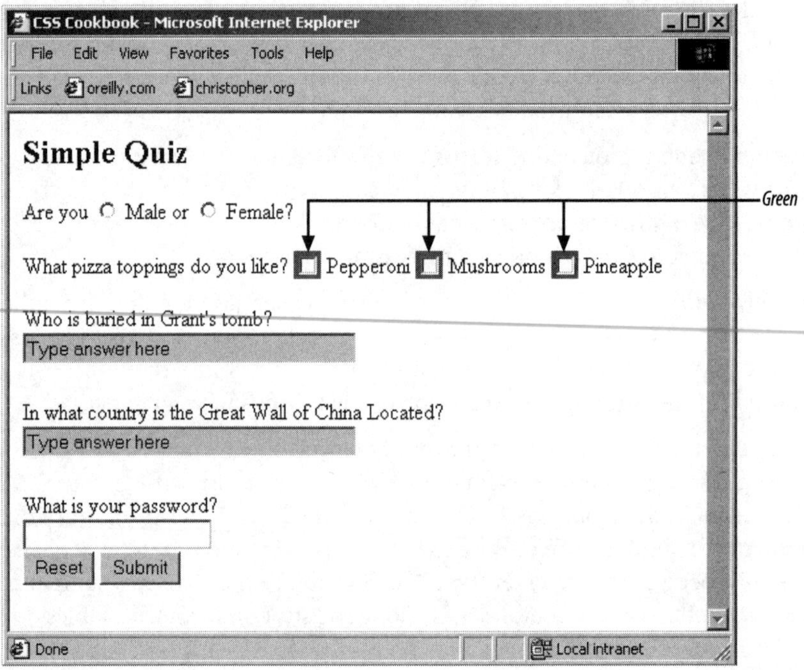

Figure 5-2. Styles applied to the input fields

Solution

Use a class selector to design the input elements of the form:

```
<h2>Simple Quiz</h2>
<form action="simplequiz.php" method="post">
<p>
```

```
  Are you
    <input type="radio" value="male" name="sex"
class="radioinput">
  Male or
    <input type="radio" value="female" name="sex"
class="radioinput">
  Female?
 </p>
<p>
 What pizza toppings do you like? <input type="checkbox" name=""
value="1" class="checkbxinput"> Pepperoni <input type="checkbox"
name="" value="mushrooms" class="checkbxinput"> Mushrooms <input
type="checkbox" name="" value="pineapple" class="checkbxinput">
 Pineapple
 </p>
 <label for="question1">Who is buried in Grant's tomb?</label>
 <input type="text" name="question1" id="question1"
class="textinput"
value="Type answer here" /><br />
 <label for="question2">In what country is the Great Wall of
China Located?</label>
 <input type="text" name="question2" id="question2"
class="textinput"
value="Type answer here" /><br />
 <label for="password">What is your password?</label>
 <input type="password" name="password" id="password"
class="pwordinput"
value="" /><br />
 <input name="reset" type="reset" id="reset" value="Reset" />
 <input type="submit" name="Submit" value="Submit"
class="buttonSubmit" />
</form>
```

Then apply CSS rules to change the presentation of the input elements:

```
.textinput {
margin-bottom: 1.5em;
width: 50%;
color: #666;
background-color: #ccc;
}
.pwordinput {
color: white;
background-color: white;
}
.radioinput {
color: green;
background-color: #ccc;
}
.checkbxinput {
color: green;
background-color: green;
}
```

Discussion

You can change the style of the active `input` field by adding the `:focus` pseudo-class. So, as a user fills out a form, the `input` field he is currently filling out will change color (see Figure 5-2):

```
input:focus {
 color: black;
 background-color: #cf0;
}
```

Opera is currently the only browser that allows radio buttons and checkboxes to be colored. Mozilla doesn't color them at all, while Internet Explorer for Windows ignores foreground color and colors the area around the widgets with the background color (as shown in Figure 5-3).

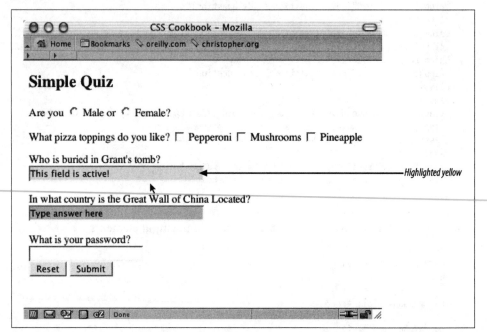

Figure 5-3. Using :focus to light up an input field

Rather than using class selectors as illustrated in the Solution, another way to stylize different kinds of input forms is through attribute selectors. For example, to style text inputs and password inputs differently you might use attribute selectors like the following:

```
input[type="text"] {
 margin-bottom: 1.5em;
 width: 50%;
 color: #666;
 background-color: #ccc;
}
```

```
input[type="password"] {
  color: white;
  background-color: white;
}
```

Although this works in most browsers, it doesn't work in Internet Explorer for Windows because this browser doesn't support attribute selectors at all. Attribute selectors currently work in Netscape Navigator 6+ and Opera 5+. If you want to ensure cross-browser support, you need to use class selectors to determine styles for different form controls.

See Also

The CSS 2.1 specification for dynamic pseudo-classes at *http://www.w3.org/TR/CSS21/selector.html#x33*; the CSS 2.1 specification for attribute selectors at *http://www.w3.org/TR/CSS21/selector.html#attribute-selectors*.

5.2   Setting Styles for textarea Elements

Problem

You want to set styles for textarea elements in a web form to change the text's color, size, weight, and other properties of the element, as in Figure 5-4.

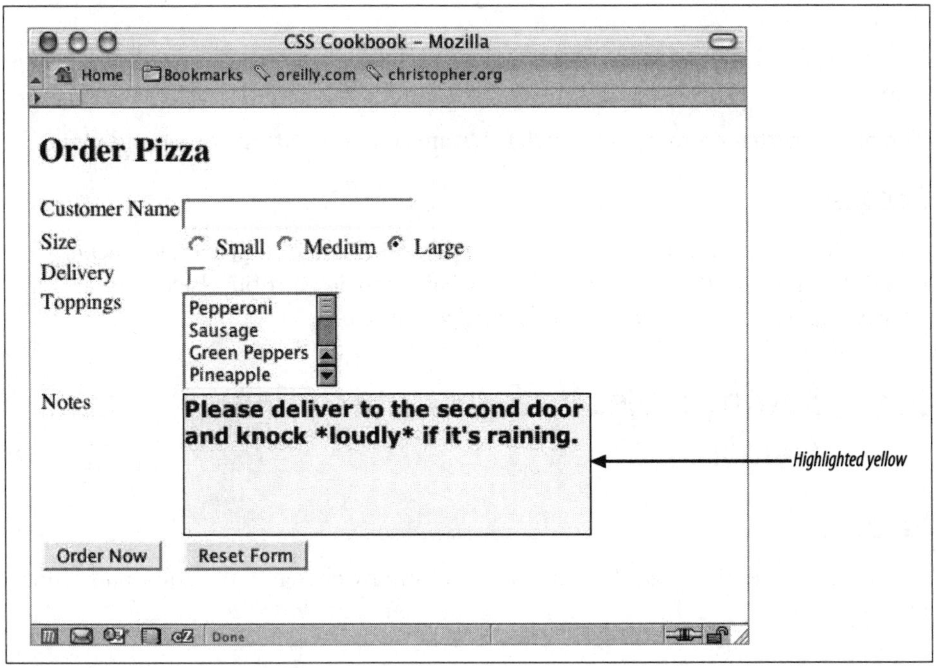

Figure 5-4. A textarea element with styles applied

Solution

Use a type selector to associate styles with textarea elements:

```
textarea {
  width: 300px;
  height: 100px;
  background-color: yellow;
  font-size: 1em;
  font-weight: bold;
  font-family: Verdana, Arial, Helvetica, sans-serif;
  border: 1px solid black;
}
```

Discussion

Associating styles to textarea elements is fairly straightforward through the use of a type selector:

```
textarea {
  background-color: blue;
}
```

By adding the :focus pseudo-class, you can change the style of the active textarea field:

```
textarea:focus {
  background-color: green;
}
```

So, as a user fills out a form, the textarea field he is currently filling out will change color.

The browsers that currently support :focus are Netscape Navigator 6+ and Opera 7.

See Also

The CSS 2.1 specification for dynamic pseudo-classes at *http://www.w3.org/TR/CSS21/selector.html#x33*; the CSS 2.1 specification for attribute selectors at *http://www.w3.org/TR/CSS21/selector.html#attribute-selectors*.

5.3 Setting Styles for Select and Option Elements

Problem

You want to alter the look of list menus in a form by changing the color and font, as in Figure 5-5.

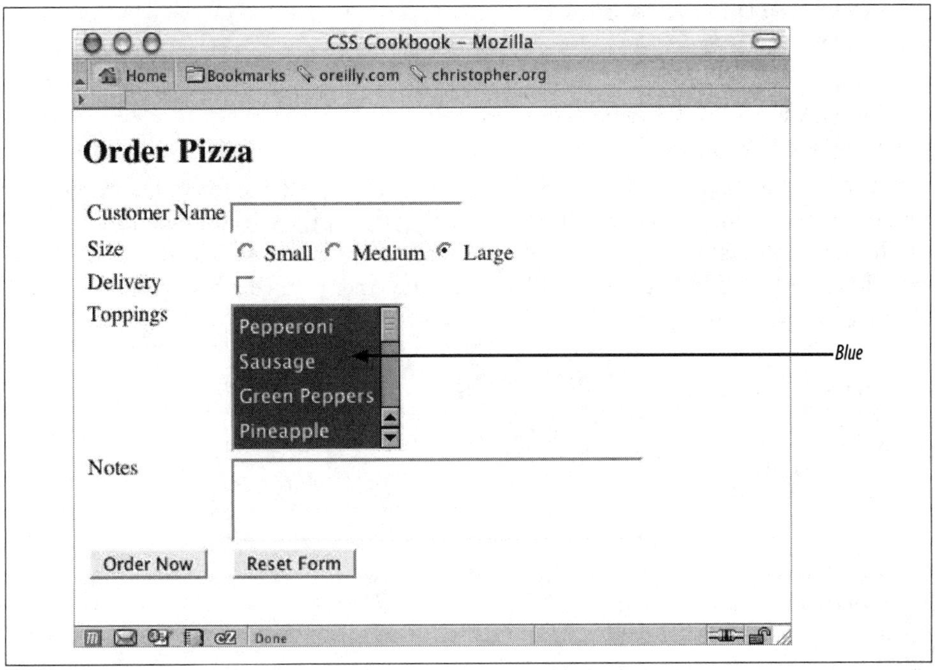

Figure 5-5. The select and option elements with styles applied

Solution

Use a type selector to associate styles with select elements:

```
select {
 color: white;
 background-color: blue;
 font-size: 0.9em;
}
option {
 padding: 4px;
}
```

Discussion

Unlike input form elements, there is only one type of select element, so associating styles to that element is straightforward and can be done through a type selector. Styling the option element is just as easy.

To stylize alternating options in a select list, first include the class attribute in the option element:

```
<select name="Topping_ID" size="6" multiple>
<option value="1">Pepperoni</option>
<option value="2" class="even">Sausage</option>
<option value="3">Green Peppers</option>
<option value="4" class="even">Pineapple</option>
```

```
<option value="5">Chicken</option>
<option value="6" class="even">Ham</option>
<option value="7">Olives</option>
<option value="8" class="even">Onions</option>
<option value="9">Red Peppers</option>
</select>
```

Then set up the CSS rules for the two sets of option elements, making sure that the option elements with an even value (as noted by the class selector even) look different from the others. For example, option elements with an even selector have a background color of red, while the "regular" option elements have a background color of blue (see Figure 5-6):

```
select {
 font-size: 0.9em;
}
option {
 color: white;
 background-color: blue;
}
option.even {
color: blue;
 background-color: red;
}
```

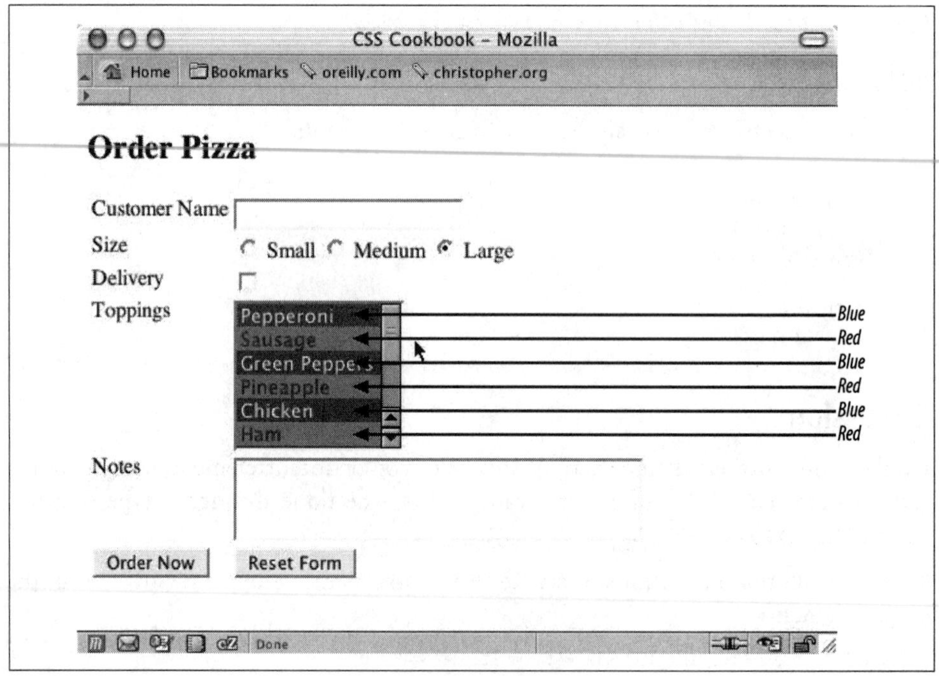

Figure 5-6. Alternating styles applied to select and option elements

See Also

Recipe 5.1 for information on how to change the color and size of `input` element text.

5.4   Creating Form Buttons

Problem

You want to stylize the color, padding, borders, and rollover effects for Submit and Reset buttons on a form. Figure 5-7 shows a form without styles applied to the buttons, and Figure 5-8 shows the form with stylized buttons.

Figure 5-7. The form buttons without styles applied

Figure 5-8. The form buttons with styles applied

Solution

First use a `class` selector to design the buttons:

```
<form action="simplequiz.php" method="post">
 <label for="question">Who is president of the U.S.?
</label>
 <input type="text" name="question" id="textfield"
```

```
value="Type answer here" /><br />
<input name="reset" type="reset"  value="Reset"
class="buttonReset" />
<input type="submit" name="Submit" value="Submit"
class="buttonSubmit" />
</form>
```

Then use CSS to stylize the buttons:

```
.buttonReset {
 color: #fcc;
 background-color: #900;
 font-size: 1.5em;
 border: 1px solid #660;
 padding: 4px;
}
.buttonSubmit {
 color: white;
 background-color: #660;
 font-size: 1.5em;
 border: 1px solid #660;
 padding: 4px;
}
```

Discussion

You also can stylize buttons using the ubiquitous rollover state. To create rollovers
for buttons, use a JavaScript function:

```
<script language="JavaScript" type="text/javascript">
function classChange(styleChange,item) {
 item.className = styleChange;
}
</script>
```

Next, add two additional CSS rules, one for the rollover state for the Reset button
and another for the Submit button:

```
.buttonResetRoll {
 color: white;
 background-color: #c00;
 font-size: 1.5em;
 border: 1px solid #660;
 padding: 4px;
}
.buttonSubmitRoll {
 color: white;
 background-color: #cc0;
 font-size: 1.5em;
 border: 1px solid #660;
 padding: 4px;
}
```

After the function is in place and the extra CSS rules are set up, place the events in the button markup so that you can toggle between the off and on states of the form buttons (see Figure 5-9):

```
<form action="simplequiz.php" method="post">
 <label for="question">Who is president of the U.S.?</label>
 <input type="text" name="question" id="textfield"
value="Type answer here" /><br />
 <input name="reset" type="reset" id="reset" value="Reset"
class="buttonReset"
onMouseOver="classChange('buttonResetRoll',this)"
onMouseOut="classChange('buttonReset',this)" />
 <input type="submit" name="Submit" value="Submit"
class="buttonSubmit"
onMouseOver="classChange('buttonSubmitRoll',this)"
onMouseOut="classChange('buttonSubmit',this)" />
</form>
```

Figure 5-9. A rollover state created through CSS and JavaScript

As noted earlier, until Internet Explorer for Windows supports attribute selectors, you'll need to use class selectors to set button styles that can be seen in all browsers. Using attribute selectors to write CSS rules for the form buttons doesn't require the extra markup in the HTML element that comes from using class selectors. For example, the attribute selector syntax for the buttons using only CSS would look something like this:

```
input[type="reset"] {
 color: #fcc;
 background-color: #900;
 font-size: 1.5em;
 border: 1px solid #660;
 padding: 4px;
}
input[type="submit"] {
 color: white;
 background-color: #660;
 font-size: 1.5em;
```

```
border: 1px solid #660;
padding: 4px;
}
```

You also can use the width property to determine the horizontal size of the button; however, Internet Explorer 4.x for Windows doesn't recognize the CSS width property on the form property.

See Also

The CSS 2.1 specification for attribute selectors at *http://www.w3.org/TR/CSS21/selector.html#attribute-selectors*.

5.5 Setting Up a Submit-Once-Only Button

Problem

You want to keep people from clicking the Submit button more than once.

Solution

First create a class for keeping the button from being displayed:

```
.buttonSubmitHide {
  display: none;
}
```

Then use the following JavaScript programmed to switch styles by class selectors:

```
<script language="JavaScript" type="text/javascript">
function classChange(styleChange,item) {
  item.className = styleChange;
}
</script>
```

Now trigger the function by using an onsubmit event to remove the Submit button from the web document:

```
<h2>Order Confirmation</h2>
<form action="login.php" method="post"
 onsubmit="classChange('buttonSubmitHide',submit);
return true">
 <div align="center">
  <p>Are you sure you want to purchase 12 cans of soda over the
Web?</p>
  <label for="uname">Final Price:</label>
  <input type="text" name="uname" id="uname" value="$7.95" />
<br />
  (includes tax, s+h extra)<br />
  <input type="submit" name="submit" value="submit"
class="buttonSubmit" />
 </div>
</form>
```

Discussion

The JavaScript function in the Solution triggers a change in which a style is applied to the element. You must use the form's onsubmit event to execute the function so that the form's action will still be executed. If the function were triggered with an onclick event on the Submit button, some browsers would execute only the class-changing function. Then, because the button is no longer visible, the user would not be able to trigger the form.

See Also

JavaScript and DHTML Cookbook (O'Reilly) for more recipes that combine JavaScript and CSS.

5.6 Designing a Web Form Without Tables

Problem

You want to include form fields and labels on rows without using an HTML table, thereby ensuring a pure CSS-enabled layout without using any markup for presentation.

Solution

First use labels in conjunction with the form fields in the markup (see Figure 5-10):

```
<form action="login.php" method="post">
 <label for="uname">Username</label>
 <input type="text" name="uname" id="uname" value="" /><br />
 <label for="pname">Password</label>
 <input type="text" name="uname" id="uname" value="" /><br />
 <label for="pname">Remember you?</label>
 <input type="checkbox" name="recall" id="recall"
class="checkbox" /><br />
 <input type="submit" name="Submit" value="Submit"
class="buttonSubmit" />
</form>
```

Then set the display and label properties for the label elements to block, float the label elements to the left, and justify the text on the right (see Figure 5-11):

```
input {
 display: block;
 width: 175px;
 float: left;
 margin-bottom: 10px;
}
label {
 display: block;
 text-align: right;
```

Figure 5-10. The form without styles applied

```
   float: left;
   width: 75px;
   padding-right: 20px;
}
.checkbox {
   width: 1em;
}
br {
   clear: left;
}
.buttonSubmit {
   width: 75px;
   margin-left: 95px;
}
```

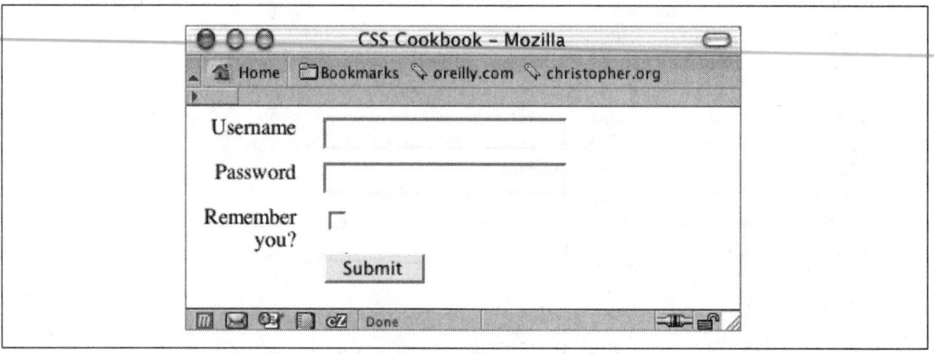

Figure 5-11. The design of the form laid out with styles

Discussion

The input and label elements are set to display: block, which displays them as block-level elements. This makes it possible to set the widths for the text in the label. Instead of resting on top of the input element, the labels are floated to the left. And because all labels have the same width, the look is uniform throughout the form.

The br tag creates a break between the label and form element sets, and clears the float from previous elements. This prevents the other elements (those that appear after the input field matched to the label) from floating as well.

See Also

The HTML 4.1 specification for the label element at *http://www.w3.org/TR/html401/ interact/forms.html#edef-LABEL*; the CSS 2.1 specification for the float property at *http://www.w3.org/TR/CSS21/visuren.html#propdef-float*; the CSS 2.1 specification for the clear property at *http://www.w3.org/TR/CSS21/visuren.html#propdef-clear*.

5.7 Sample Design: A Login Form

Login forms are all over the Web. For instance, you need a login and a password to check your email on the Web, order books from Amazon.com, and even pay that parking ticket online.

Only a few components of a login form are visible to the user: the input field's Submit button and labels as well as the username and password fields themselves. Here is the markup of the form to be stylized (Figure 5-12 shows the input field without styles applied):

```
<form action="login.php" method="post">
 <label for="uname">Username</label>
 <input type="text" name="uname" id="uname" value="" /><br />
 <label for="pword">Password</label>
 <input type="text" name="pword" id="pword" value="" /> <br />
 <input type="submit" name="Submit" value="Submit" />
</form>
```

Figure 5-12. The login form without styles

First, add a character after the text in the label element. Use the :after pseudo-class property to autogenerate the character:

```
label:after {
 content: ": ";
}
```

Next, to make the labels stick out from the form fields, change the background color of the labels and the weight of the font. Through CSS, change the labels so that they have a gray background and black text set in bold type (see Figure 5-13):

```
label {
 background-color: gray;
 color: black;
 font-weight: bold;
}
```

Figure 5-13. Styles for color applied to the label elements

Now, place some padding around the text and change the text to uppercase (see Figure 5-14):

```
label {
 background-color: gray;
 color: black;
 font-weight: bold;
 padding: 4px;
 text-transform: uppercase;
}
```

Figure 5-14. Text transformed to uppercase letters

As you can see, the labels need to be toned down because they compete for attention with the input fields. To reduce their visual impact, shrink the size of the text while keeping the weight of the font set to bold. Also, set the typeface of the labels to Verdana, which renders legibly even in small sizes (see Figure 5-15):

```
label {
 background-color: gray;
```

```
  color: black;
  font-weight: bold;
  padding: 4px;
  text-transform: uppercase;
  font-family: Verdana, Arial, Helvetica, sans-serif;
  font-size: xx-small;
}
```

Figure 5-15. The text refined in the label element

Now it's time to style the input fields. Because the form has two types of input fields, differentiate them by placing a class attribute in the Submit button. This technique enables you to style the input fields and the Submit button differently. If you didn't do this, styles that are intended just for the form fields would also be applied to the Submit button. Using the class selector, you can override or change the properties intended for one element so that they aren't applied to all elements:

```
<input type="submit" name="Submit" value="Submit"
class="buttonSubmit" />
```

To bring in some whitespace around the form elements, set the input fields to display as block-level elements and apply a margin to the bottom (see Figure 5-16):

```
input {
  display: block;
  margin-bottom: 1.25em;
}
```

Next, extend the width of the input box to 150 pixels and place a one-pixel border around the box so that the default bevel rendering that occurs in most browsers goes away. Indicate a slight depth to the page by adding a two-pixel border on the right and bottom of the input box (see Figure 5-17):

```
input {
  display: block;
  margin-bottom: 1.25em;
  width: 150px;
  border: solid black;
  border-width: 1px 2px 2px 1px;
}
```

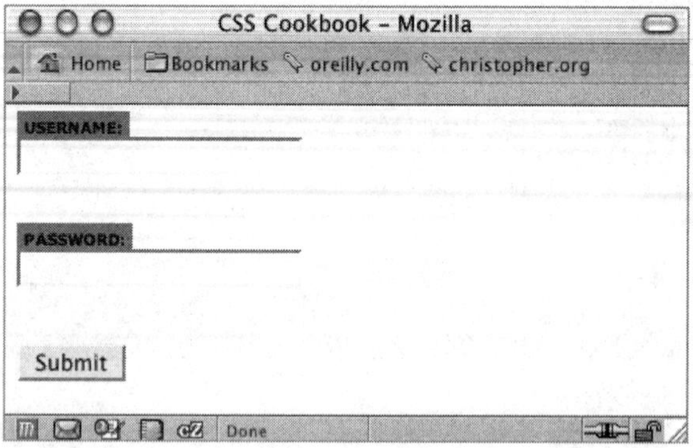

Figure 5-16. The input elements sliding under the labels

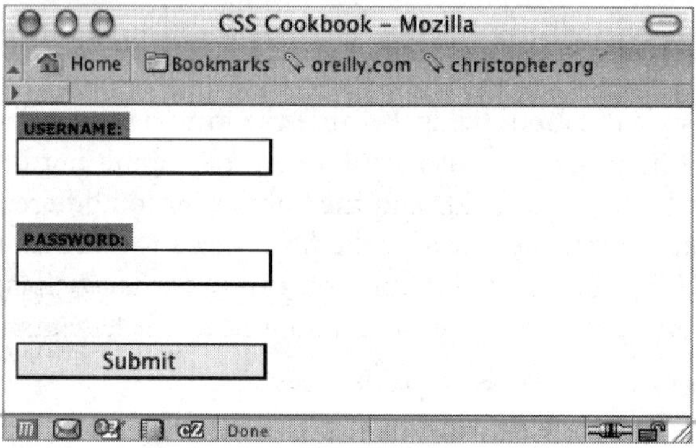

Figure 5-17. The modified input fields

With the main input fields in place, now it's time to apply styles to the Submit button. Because you don't want the Submit button to look like the regular input text fields, use a class selector.

Start by changing the size and position of the Submit button. First, shrink the width of the button by 75 pixels (which is one-half the size of the input fields). Then slide the button to the right by setting the left side margin to 75 pixels (see Figure 5-18):

```
.buttonSubmit {
  width: 75px;
  margin-left: 75px;
}
```

Next, change the Submit button's background to green with a green border, and convert the text to uppercase by using the text-transform property (see Figure 5-19):

```
.buttonSubmit {
  width: 75px;
  margin-left: 75px;
  color: green;
```

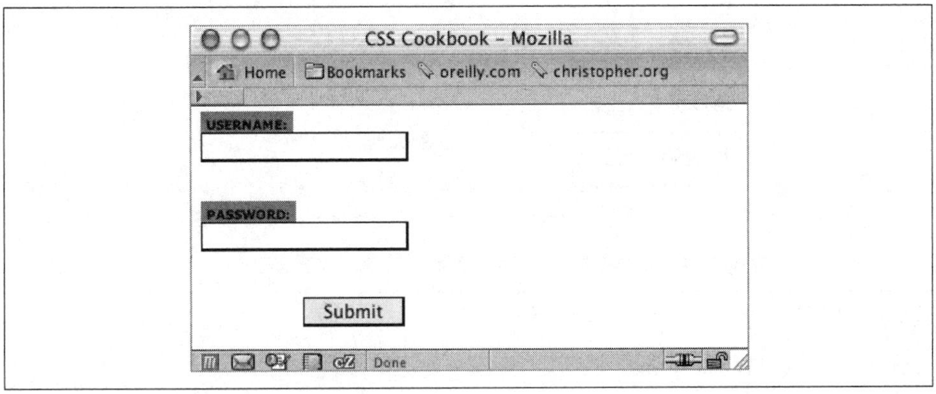

Figure 5-18. The refined Submit button

```
text-transform: uppercase;
border: 1px solid green;
}
```

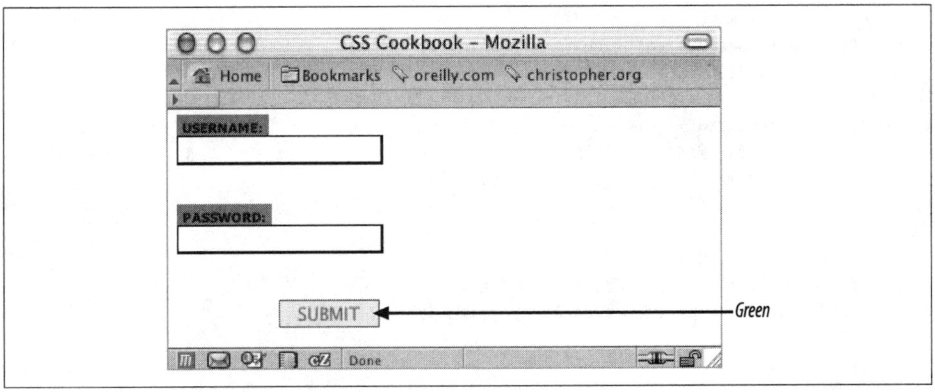

Figure 5-19. The green Submit button in uppercase letters

To add the final touch, hide the br element from the display because the br introduces extra whitespace to the form. Figure 5-20 shows the result.

```
br {
  display: none;
}
```

5.8   Sample Design: A Registration Form

For some forms you might want to place the form elements into a two-column table, with the labels in one column and the fields in the other. Example 5-1 provides the code. Figure 5-21 shows the form and tables without styles applied.

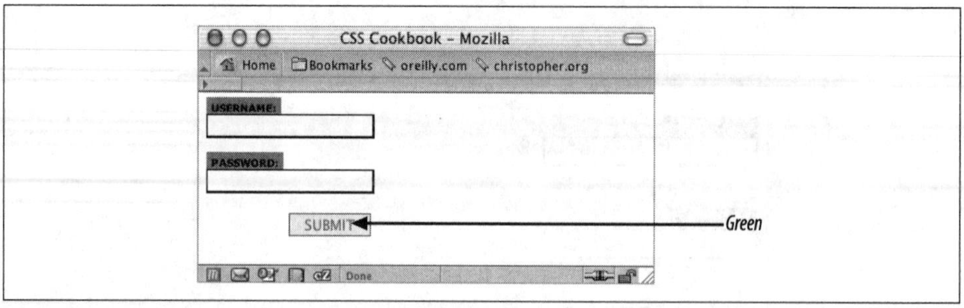

Figure 5-20. The login form styles finalized

Example 5-1. Stylized long form

```
<form action="registration.cfm" method="post">
  <table cellspacing="0">
    <tr class="header">
      <th colspan="2">Account Information</th>
    </tr>
    <tr class="required">
      <th scope="row">Login Name*</th>
      <td><input name="uname" type="text" size="12"
maxlength="12" /></td>
    </tr>
    <tr class="required">
      <th scope="row">Password*</th>
      <td><input name="pword" type="text" size="12"
maxlength="12" /></td>
    </tr>
    <tr class="required">
      <th scope="row">Confirm Password* </th>
      <td><input name="pword2" type="text" size="12"
maxlength="12" /></td>
    </tr>
    <tr class="required">
      <th scope="row">Email Address*</th>
      <td><input name="email" type="text" /></td>
    </tr>
    <tr class="required">
      <th scope="row">Confirm Email*</th>
      <td><input type="text" name="email2" /></td>
    </tr>
    <tr class="header">
      <th colspan="2">Contact Information</th>
    </tr>
    <tr class="required">
      <th scope="row">First Name* </th>
      <td><input name="fname" type="text" size="11" /></td>
    </tr>
    <tr class="required">
      <th scope="row">Last Name* </th>
      <td><input name="lname" type="text" size="11" /></td>
    </tr>
```

Example 5-1. Stylized long form (continued)

```
    <tr class="required">
      <th scope="row">Address 1*</th>
      <td><input name="address1" type="text" size="11" /></td>
    </tr>
    <tr>
      <th scope="row">Address 2 </th>
      <td><input type="text" name="address2" /></td>
    </tr>
    <tr class="required">
      <th scope="row">City* </th>
      <td><input type="text" name="city" /></td>
    </tr>
    <tr class="required">
      <th scope="row">State or Province*</th>
      <td><select name="state">
        <option selected="selected"
disabled="disabled">Select...</option>
        <option value="alabama">Alabama</option>
      </select></td>
    </tr>
    <tr class="required">
      <th scope="row">Zip*</th>
      <td><input name="zipcode" type="text" id="zipcode"
size="5" maxlength="5" /></td>
    </tr>
    <tr class="required">
      <th scope="row">Country*</th>
      <td><input type="text" name="country" /></td>
    </tr>
    <tr class="required">
      <th scope="row">Gender*</th>
      <td> <input type="radio" name="sex" value="female" />
        Female
        <input type="radio" name="sex" value="male" />
        Male </td>
    </tr>
    <tr class="header">
      <th colspan="2">Misc. Information</th>
    </tr>
    <tr>
      <th scope="row"> Annual Household Income </th>
      <td>
       <select name="income" size="1" >
         <option selected="selected" disabled="disabled">
Select...</option>
         <option value="notsay">I'd rather not say</option>
       </select> </td>
    </tr>
    <tr>
      <th scope="row">Interests</th>
      <td><input name="interests" type="checkbox"
value="shopping-fashion" />
```

Example 5-1. Stylized long form (continued)

```
          Shopping/fashion
          <input name="interests" type="checkbox"
value="sports" />
          Sports
          <input name="interests" type="checkbox"
value="travel" />
          Travel</td>
    </tr>
    <tr>
      <th scope="row">Eye Color</th>
      <td><input name="eye" type="checkbox" value="red" />
      Red
      <input name="eye" type="checkbox" value="green" />
      Green
      <input name="eye" type="checkbox" value="brown" />
      Brown
      <input name="eye" type="checkbox" value="blue" />
      Blue Gold</td>
    </tr>
  </table>
  <input type="submit" name="Submit" value="Submit"
id="buttonSubmit" />
  <input type="reset" name="Submit2" value="Reset"
id="buttonReset" />
</form>
```

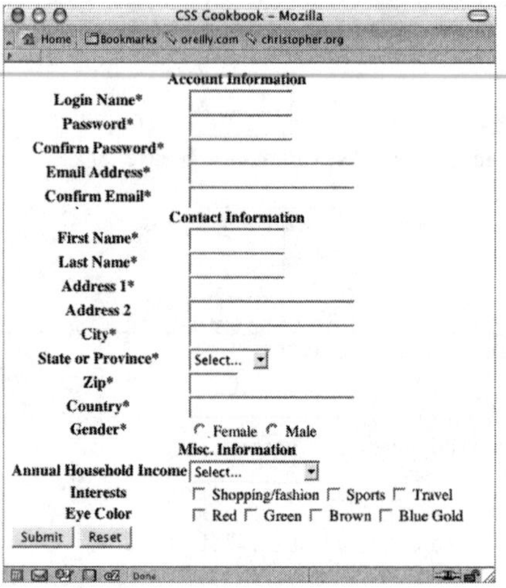

Figure 5-21. The form and table without styles applied

The first element to style is the table element. Set the border model as well as the text color and border around the table itself (see Figure 5-22):

```
table {
  border-collapse: collapse;
  color: black;
  border: 1px solid black;
}
```

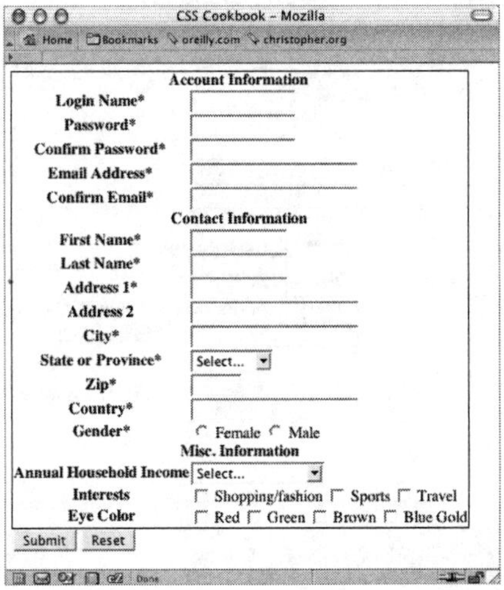

Figure 5-22. A border placed around the table

Next, tackle the table header cells, which are located in the left column (see Figure 5-23). The table header cells is set to a width of 200 pixels, while the content inside the cell is aligned to the left, set to Verdana and sized to 0.7 em units:

```
th {
  width: 200px;
  text-align: right;
  vertical-align: top;
  border-top: 1px solid black;
  font-family: Verdana;
  font-size: 0.7em;
}
```

Adjust the padding of the header cells (see Figure 5-24):

```
th {
  width: 200px;
  text-align: right;
  vertical-align: top;
  border-top: 1px solid black;
  font-family: Verdana;
  font-size: 0.7em;
  padding-right: 12px;
  padding-top: 0.75em;
  padding-bottom: 0.75em;
}
```

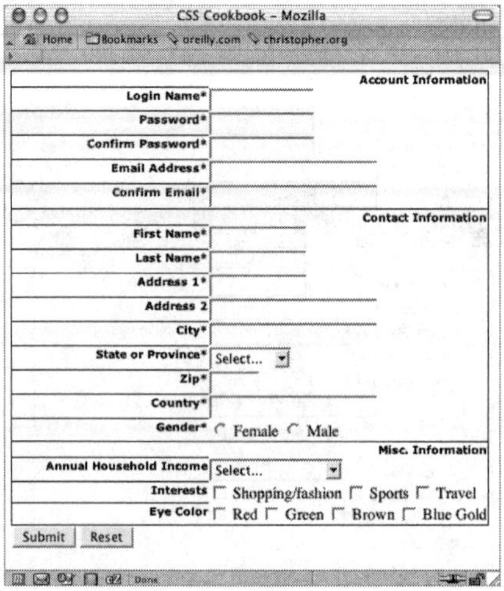

Figure 5-23. Refined table header cells

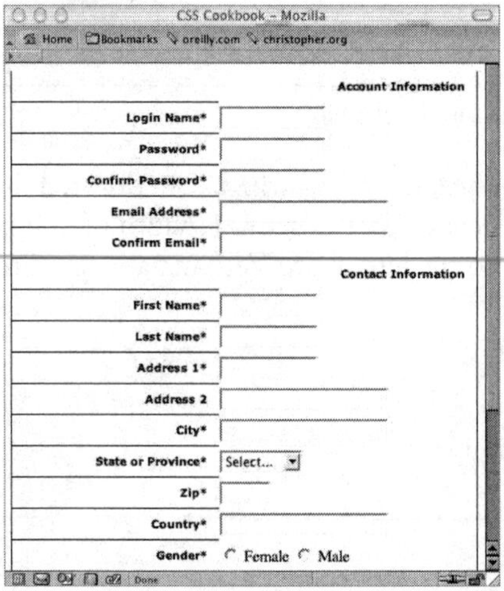

Figure 5-24. Padding applied to the table header cells

Next, apply styles to the right table cells. To underscore the difference between the left and right columns, convert the right table cell background to black. Also, set a gray border to the left to soften the transition when reading the rows left to right (see Figure 5-25):

```
td {
  vertical-align: middle;
  background-color: black;
  border-bottom: 1px solid white;
```

```
    color: white;
    border-left: 4px solid gray;
    padding: 4px;
    font-family: Verdana;
    font-size: .7em;
}
```

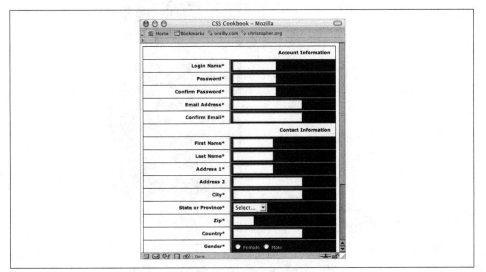

Figure 5-25. The stylized right column table cells

Certain fields are required to execute the registration, so change the color of the text labels for those fields. This change in color will indicate at a glance which fields are required (see Figure 5-26):

```
.required {
    color: red;
}
```

Note that the CSS rule states that the color is red, but for printing purposes the color will come out a shade of gray.

Adjust the form headers that indicate the different sections of the form by making the text uppercase and slightly larger than the other text in the form (see Figure 5-27):

```
.header th {
    text-align: left;
    text-transform: uppercase;
    font-size: .9em;
}
```

Slide the form headers so that they rest on top of the second column. To determine where to place the headers, add the size of the left column (200 pixels), the padding

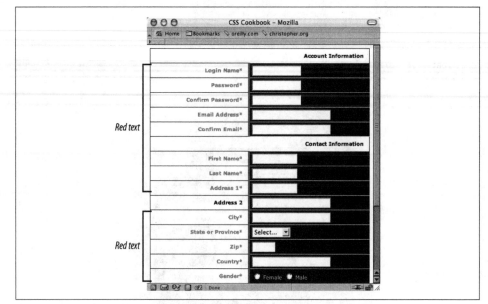

Figure 5-26. The required fields marked with red text

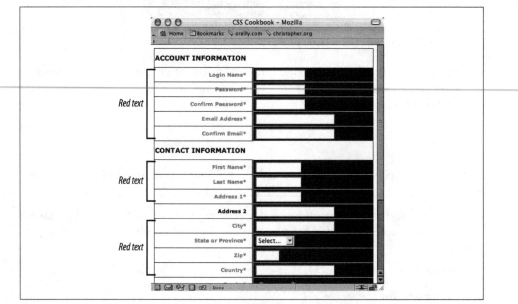

Figure 5-27. The refined form section headers

of the right column (4 pixels), the width of the border on the left of the right column (4 pixels), and the padding of the right column (12 pixels):

```
.header th {
  text-align: left;
```

```
        text-transform: uppercase;
        font-size: .9em;
        padding-left: 220px;
}
```

Then add a touch of visual appeal by applying thicker borders to the top and bottom of the header (see Figure 5-28):

```
.header th {
        text-align: left;
        text-transform: uppercase;
        font-size: .9em;
        padding-left: 220px;
        border-bottom: 2px solid gray;
        border-top: 2px solid black;
}
```

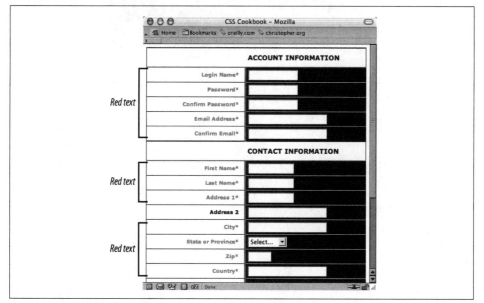

Figure 5-28. Padding added to the section headers

For the finishing touch, move the Submit and Reset buttons so that they fall under the form fields, just like the section headings, by assigning the left side of the margin to be 220 pixels (see Figure 5-29):

```
#buttonSubmit {
        margin-left: 220px;
        margin-top: 4px;
}
```

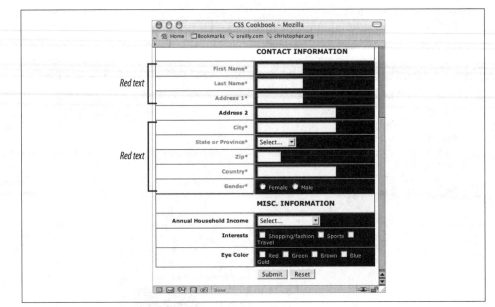

Figure 5-29. The Submit and Reset buttons moved into place

CHAPTER 6

Tables

6.0   Introduction

Print designers use grids to create compelling layouts. Using such a structure makes it easy to place elements into all sorts of layouts, from the front page of a newspaper to a movie poster to the cover of this book. It also makes the designs visually more appealing.

When print designers began gravitating toward the Web, they found the lack of structure frustrating. At most, designers initially could only float images to the left or right until Netscape invented the center tag. In fact, it wasn't until HTML tables were used as grids that the web-design industry took off. Even still, available tools had their limitations and as such designers overused tables to structure entire web pages.

With CSS-enabled designs, web developers learned they could forego the practice of manipulating tables to hold designs. However, they also learned that styling tabular data, such as a calendar, could still be challenging.

This chapter teaches you how to make your tables look better by stylizing table headers, setting borders for a table and for its cells, and reducing gaps with images in table cells. The sample design at the end of the chapter takes you through the steps required to stylize a calendar.

6.1   Setting the Cell Spacing

Problem

You want to change the space between the table border and cell borders.

Solution

Use the cellspacing table attribute:

```
<table cellspacing="15">
 <tr>
   <th colspan="2">
    General Demographic Characteristics of Tallahassee, FL
   </th>
 </tr>
 <tr>
   <th>
   </th>
   <th>
    Estimate
   </th>
 </tr>
 <tr>
   <td>
    Total population
   </td>
   <td>
    272,091
   </td>
 </tr>
</table>
```

Discussion

The CSS 2.1 specification describes a standard mechanism to manipulate the cellspacing table attribute through the use of the border-spacing property when the border-collapse value is set to separate:

```
border-collapse: separate;
border-spacing: 15px;
```

However, implementation of this part of the specification isn't visible in Internet Explorer for Windows. (It does work in Netscape Navigator 7+.) Using the cellspacing attribute is currently the best solution that works in Internet Explorer for Windows, Netscape Navigator, Safari, and Opera browsers.

See Also

Recipe 6.2 on setting table borders and cell padding; the CSS 2.1 specification for border-collapse at *http://www.w3.org/TR/CSS21/tables.html#propdef-border-collapse*; the CSS 2.1 specification for border-spacing at *http://www.w3.org/TR/CSS21/tables.html#propdef-border-spacing*.

6.2   Setting the Borders and Cell Padding

Problem

You want to set the borders and the amount of space within table cells to create a stronger visual display than the default rendering of a table, as in Figure 6-1, for example.

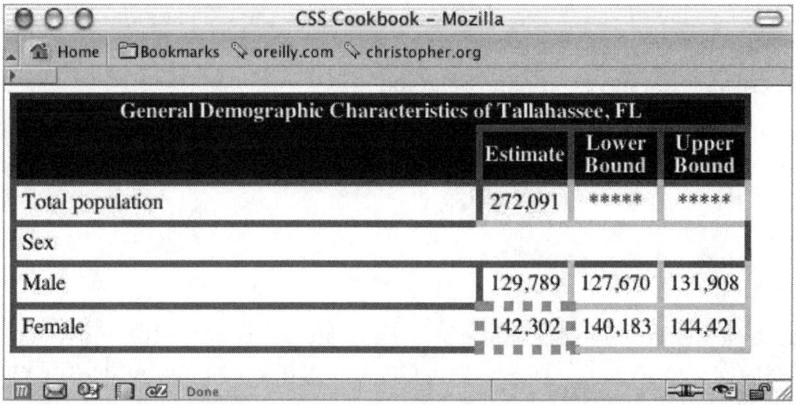

Figure 6-1. Borders and padding applied to the table and table cells

Solution

Use the padding property to address the amount of space between the content in the cell and the edges of the cell. Use the border property to set the borders on both the table and its cells:

```
table {
  border-collapse: collapse;
  border: 5px solid #444;
}
td {
  padding: 4px;
}
th {
  color: white;
  background-color: black;
}
td, th+th {
  border: 5px solid #666;
}
td+td {
  border: 5px solid #ccc;
  text-align: center;
}
```

```
td#winner {
  border: 7px dotted #999;
}
```

Discussion

There are two border models for HTML tables: collapse and separate. At the time of writing, the collapse model is more widely implemented by browsers and thus more used by designers.

All browsers today default to the collapse model. As the CSS standard doesn't specify that behavior, you should explicitly set the collapse model in your style sheets lest a future browser not have the same defaults.

The collapse model for a table is set by default. Just in case a browser might start using another border model, you can specifically set the border model using the border-collapse property set to collapse:

```
table {
  border-collapse: collapse;
}
```

The table element's border attribute specifies borders for the table and its enclosing cells. You can specify CSS's border property through a separate border thickness for the table and individual cells.

If you do apply a border to a cell that runs counter to a previous CSS rule, you must follow these four CSS specification rules for conflict resolution:

- If border-style is set to hidden, all other border styles are concealed.
- If border-style is set to none, any other border style wins.
- Unless a cell has border-style set to hidden or has border-style set to none, a thicker border overrides the narrower borders. If adjoining cells have the same width, the style of the border will be determined in the following order: double, solid, dashed, dotted, ridge, outset, groove, inset.
- If adjoining cells have a different color while possessing the same style and width, the border color will be determined in the following order: cell, row, row group, column, column group, and then table.

The other border model is separate, in which every cell contains its own borders and can be styled independently of other cell borders. Within the separate model, the border-spacing property is used to set the horizontal and vertical space respectively between cells:

```
table#runoffdata {
  border-collapse: separate;
  border-spacing: 4px 4px;
}
```

If the `border-collapse` property is set to `separate`, then any styles set for rows, columns, or groups of table cells aren't applied. Also, styles for table cells that don't contain content can be displayed or hidden using the `empty-cells` property with the value of `show` or `hide`, respectively.

While the separate border model gives more control to web developers, as of this writing separate is supported only in Mozilla and Netscape 6+, not in Internet Explorer. Therefore most web designers stick to the collapse model.

See Also

The CSS 2.1 specification about border models at *http://www.w3.org/TR/CSS21/tables.html#propdef-border-collapse*; for more discussion on tables, see Chapter 11 in *Cascading Style Sheets: The Definitive Guide* (O'Reilly).

6.3   Setting the Styles Within Table Cells

Problem

You want to stylize links within a table cell to make them appear visually different from the rest of the page.

Solution

Use a descendant selector (sometimes referred to as a *contextual selector*) to manipulate the styles for content in a table cell:

```
td a {
  display: block;
  background-color: #333;
  color: white;
  text-decoration: none;
  padding: 4px;
}
```

Discussion

By using the type and descendent selectors—the `td a` in the CSS rule—to apply the styles, you reduce the amount of markup needed to perfect your designs and you reduce the document's file sizes. The style affects only the a elements within the table cells, td.

If you need more control over the design of the content within a table cell, use a class selector:

```
<td class="navText">
<a href="/">Home</a>
</td>
```

You then can apply the CSS rules to the cell's content through a combination of class and descendant selectors:

```
td.navText {
  font-size: x-small;
}
```

See Also

The CSS 2.1 specification regarding type selectors at *http://www.w3.org/TR/CSS21/selector.html#type-selectors*; *http://www.w3.org/TR/CSS21/selector.html#descendant-selectors* for information about descendant selectors.

6.4 Removing Gaps from Table Cells with Images

Problem

You want to get rid of space in a table cell that contains only an image. You want to go from Figure 6-2 to Figure 6-3.

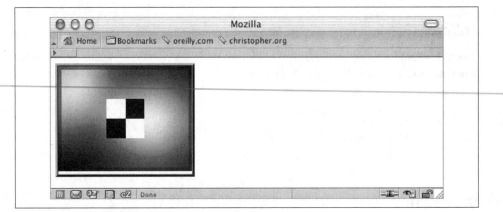

Figure 6-2. A gap appearing below an image in a table cell

Solution

Set the image to be displayed as a block-level element:

```
td img {
  display: block;
}
```

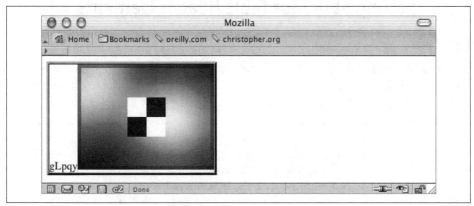

Figure 6-3. Displaying an image in a table cell as a block-level element

Discussion

We set the element to block content because the whitespace at the bottom of the image occurs because the image element is supposed to contain inline content, possibly text. The browser puts the image on the baseline used for text content even if there is no text in the content. This baseline isn't at the bottom of the cell because some letters (e.g., g, p, q, and y) have descenders that hang below that baseline (see Figure 6-4).

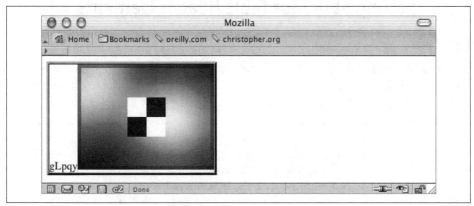

Figure 6-4. The lowercase letters g, p, q, and y

You can't get rid of the descender space, because the baseline is a percentage of the total font size. Therefore the only way to place images without a baseline is to set the display property for the image to block as shown in the Solution.

A Document Type Definition (DTD) is a formal statement that defines the relationship of elements used in a web page. For example, there are differences in the HTML2 DTD compared to the HTML 4.1 DTD. Those differences are spelled out in their own DTD. A browser can determine which DTD to use when rendering a page by a small statement that precedes any markup in a web page.

There are certain DOCTYPEs that will put the browser into standards mode instead of quirks mode.

Having the browser in standards mode ensures the gap between images and table cell borders. Use alternative DOCTYPES that trigger quirks mode but that still validate to avoid this gap or if you simply want to avoid standards mode. For more information, see a chart comparing DOCTYPEs and browsers at *http://www.webstandards. org/learn/reference/doctype_switch.html.*

There might be times when setting the image's display to block isn't the best solution to removing whitespace around an image in a table cell. If that turns out to be the case, another method to remove the space is to set the image's vertical-align property to bottom as long as the image is taller than the line box.

See Also

The CSS 2.1 specification for the display property at *http://www.w3.org/TR/CSS21/ visuren.html#propdef-display*; "quirks" mode at *http://www.mozilla.org/docs/web-developer/quirks/*; "almost standards" mode at *http://devedge.netscape.com/viewsource/ 2002/almost-standards/.*

6.5 Setting Styles for Table Header Elements

Problem

You want to modify the default bold look of table header cells to grab the viewer's attention; Figure 6-5 shows a table with traditional table headers, and Figure 6-6 shows a stylized version of the same table.

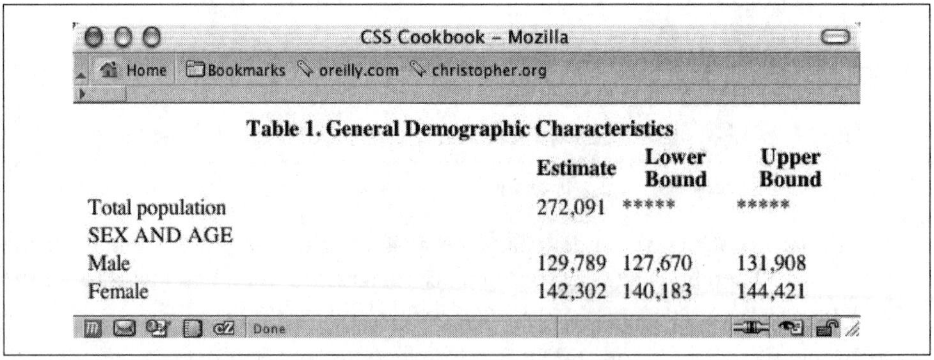

Figure 6-5. The table as it appears before styles are applied to the table headers

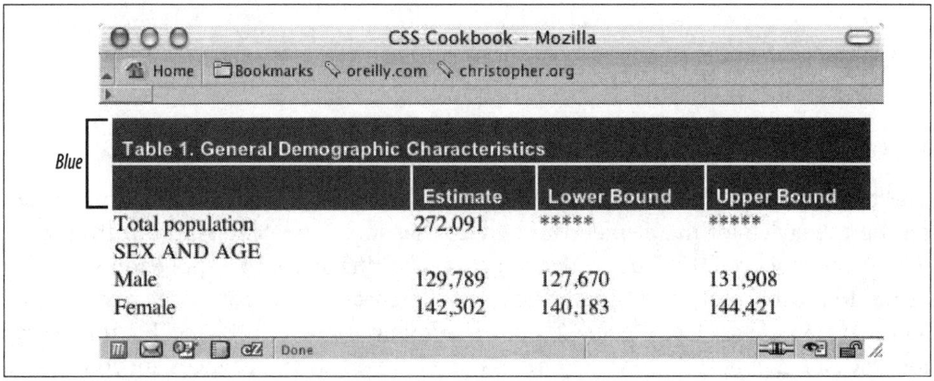

Figure 6-6. Styles applied to the table headers

Solution

Use the th element selector to stylize the table header:

```
th {
  text-align: left;
  padding: 1em 1.5em 0.1em 0.5em;
  font-family: Arial, Helvetica, Verdana, sans-serif;
  font-size: .9em;
  color: white;
  background-color: blue;
  border-right: 2px solid blue;
}
```

For tables with multiple rows of th elements that require different styles, use a class selector to differentiate the rows:

```
.secondrow th {
/* Use a lighter shade of blue in the background */
  background-color: #009;
}
```

Put the appropriate rows into that class:

```
<tr>
<th colspan="4">
Table 1. General Demographic Characteristics
</th>
</tr>
<tr class="secondrow">
<th>
 
</th>
<th>
Estimate
</th>
<th>
Lower Bound
</th>
```

```
<th>
    Upper Bound
</th>
</tr>
```

Discussion

The th element characterizes the contents of the cell as header information. When setting the styles for the element, use styles that make the cell stand out from content in the table cell, td. You can generate contrasting styles by simply adjusting any of the following properties: font-family, background-color, font-size, font-weight, and text alignment. (See Recipe 1.1 for specifying fonts and Recipe 1.2 for setting font measurements and sizes.) Regardless of what you adjust, chances are you will be improving the look of the table headers.

In terms of stylizing stacks of rows, no matter-of-fact solution that did not require a class or id selector was available at the time of this writing. CSS 3 introduces the :nth-child pseudoclass, which makes styling for alternating table rows practical. However, at the time of this writing, it's only a Candidate Recommendation and support is nonexistent.

See Also

The :nth-child pseudoclass specification at *http://www.w3.org/TR/2001/CR-css3-selectors-20011113/#nth-child-pseudo*.

6.6   Sample Design: An Elegant Calendar

Great for organization, calendars enable us to schedule lunches, remember birthdays, and plan honeymoons. As designers, we can think of all those months, dates, and appointments as tabular data.

If you display your calendar as an HTML table, chances are the table looks rather plain, and if it contains numerous events then it probably looks somewhat convoluted as well. In this design, we use CSS to create a calendar that is more legible than what you could create using vanilla HTML.

First, take a look at Figure 6-7, which shows the markup for the calendar without styles.

Next, look at the markup itself to see how it's set up. As you learned in Recipe 6.1, the cellspacing attribute needs to be set in the table element:

```
<table cellspacing="0">
```

Now, set the first three rows of table headers, th, containing the year, month, and days, in their own rows within their own table headers:

```
<tr>
<th colspan="7" id="year">
```

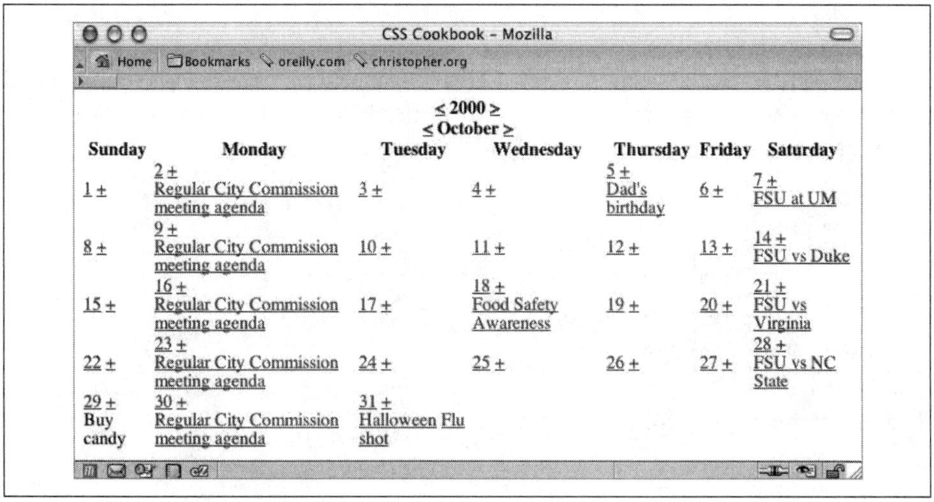

Figure 6-7. The calendar without styles

```
    <a href="year.html?previous">&lt;</a> 2000 <a
href="year.html?next">&gt;</a>
  </th>
 </tr>
 <tr>
  <th colspan="7" id="month">
    <a href="month.html?previous">&lt;</a> October <a
href="month.html?next">&gt;</a>
  </th>
 </tr>
  <tr id="days">
  <th>Sunday</th>
  <th>Monday</th>
  <th>Tuesday</th>
  <th>Wednesday</th>
  <th>Thursday</th>
  <th>Friday </th>
  <th>Saturday</th>
 </tr>
```

The first date is October 1, which in this calendar falls on a Sunday. To signify that Sundays and Saturdays are days of the weekend, use a class selector in the td element.

In each date of the month there is a link on the date itself (which would, in theory, take the user to a detailed listing of the day) as well as a link to add more events to the day. Wrap these two links in a div element so that when new events are added there is a clear division between the two sections in the table cell:

```
<tr>
 <td class="weekend">
  <div>
   <a href="1.html" class="date">1</a>
   <a href="add.html" class="addevent">+</a>
```

```
    </div>
   </td>
```

The next date, October 2, has an event listed. The event is marked up as a link and placed below the div containing the date and the addevent links (because October 2 is a weekday, the weekend class isn't applied to the td element):

```
   <td>
    <div>
     <a href="2.html" class="date">2</a>
     <a href="add.html" class="addevent">+</a>
    </div>
    <a href="16.html?id=1" class="event">Regular City
   Commission meeting agenda</a>
    </td>
```

The rest of the markup follows a similar structure:

```
   <td>
    <div>
     <a href="3.html" class="date">3</a>
     <a href="add.html" class="addevent">+</a>
    </div>
   </td>
   <td>
     <div>
      <a href="4.html" class="date">4</a>
      <a href="add.html" class="addevent">+</a>
     </div>
   </td>
   <td>
    <div>
      <a href="5.html" class="date">5</a>
      <a href="add.html" class="addevent">+</a>
     </div>
     <a href="5.html?id=1" class="event">Dad's birthday</a>
    </td>
   <td>
     <div>
      <a href="6.html" class="date">6</a>
      <a href="add.html" class="addevent">+</a>
     </div>
   </td>
   <td class="weekend">
     <div>
      <a href="7.html" class="date">7</a>
      <a href="add.html" class="addevent">+</a>
     </div>
     <a href="7.html?id=1" class="event">FSU at UM</a>
    </td>
   </tr>

   [...]

   <tr>
```

```
<td class="weekend">
  <div>
    <a href="29.html" class="date">29</a>
    <a href="add.html" class="addevent">+</a>
  </div>
  <div class="event">Buy candy</div>
</td>
<td>
  <div>
    <a href="30.html" class="date">30</a>
    <a href="add.html" class="addevent">+</a>
  </div>
  <a href="16.html?id=1" class="event">Regular City
Commission meeting agenda</a>
</td>
<td>
  <div>
    <a href="31.html" class="date">31</a>
    <a href="add.html" class="addevent">+</a>
  </div>
  <a href="31.html?id=1" class="event">Halloween</a>
  <a href="31.html?id=2" class="event">Flu shot</a>
</td>
<td>
  <div class="emptydate"> </div>
</td>
<td>
  <div class="emptydate"> </div>
</td>
<td>
  <div class="emptydate"> </div>
</td>
<td class="weekend">
  <div class="emptydate"> </div>
</td>
</tr>
</table>
```

With the calendar marked up, you can begin setting up the styles. First, apply the styles to the table and links. The width of the table is set to 100% and the border model (see Recipe 6-2) is set to collapse, the common model web designers are used to and most browsers get right in their CSS implementations; the underline decoration is turned off (see Figure 6-8):

```
table {
 width: 100%;
 border-collapse: collapse;
}
td a:link, td a:visited {
 text-decoration: none;
}
```

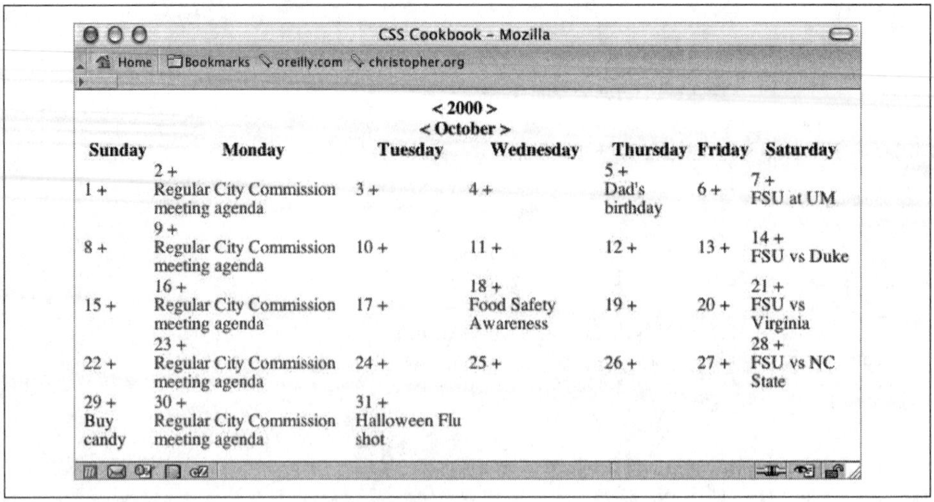
CSS Cookbook - Mozilla
Home
Bookmarks
oreilly.com
christopher.org
< 2000 >
< October >
Sunday Monday Tuesday Wednesday Thursday Friday Saturday
1 + 2 + Regular City Commission meeting agenda 3 + 4 + 5 + Dad's birthday 6 + 7 + FSU at UM
8 + 9 + Regular City Commission meeting agenda 10 + 11 + 12 + 13 + 14 + FSU vs Duke
15 + 16 + Regular City Commission meeting agenda 17 + 18 + Food Safety Awareness 19 + 20 + 21 + FSU vs Virginia
22 + 23 + Regular City Commission meeting agenda 24 + 25 + 26 + 27 + 28 + FSU vs NC State
29 + Buy candy 30 + Regular City Commission meeting agenda 31 + Halloween Flu shot

Figure 6-8. Underline decoration of the links removed

Next, set up the styles for the first three rows of the table. The rows are marked with ID selectors because you want the styles to show up only once in the document. Stylize these rows in a straightforward manner using the monospace font for the heading font and then decreasing the font sizes, with the month sized the largest (see Figure 6-9):

```
#year {
 font-family: monospace;
 font-size: 1.5em;
 padding: 0;
 margin: 0;
}
#month {
 font-family: monospace;
 font-size: 2em;
 padding: 0;
 margin: 0;
}
#days {
 background-color: black;
 color: white;
 font-family: monospace;
 width: 75px;
}
```

Now it's time to stylize the dates and add event links in each cell. To reproduce the box date effect seen in most calendars, place a border to the right and bottom of the text and float the content to the left.

You want the add event links to be close to the dates. Floating the link to the right means the link will be positioned next to the date of the following day. By floating

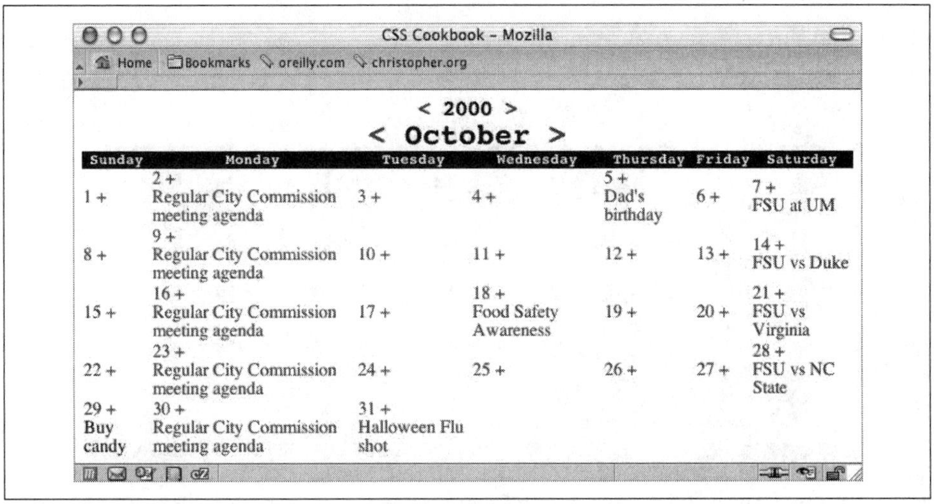

Figure 6-9. Styling the first three rows

the add event link to the left, you are telling the user that the plus sign means add an event for that particular day (see Figure 6-10):

```
.date {
  border-right: 1px solid black;
  border-bottom: 1px solid black;
  font-family: monospace;
  text-decoration: none;
  float: left;
  width: 1.5em;
  height: 1.5em;
  background-color: white;
  text-align: center;
}
.addevent {
  display: block;
  float: left;
  width: 1em;
  height: 1em;
  text-align: center;
  background-color: #666;
  color: white;
  font-weight: bold;
  text-decoration: none
}
```

Now it's time to look at how the event listings can be stylized. Because the previous links are floated, you need to create a visible break and move the events below the date.

Setting the clear property to both achieves this visual break. The clear property is used to indicate which sides of an element should not be positioned next to a floated

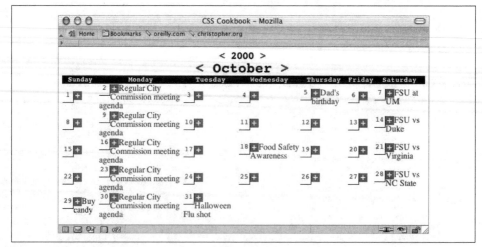

Figure 6-10. Styles introduced to the date and add event links

element. In this case, you don't want the left side to run next to the date and add event links. However, just in case the design changes in the future and the dates are positioned on the opposite side, use a value of both instead of left.

Next, change the display of the link to block and place padding on the bottom (see Figure 6-11). You're making these changes to prevent multiple events in a table cell from running into each other. Also, the padding acts as a nice visual buffer, allowing the eye to easily discern between two events:

```
.event {
  clear: both;
  padding-left: 1em;
  padding-bottom: .75em;
  display: block;
}
```

To each table cell, apply a width of 14%. You're using 14% because 7 (representing the seven sections of the calendar, or days of the week) goes into 100 (representing 100% of the viewport) approximately 14 times. Also, place a white border on all sides of the cell and position all the content to the top with the vertical-align property (see Figure 6-12):

```
td {
  width: 14%;
  background-color: #ccc;
  border: 1px solid white;
  vertical-align: top;
}
```

Figure 6-11. Event links treated like block-level elements

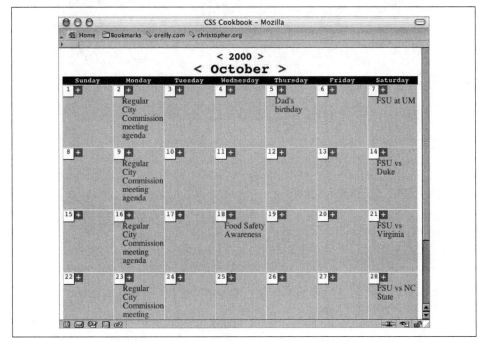

Figure 6-12. The content in each of the cells moved to the top

Make the background color of the weekend dates darker than that used for the week-day dates (see Figure 6-13):

```
.weekend {
  background-color: #999;
}
```

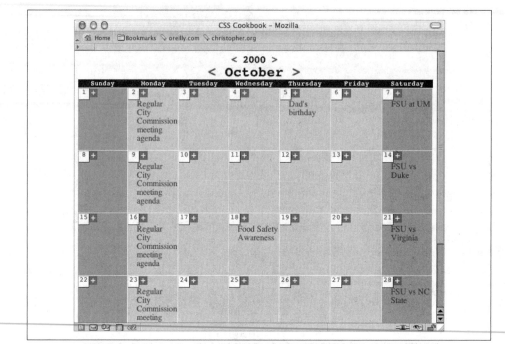

Figure 6-13. The weekend days marked with a darker gray background color

Slightly gray-out the look of the remaining days in the calendar (see Figure 6-14):

```
.emptydate {
  border-right: 1px solid #666;
  border-bottom: 1px solid #666;
  font-family: monospace;
  text-decoration: none;
  float: left;
  width: 1.5em;
  height: 1.5em;
  background-color: #ccc;
  text-align: center;
}
```

For the current day (in this example the current day is the 27th), place a two-pixel black border around the box:

```
#today {
  border: 2px solid black;
}
```

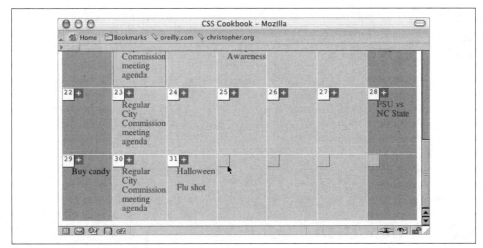

Figure 6-14. Empty dates for the next month stylized

And with that, the calendar is complete, as shown in Figure 6-15.

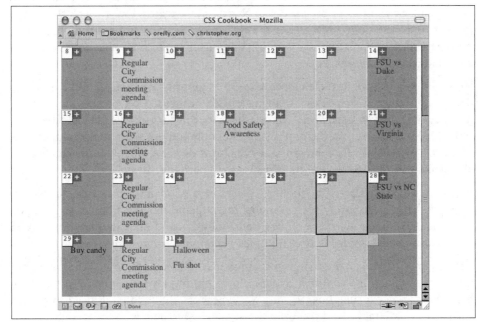

Figure 6-15. The current date in the calendar with a darker border

CHAPTER 7

Page Layouts

7.0   Introduction

One of the last frontiers in creating a truly CSS-enabled presentation is the layout. For a long time, web developers have been using HTML tables to create their layouts, often nesting tables to create multicolumn, multilevel layouts. Nested HTML tables render well in older browsers like Netscape Navigator 4 where CSS support, if present, is barely noticeable and is mostly wrong. If your audience uses an older browser and visual presentation is a key component of the site's success, you should consider using HTML tables.

However, if your audience uses a browser that supports CSS, you should use CSS to design your layouts. As a design language, CSS is focused on presentation, which includes helping web developers control the layout of their pages. HTML tables and other HTML elements, on the other hand, are tools you use to mark up content. The ideal is to have HTML represent the structure of the content at an intellectual abstract level and CSS say how to present it for a particular device.

Furthermore, with CSS you diminish file sizes and maintenance headaches. For example, by stripping away presentational markup and moving a design to CSS, you can reduce the file size of a web page tremendously. And once the design is in CSS syntax, creating site-wide changes becomes a snap.

This chapter discusses the many ways in which you can create column layouts—including simple one-column layouts, four-column layouts, and everything in between. It also explains how to start working with CSS if you still need to build a site using HTML tables and you want to use CSS just to help with the layout chores.

7.1 Developing Hybrid Layouts Using HTML Tables and CSS

Problem

You want to build a page layout that possesses the rigid structure of an HTML table while leveraging the ability to control its appearance through CSS.

Solution

Use one HTML table to control the layout of the entire page. Then, in each table row element, tr, insert an id attribute (see Figure 7-1):

```
<table width="600" cellspacing="0" align="center">
 <tr>
  <th colspan="5" id="header">
   <h1>Business Web Site</h1>
  </th>
 </tr>
 <tr id="navSite">
  <td width="120"><a href="/">Home</a></td>
  <td width="120"><a href="/products/">Products</a></td>
  <td width="120"><a href="/services/">Services</a></td>
  <td width="120"><a href="/aboutus/">About Us</a></td>
  <td width="122"><a href="/contact/">Contact</a></td>
 </tr>
 <tr id="content">
  <td colspan="3">
   <img src="dot_darkgrey.gif" width="300" height="200">
   <h2><a href="/products/">Epsum factorial non</a></h2>
    <p>Lorem ipsum dolor sit <a href="/products/">amet</a>,
consectetuer adipiscing elit. Li Europan lingues es membres del
sam familie. Lor separat existentie es un myth. Por scientie,
musica, sport etc., li tot Europa usa li sam
vocabularium.</p>
    <p>Li lingues differe solmen in li grammatica, li
pronunciation e li plu commun vocabules. Omnicos directe al
desirabilitá de un nov lingua franca.</p>
  </td>
  <td colspan="2" >
   <img src="dot_darkgrey.gif" width="150" height="100">
   <h3><a href="/services/">deposit quid pro</a></h3>
   <p>Lorem ipsum <a href="/services/">dolor</a> sit amet,
consectetuer adipiscing elit.</p>
   <img src="dot_darkgrey.gif" width="150" height="100">
   <h3><a href="/services/">sommun paroles</a></h3>
   <p>Lorem ipsum dolor sit amet, <a href="/services/">
consectetuer</a> adipiscing elit.</p>
  </td>
 </tr>
 <tr id="footer">
```

```
 <td colspan="5">
  Copyright 2003 Lorem ipsum dolor sit amet.
 </td>
</tr>
</table>
```

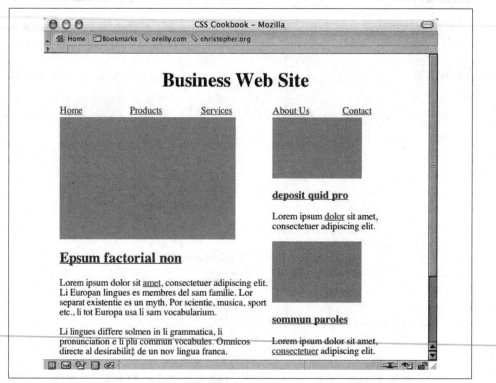

Figure 7-1. The default rendering of the table

Next, for table cells that act as page columns, insert id attributes for each column. For example, this Solution comprises two columns, a left and a right, which are marked with the values contentLeft and contentRight, respectively:

```
<table width="600" cellspacing="0" align="center">
 <tr>
  <th colspan="5" id="header">
   <h1>Business Web Site</h1></th>
 </tr>
 <tr id="navSite">
  <td width="120"><a href="/">Home</a></td>
  <td width="120"><a href="/products/">Products</a></td>
  <td width="120"><a href="/services/">Services</a></td>
  <td width="120"><a href="/aboutus/">About Us</a></td>
  <td width="122"><a href="/contact/">Contact</a></td>
 </tr>
 <tr>
```

```
  <td colspan="3" id="contentLeft">
   <img src="dot_darkgrey.gif" width="300" height="200">
   <h2><a href="/products/">Epsum factorial non</a></h2>
    <p>Lorem ipsum dolor sit <a href="/products/">amet</a>,
consectetuer adipiscing elit. Li Europan lingues es membres del
sam familie. Lor separat existentie es un myth. Por scientie,
musica, sport etc., li tot Europa usa li sam
vocabularium.</p>
    <p>Li lingues differe solmen in li grammatica, li
pronunciation e li plu commun vocabules. Omnicos directe al
desirabilitá de un nov lingua franca.</p>
  </td>
  <td colspan="2" id="contentRight">
   <img src="dot_darkgrey.gif" width="150" height="100">
   <h3><a href="/services/">deposit quid pro</a></h3>
   <p>Lorem ipsum <a href="/services/">dolor</a> sit amet,
consectetuer adipiscing elit.</p>
   <img src="dot_darkgrey.gif" width="150" height="100">
   <h3><a href="/services/">sommun paroles</a></h3>
   <p>Lorem ipsum dolor sit amet, <a href="/services/">
consectetuer</a> adipiscing elit.</p>
  </td>
 </tr>
 <tr id="footer">
  <td colspan="5">
   Copyright 2003 Lorem ipsum dolor sit amet.
  </td>
 </tr>
</table>
```

Finally, use id selectors to apply styles to the HTML table (see Figure 7-2):

```
body {
 color: #333;
}
table {
 border: 0;
 padding: 0;
}
td {
 vertical-align: top;
}
th#header  {
 text-align: left;
 font-family: Georgia, Times, "Times New Roman", serif;
 font-style: italic;
 background-color: #036;
 border-bottom: 1px solid #369;
}
th#header h1 {
 margin: 0;
 padding: 10px 0 0 0;
 font-size: 3em;
 color: #ccc;
```

Figure 7-2. The stylized HTML table layout

```
}
tr#navSite td {
 font-weight: bold;
}
tr#navSite td {
 background-color: #036;
 border-left: 10px solid #369;
}
tr#navSite td a:link, tr#navSite td a:visited {
 padding-left: .5em;
 background-color: #036;
 color: #fff;
 text-decoration: none;
 width: 100%;
}
td#contentLeft h2 {
 padding: 0;
 margin: 0.25em 0 0 0;
}
td#contentRight h3 {
 padding: 0;
 margin: 0.25em 0 0 0;
}
```

```
td#contentLeft, td#contentRight {
 padding-top: 1em;
 padding-bottom: 2.5em;
 font-family: Verdana, Arial, Helvetica, sans-serif;
 font-size: small;
}
td#contentLeft p, td#contentRight p {
 padding-right: 1.5em;
 padding-bottom: 0;
 margin: 0 0 0.75em 0;
}
tr#footer td {
 text-align: center;
 border-top: 1px solid #999;
 padding-bottom: 1.5em;
}
```

Discussion

This Solution applies styles through the id attributes on HTML elements. If you determine that you need more control over the content in a table cell, put a div element around the sections of the content or apply another id attribute in the markup inside the cell. For example, if you need to stylize a registration form at the top of a table cell differently from the content below it, use the following code:

```
<td colspan="3" id="contentRight">
 <form action="login.php" method="post" id="form">
  <label for="uname">Username</label>
  <input type="text" name="uname" id="uname" value="" /><br />
  <label for="pname">Password</label>
  <input type="text" name="pname" id="pname" value="" /><br />
  <input type="submit" name="Submit" value="Submit"
class="buttonSubmit" />
 </form>
 [...]
</td>
```

Working with a scaled-back version of an HTML table is a potential path to take if you want to become familiar with CSS as a presentation technology. By using a basic HTML table as the framework for a web document, you reap the benefits of using CSS to stylize content in the table cells. As you gain experience in CSS, you will find it easier to transition to the process of rendering the whole page, including the layout.

See Also

Chapter 6 for more information on how to stylize HTML tables, mostly geared toward presentation of tabular data; "Designing with Web Standards" by Jeffrey Zeldman (New Riders); "Web Page Reconstruction with CSS" at *http://www.digital-web.com/tutorials/tutorial_2002-06.shtml*, which discusses the reconstruction of a page layout from HTML tables to a CSS-enabled layout.

7.2   Building a One-Column Layout

Problem

You want to build a layout that consists of one main column, as in Figure 7-3.

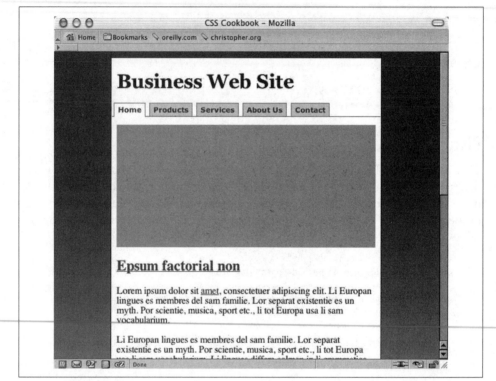

Figure 7-3. One-column page reinforced by increased margin

Solution

Apply a percentage value to the left and right margins of the web document's body element:

```
body {
 margin-left:15%;
 margin-right: 15%;
 }
```

Discussion

When you apply a percentage value to the left and right margins of the body, the column width becomes flexible. This allows the content to stretch to the width of the user's browser.

To create a fixed-width column, use the `width` property for the body element:

```
body {
  width: 600px;
}
```

This technique aligns the column to the left side of the user's browser. If you want to center a column with a fixed width, wrap a `div` element around the entire contents of the web document with a specific, unique `id` attribute such as a `frame`:

```
<div id="frame">
  [...]
</div>
```

Then, in the CSS rules, apply a 50% value to the left padding of the body:

```
body {
  width: 600px;
  padding-left: 50%;
}
```

Through an `id` selector, set the width of the column, then set a negative left margin equal to half the column width:

```
#frame {
  /* set the width of the column */
  width: 600px;
  margin-left: -300px;
}
```

You might think to just set the left and right margins to `auto`:

```
#frame {
  width: 600px;
  margin-left: auto;
  margin-right: auto;
}
```

This straightforward approach doesn't work in Internet Explorer for Windows, however. The Solution uses a workaround that works on all major browsers.

See Also

Recipe 2.3 on centering elements in a web document; Recipe 3.8 on horizontal tab navigation.

7.3   Building a Two-Column Layout

Problem

You want to create a two-column layout with columns that resize to the width of the browser, as in Figure 7-4.

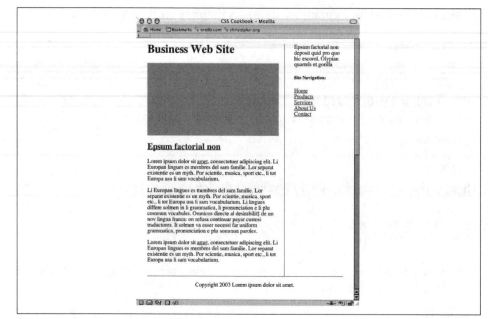

Figure 7-4. Two-column layout achieved through CSS

Solution

First, mark up the content with div elements using the id attributes that contain appropriate values (see Figure 7-5).

For demonstration purposes the values of the id attributes are used to show where the content is displayed when CSS is used. Semantic values would be preferred, like mainContent or sidebar, instead of using values that represent their placement on the page:

```
<div id="columnLeft">
 [...]
</div>
<div id="columnRight">
 [...]
</div>
<div id="footer">
 [...]
</div>
```

Then, in CSS, use the float property to move the contents of the left column to the left, and set a width that is two-thirds the web document's width:

```
#columnLeft {
  float: left;
  width: 67%;
  background:#fff;
  margin-top: 0;
```

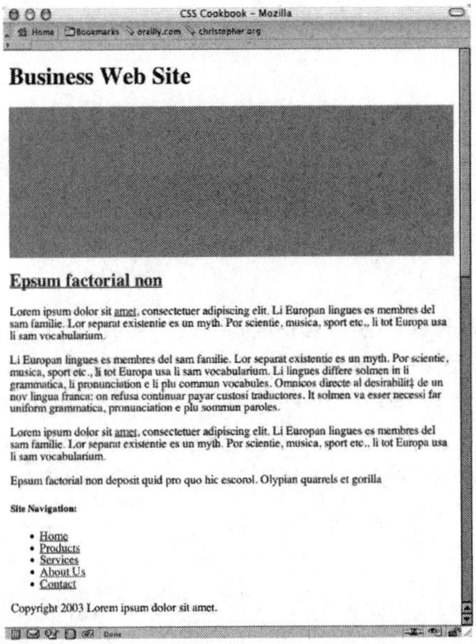

Figure 7-5. The default rendering of the page

```
  margin-right: 1.67em;
  border-right: 1px solid black;
  padding-top: 0;
  padding-right: 1em;
  padding-bottom: 20px;
}
```

The right column wraps around the contents of the left column. On the right column, set the top of the margin and padding to 0, allowing the column and the first element in it to become level with the left column:

```
#columnRight {
 padding-left: 2em;
 margin-top: 0;
 padding-top: 0;
}
h1 {
 margin-top: 0;
 padding-top: 0;
}
```

To display the footer at the bottom of the web document, set the clear property to both:

```
#footer {
 clear: both;
 padding-bottom: 1em;
```

```
    border-top: 1px solid #333;
    text-align: center;
}
```

Discussion

The float property is similar to the align attribute that is used in HTML to allow text and other elements to flow around an image:

```
<img src="this.jpg" width="250" height="150" hspace="7" vspace="7"
alt="example" align="right">
```

Once the image has been set to align to either the right or left, the content around the image flows to the opposite side of the image's alignment. For example, an image aligned to the right forces content to flow around the image on the left side, as shown in Figure 7-6. With CSS, floats provide a similar function, except they offer more exacting control over the presentation by using borders, margins, padding, and other properties.

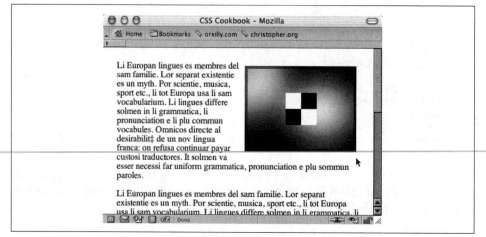

Figure 7-6. Text wrapping around an image set to right alignment

To make sure the content that comprises the footer is placed at the bottom of the columns, set the clear property to a value of both. When you set the value to both, the browser understands that the content of the footer isn't flowing around the floated left column and positions it below (or past) any floated elements.

The only caveat to this technique for creating a two-column layout is that the content in the left column needs to be longer than the content in the right column. Because the content in the left column appears first in the document, the content in the right column wraps around the left column. Too much content in the column that doesn't float results in the anomaly shown in Figure 7-7.

Figure 7-7. Unwanted wrapping of text under the left column

A method for fixing this problem is to set of the left margin or padding on the right column element so that the column width is at least maintained after the content flows below the float:

```
#mainColumn {
 width: 400px;
 /* Enough padding to compensate for the left column */
 padding-left: 200px;
}
#navigation {
 float: left;
 width: 175px;
}
```

See Also

Recipe 7.4 for a two-column layout with fixed widths; Jeffrey Zeldman's "From Table Hacks to CSS Layout: A Web Designer's Journal" for a background on this Solution at *http://www.alistapart.com/articles/journey/*.

7.4 Building a Two-Column Layout with Fixed-Width Columns

Problem

You want to create a two-column layout with fixed-width columns.

Solution

First, mark up the content with `div` elements using the `id` attributes that contain appropriate values representing their placement on the page (see Figure 7-8):

```
<div id="header">
 [...]
</div>
<div id="columnLeft">
 [...]
</div>
<div id="columnRight">
 [...]
</div>
<div id="footer">
 [...]
</div>
```

Using the `float` property, set the width of the left column to a length unit rather than to percentages. Also, set the width of the entire document to a length unit (see Figure 7-9):

```
body {
  margin: 0;
  padding: 0;
  font-family: Georgia, Times, "Times New Roman", serif;
  color: black;
  width: 600px;
  border-right: 1px solid black;
}
#header {
  background-color: #666;
  border-bottom: 1px solid #333;
}
#columnLeft {
  float: left;
  width: 160px;
```

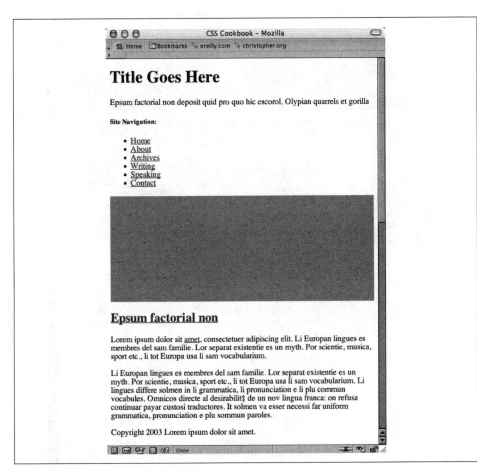

Figure 7-8. The default rendering of the page

```
  margin-left: 10px;
  padding-top: 1em;
}
#columnRight {
  padding-top: 1em;
  margin: 0 2em 0 200px;
}
#footer {
  clear: both;
  background-color: #ccc;
  padding-bottom: 1em;
  border-top: 1px solid #333;
  padding-left: 200px;
}
```

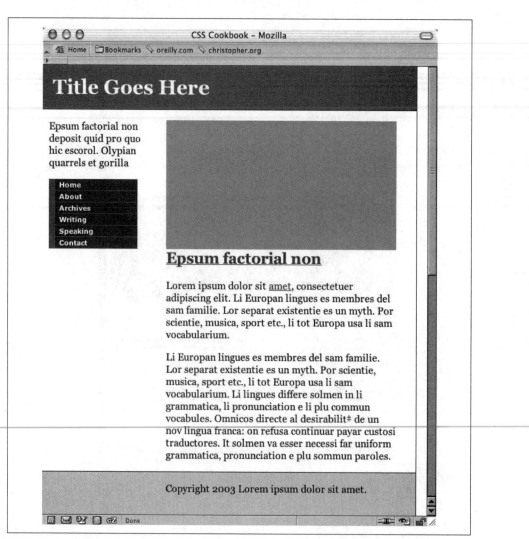

Figure 7-9. The two-column layout enabled by CSS

Discussion

By default, block-level elements stretch to the width of their containers. If the browser window is small, the block-level elements shrink—in other words, text inside the content wraps into narrow columns.

However, when you use length units rather than percentages, the width of the columns becomes fixed. Even as a browser window shrinks or expands, the column widths remain fixed.

To keep the width of the left column fixed while enabling the main column to stretch, simply remove the width property assigned to the body element.

See Also

Recipe 7.3 on creating a two-column layout with flexible-width columns.

7.5 Creating a Flexible Multicolumn Layout with Floats

Problem

You want to create a three-column layout with columns that resize to the width of the browser, as shown in Figure 7-10.

Figure 7-10. Three-column layout achieved through CSS

Solution

First, mark up the content with div elements using the id attributes that contain appropriate values representing their placement on the page (see Figure 7-11):

```
<div id="header">
 [...]
</div>
<div id="columnLeft">
 [...]
</div>
<div id="columnMain">
```

```
  [...]
</div>
<div id="columnRight">
 [...]
</div>
<div id="footer">
 [...]
</div>
```

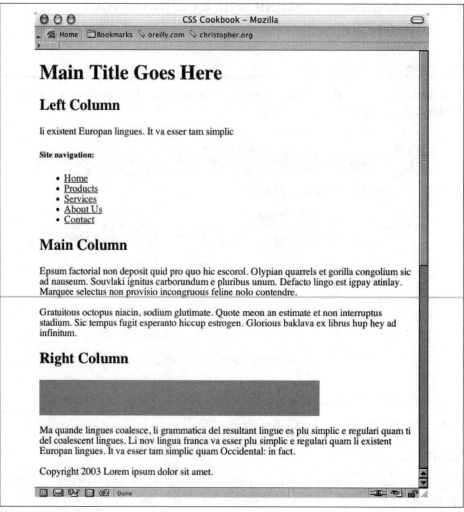

Figure 7-11. The default rendering of the page

Next, set each column to float to the left, making sure that the width is a percentage. All three values of the columns should equal 100% (see Figure 7-12):

```
#columnRight {
 width: 33%;
 float: left;
 background: white;
 padding-bottom: 1em;
}
#columnLeft {
 width: 20%;
 float:left;
 background: white;
 padding-bottom: 1em;
 text-align: justify;
}
#columnMain {
 width:47%;
 float:left;
 background: white;
 padding-bottom: 1em;
}
#footer {
 clear: both;
 padding-bottom: 1em;
 border-top: 1px solid #333;
 text-align: center;
}
```

Figure 7-12. An increased width for the main column forcing the right column to wrap underneath

Discussion

This technique works because all columns are set to float to the left and their widths aren't larger than 100%. Setting the floats to the right can flip the columns, but the result is the same.

Be sure to apply margins and padding to the elements within the columns (unless you account for their widths when sizing the columns). If you don't, the columns will expand beyond 100%, forcing one or more columns to wrap underneath each other, as shown in Figure 7-12.

See Also

Recipe 7.6 on creating a three-column layout with fixed-width columns; *http://www. realworldstyle.com/nn4_3col_header.html* for information on creating a three-column layout with one flexible- column and two fixed-width columns.

7.6 Creating a Fixed-Width Multicolumn Layout with Floats

Problem

You want to create a three-column layout with fixed-width columns.

Solution

First, mark up the content with div elements using the id attributes that contain appropriate values representing their placement on the page (see Figure 7-13):

```
<div id="header">
 [...]
</div>
<div id="columnMain">
 [...]
</div>
<div id="columnLeft">
 [...]
</div>
<div id="columnRight">
 [...]
</div>
<div id="footer">
 [...]
</div>
```

Next, wrap the div elements that compose the main and left columns in another div element and set the value of the id attribute to enclose. Also, wrap another div element around the entire set of div elements, setting the value to frame:

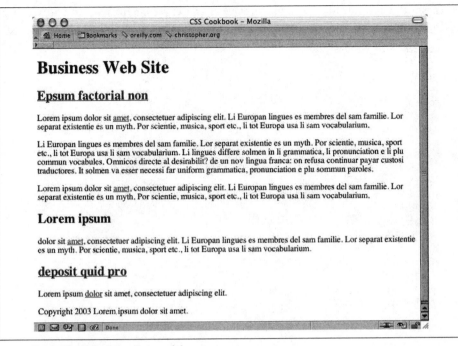

Figure 7-13. The default rendering of the page

```
<div id="frame">
 <div id="header">
  [...]
 </div>
 <div id="enclose">
  <div id="columnMain">
   [...]
  </div>
  <div id="columnLeft">
   [...]
  </div>
 </div>
 <div id="columnRight">
  [...]
 </div>
 <div id="footer">
  [...]
 </div>
<div>
```

Set the width of the page using an id selector for the "frame" div element:

```
#frame {
 margin-left: 20px;
 width: 710px;
}
```

Next, set the column div elements as well as the div element with the id value of enclose to float (see Figure 7-14):

```
#columnMain {
  float: right;
  width: 380px;
}
#columnLeft {
  float: left;
  width: 150px;
}
#columnRight {
  float: right;
  width: 120px;
}
#enclose {
  float:left;
  width:560px;
}
#footer {
  clear: both;
  padding-top: 1em;
  text-align: center;
}
```

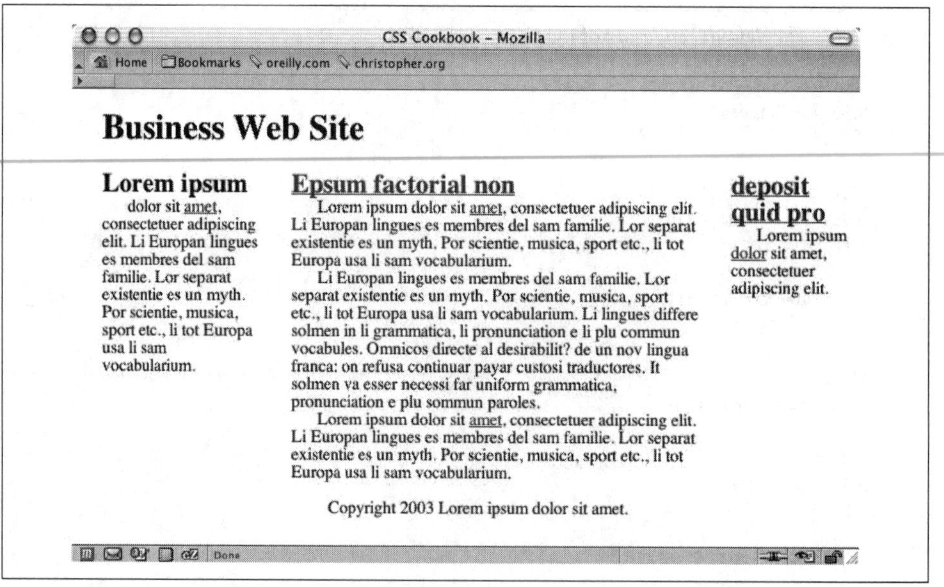

Figure 7-14. Three-column layout with fixed column widths

Discussion

Because the width of the columns is set in pixels, the columns are fixed. To display the columns, you need an extra div element wrapped around the main and left columns. With this extra div element, which contains an id attribute value of enclose, the main and left columns as a whole are set to float to the left. And inside the "enclose" div, the main column is aligned to the right while the left column is aligned to the left.

See Also

Recipe 7.5 on creating a three-column layout with flexible columns.

7.7 Creating a Flexible Multicolumn Layout with Positioning

Problem

You want to create a four-column layout with columns that resize to the width of the browser as shown in Figure 7-15.

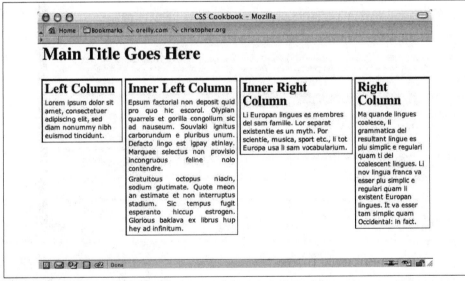

Figure 7-15. Four-column layout with percentage-based widths

Solution

First, mark up the content with div elements using the id attributes that contain appropriate values representing their placement on the page (see Figure 7-16):

```
<div id="header">
 [...]
</div>
<div id="columnLeft">
```

```
  [...]
</div>
<div id="columnInnerLeft">
 [...]
</div>
 [...]
<div id="columnInnerRight">
  [...]
</div>
 [...]
<div id="columnRight">
 [...]
</div>
```

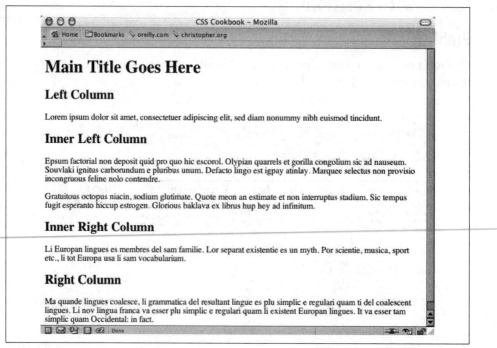

Figure 7-16. The default rendering of the content

Next, use the position property in each column, setting the value to absolute while setting the placement of the columns with the left and top properties:

```
#columnLeft {
 position: absolute;
 left:1%;
 width:20%;
 top: 4em;
 background:#fff;
}
#columnInnerLeft {
 position: absolute;
```

```
    left: 22%;
    width: 28%;
    top: 4em;
    background: #fff;
    text-align: justify;
    border-width: 0;
}
#columnInnerRight {
    position: absolute;
    left: 51%;
    width: 28%;
    top: 4em;
    background: #fff;
}
#columnRight {
    position: absolute;
    left: 80%;
    width: 19%;
    top: 4em;
    background: #fff;
}
```

Discussion

By setting the `position` property to `absolute` you take the element completely out of the flow of the document. When an element is set to `float`, other elements in a page can flow around the "floated" element. When an element is set to `absolute`, that element is treated like a ghost.

The default rendering of an element when positioned absolutely is to the upper left corner of its closest positioned ancestor or the initial containing block. (In other words, to position a child element set to `absolute` within the parent element, first apply a `position` property and value to its parent element.) If other elements are on the page, this creates an overlap of the content, as shown in Figure 7-17.

To avoid this problem, use four additional CSS properties that allow the element to be moved into any location: `top`, `left`, `bottom`, and `right`. Be sure to set the values of the columns to percentages to maintain flexible widths as a user's browser resizes.

Also use percentages as the values for the `left` property to mark the distance away from the left side of a browser's viewport. However, use em units as the values for the `top` property to compensate for the height of the heading. If you want to use an image for the heading, change the values for `top` to pixels, making sure there is enough room for the graphic header.

While this technique grants freedom in the placement of elements, there are drawbacks to using `absolute` to position elements. In some circumstances, Netscape Navigator 4 loses the location of positioned elements when you resize the window.

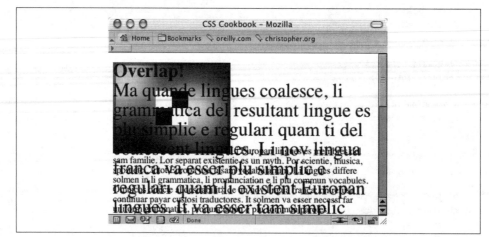

Figure 7-17. Text overlapping an image and other text in a web document

While the placement of columns next to each other can be carried out easily with this technique, the placement of a footer at the bottom of the columns is hard to do unless you know where the columns exactly end at the bottom of the page.

See Also

The CSS 2.1 specification on the position property at *http://www.w3.org/TR/CSS21/visuren.html#propdef-position*; the CSS 2.1 specification on positioning elements set to absolute at *http://www.w3.org/TR/CSS21/visuren.html#position-props*; read more about containing blocks at *http://www.w3.org/TR/2003/WD-CSS21-20030915/visudet.html#containing-block-details*.

7.8 Creating a Fixed-Width Multicolumn Layout with Positioning

Problem

You want to create a four-column layout with fixed-width columns.

Solution

First, mark up the content with div elements using the id attributes that contain appropriate values representing their placement on the page:

```
<div id="header">
 [...]
</div>
<div id="columnLeft">
 [...]
</div>
```

```
<div id="columnInnerLeft">
 [...]
</div>
 [...]
<div id="columnInnerRight">
  [...]
</div>
 [...]
<div id="columnRight">
 [...]
</div>
```

Next, use the position property in each column, setting the value to absolute while setting the placement of the columns with the left and top properties, making sure to use pixels for the units:

```
#columnLeft {
 position: absolute;
 left:5px;
 width:190px;
 top: 44px;
 background:#fff;
}
#columnInnerLeft {
 position: absolute;
 left: 205px;
 width: 190px;
 top: 44px;
 background: #fff;
 text-align: justify;
 border-width: 0;
}
#columnInnerRight {
 position: absolute;
 left: 405px;
 width: 190px;
 top: 44px;
 background: #fff;
}
#columnRight {
 position: absolute;
 left: 605px;
 width: 190px;
 top: 44px;
 background: #fff;
}
```

Discussion

Setting the width of the columns as well as the left and top properties to length units creates the fixed-width columns. This Solution is just as easy with two to three or more columns. Remember that anything more than four or five columns might be impractical.

See Also

Recipe 7.4 on creating a fixed-width two-column layout; Recipe 7.6 on creating a fixed-width multicolumn layout with floats.

7.9 Designing an Asymmetric Layout

Problem

You want to create a flexible, asymmetric or organic layout as seen in Figure 7-18.

Figure 7-18. The asymmetric placement of the content

Solution

First, mark up the content with div elements using the id attributes that contain appropriate values representing their placement on the page:

```
<div id="header">
 [...]
</div>
<div id="columnSmall">
 [...]
</div>
<div id="columnMain">
 [...]
```

```
</div>
<div id="columnMedium">
[...]
</div>
```

Next, use the position property in each column, setting the value to absolute while setting the placement of the columns with the left and top properties using percentages. Also, use percentage values for positioning a background image (see Figure 7-19):

```
body {
 margin:5px 0 0 5px;
 background-image: url(flower5.jpg);
 background-position: 50% 35%;
 background-repeat: no-repeat;
 }
#header {
 position: absolute;
 left: 65%;
 top: 50%;
 width: 125px;
 font-size: small;
 }
#columnSmall {
 position: absolute;
 left: 35%;
 width: 15%;
 top: 1%;
 background: #fff;
font-size: small;
 }
#columnMain {
 position: absolute;
 left: 5%;
 width: 45%;
 top: 40%;
 background: #fff;
 text-align: justify;
 border-width: 0;
 font-size: large;
 }
#columnMedium {
 position: absolute;
 left: 80%;
 width: 20%;
 top: 10%;
 background: #fff;
 }
```

Discussion

Although web sites seem to use traditional column layouts, CSS enables web developers to come up with new ways to present their documents. Through the position,

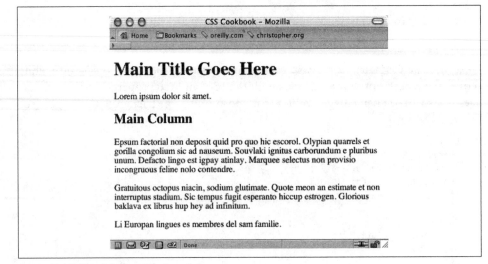

Figure 7-19. The default rendering of the page

top, and left properties, you can break up the content into chunks, stylize them separately, and place them in unique arrangements.

The background image moves with the content if the browser window is resized because you used a percentage value to set the position of the background image.

Instead of changing the values for the position, top, and left properties by hand, you can more easily place div elements with a WYSIWYG application such as Macromedia Dreamweaver.

If you want to create an asymmetric or organic layout with fixed-width columns instead of making this layout resizable, use length units to dictate the exact position of both the content and the background image:

```
body {
  margin:5px 0 0 5px;
  background-image: url(flower5.jpg);
  background-position: -400px -200px;
  background-repeat: no-repeat;
}
#header {
  position: absolute;
  left: 500px;
  top: 200px;
  width: 125px;
  font-size: small;
}
#columnLeft {
  position: absolute;
  left: 200px;
  width: 125px;
  top: 10px;
```

```
  background:#fff;
  font-size: small;
}
#columnInnerLeft {
  position: absolute;
  left: 50px;
  width: 375px;
  top: 175px;
  background: #fff;
  text-align: justify;
  border-width: 0;
  font-size: large;
}
#columnInnerRight {
  position: absolute;
  left: 600px;
  width: 150px;
  top: 50px;
  background: #fff;
}
```

See Also

Recipes 2.4 and 2.5 for setting background images on a web page; for more information about Macromedia Dreamweaver see *http://www.dreamweaver.com*.

CHAPTER 8

Print

8.0 Introduction

If you were to try to print out a web page exactly as it appears on your screen, chances are you would end up wasting a lot of ink and paper printing unnecessary page elements, or worse yet, the content you printed would be illegible.

That's why links to "printer-friendly" versions of web pages are all over the Internet, especially on news and business sites. When you click this kind of link, you are given a web page design or shell that contains the same text as what you see on your screen, but in a minimal version that is, well, friendlier (or easier) to print.

To create this printer-friendly version of the text, you traditionally would either have to manually convert the web page content to a new, stripped-down page, or use a script dynamically to generate a separate page design. With CSS, however, you can "automagically" redesign documents when they are printed, thereby eliminating the need to code a separate, printer-friendly version as well as saving on server resources typically required to generate the page.

Support for print-media CSS is fairly commonplace these days. Currently, the browsers that support this aspect of the technology include Internet Explorer 4+ for Windows, Internet Explorer 4.5+ for Macintosh, Navigator 6+, Safari, and Opera.

There are print-only properties associated with CSS. However, these properties have limited support among the browsers on the market; Opera 5 and 7 are the only browsers that support more than two of these kinds of properties (15 printing properties out of the 16 in the specification). Because of this reality and the nature of this book to focus on practical, cross-browser nature of CSS, the recipes in this chapter are geared to styling the contents of the page rather than dealing with the theory of CSS printing properties. For more information on CSS printing properties, see Chapter 14 of *Cascading Style Sheets: The Definitive Guide* (O'Reilly).

This chapter teaches the basics of how to tell the browser which style sheet to use when sending a document to print. It also discusses how to switch graphics from web to print CSS, as well as how to develop a document for printing.

8.1 Creating a Printer-Friendly Page

Problem

You want to create a printer-friendly page without having to manually or dynamically generate another web page.

Solution

Create a separate style sheet that dictates how a page looks when printed. Then associate the style sheet and set the media property to print:

```
<link rel="stylesheet" type="text/css" href="adv.css"
media="screen">
<link rel="stylesheet" type="text/css" href="print.css"
 media="print">
```

If you're writing a web page in valid XHTML, you need to include a space and a forward slash before the closing bracket at the end of an empty element such as link:

```
<link rel="stylesheet" type="text/css" href="adv.css"
media="screen" />
<link rel="stylesheet" type="text/css" href="print.css"
media="print" />
```

Discussion

You can use style sheets to dictate the presentation of documents in a wide range of media. By default, the value for the media attribute is all. Without the attribute, the user agent will apply the CSS rules in the style sheet to all media.

Although the most common attribute you probably have encountered is screen, which is used mainly for displaying documents on color monitors, the CSS 2.1 specification actually defines a total of ten media types, as shown in Table 8-1.

Table 8-1. Media types for CSS

Media type	Description
all	Suitable for all devices
braille	Intended for Braille tactile feedback devices
embossed	Intended for paged Braille printers
handheld	Intended for handheld devices (typically small-screen, limited-bandwidth devices)
print	Intended for paged material and for documents viewed on-screen in print preview mode
projection	Intended for projected presentations—for example, projectors

Table 8-1. Media types for CSS (continued)

Media type	Description
screen	Intended primarily for color computer screens
speech	Intended for speech synthesizers
tty	Intended for media using a fixed-pitch character grid (such as teletypes, terminals, or portable devices with limited display capabilities)
tv	Intended for television-type devices (with low-resolution, limited-scrollable color screens and available sound)

You can use one style sheet for all media:

```
<link rel="stylesheet" type="text/css" href="uber.css"
media="all" />
```

Or you can use one style sheet for several (but not all) media. For instance, to use one style sheet for both projection and print media, simply separate the media values with a comma:

```
<link rel="stylesheet" type="text/css" href="print.css"
 media=" print,projection " />
```

In the preceding code, the print.css style sheet is used for projection and print media when rendering the web document.

You can use other methods besides link to assign media types. One method is @import, as shown in the following line, which specifies the style sheet for both print and projection media:

```
@import url(print.css) print,projection;
```

The @import rule needs to be placed within a style element or within an external style sheet.

Another method you can use to associate and dictate style sheets and media types is @media, which enables you to write blocks of CSS rules that can be set for different media, all in *one* style sheet:

```
<style type="text/css">
@media print {
 body {
   font-size: 10pt;
   background-color: white;
   color: black;
 }
}
@media screen {
 body {
   font-size: medium;
   background-color: black;
   color: white;
 }
}
</style>
```

See Also

Media Types in Section 7 of the CSS 2.1 Working Draft, *http://www.w3.org/TR/CSS21/media.html*.

8.2 Making a Web Form Print-Ready

Problem

You need to have a form that users can fill out online, or that they can print and then fill out offline, as shown in Figure 8-1.

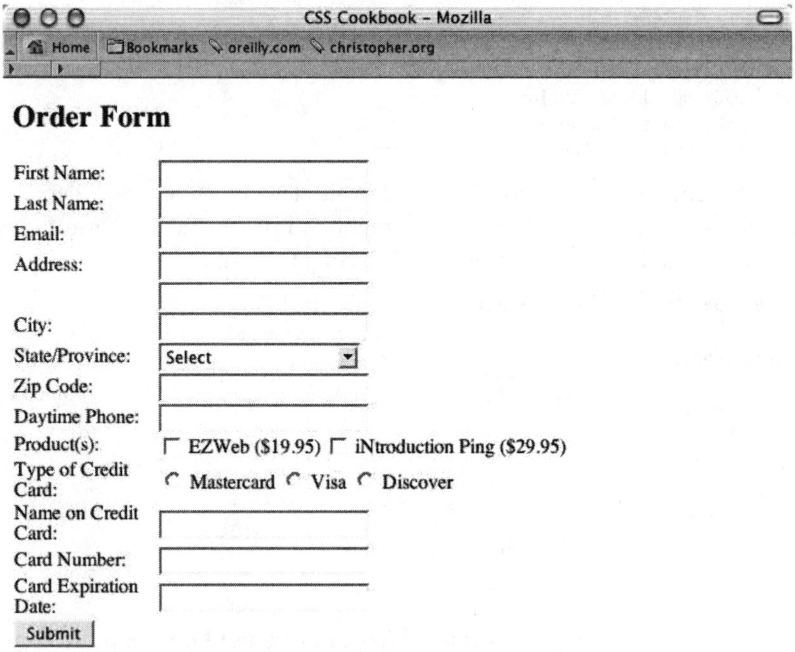

Figure 8-1. An online form

Solution

First, create a print media style sheet and a `class` selector that transforms the `form` elements so that they display black text and feature a one-pixel border on the bottom. For example, the following HTML code for an `input` text element:

```
<label for="fname">First Name</label>
<input class="fillout" name="fname" type="text" id="fname" />
```

requires the following CSS rule:

```
<style type="text/css" media="print ">
.fillout {
 color: black;
 border-width: 0;
 border: 1px solid #000;
 width: 300pt;
}
</style>
```

For drop-down menus, hide the select element altogether and add some additional markup to help produce the bottom border:

```
<label for="bitem">Breakfast Item</label>
<select name="bitem" size="1">
 <option selected="selected">Select</option>
 <option>Milk</option>
 <option>Eggs</option>
 <option>Orange Juice</option>
 <option>Newspaper</option>
 </select><span class="postselect">  </span>
```

Then, in the CSS rules, convert the inline span element to a block element. This enables you to set the width of the span element and places the border at the bottom to equal that of the input elements in the preceding CSS rule:

```
<style type="text/css" media="print">
select {
 display: none;
}
.postselect {
 display: block;
 width: 300pt;
 height: 1em;
 border: none;
 border-bottom: 1px solid #000;
}
</style>
```

For elements such as a Submit button, which can't be used on the printed page, set the display property to none. You can see the finished product in Figure 8-2.

Discussion

Lines on an order form tell users they can fill out the form. By using the border property, you can easily create these lines in a browser, making web forms useful both online and offline.

For select elements, the workaround is somewhat of a hack that involves interfering with the ideal semantic markup; it still works and is valid HTML. Place a span element after the select element:

Order Form

```
┌─────────────────────────────────────────────────────────────────┐
│  ⊙ ⊙ ⊙              CSS Cookbook – Mozilla                    ⊖  │
│  ⌂ Home  ⌷Bookmarks  ⬙ oreilly.com  ⬙ christopher.org            │
│  ▶  ▶                                                             │
│                                                                   │
│  Order Form                                                       │
│                                                                   │
│            First Name:   _____      │
│            Last Name:    _____      │
│               Email:     _____      │
│             Address:     _____      │
│                          _____      │
│                 City:    _____      │
│        State/Province:   _____      │
│            Zip Code:     _____      │
│        Daytime Phone:    _____      │
│          Product(s):  ⊓ EZWeb ($19.95)  ⊓ iNtroduction Ping ($29.95)│
│    Type of Credit Card: ⊙ Mastercard ⊙ Visa ⊙ Discover           │
│    Name on Credit Card:  _____      │
│          Card Number:    _____      │
│      Card Expiration Date: _____      │
│                                                                   │
│  ▥ ⊠ ⊙ □ ⊄ Done                                      ⊷⊏⌨ //     │
└─────────────────────────────────────────────────────────────────┘
```

Figure 8-2. The same form primed for printing

```
<select name="bitem" size="1">
 <option selected="selected">Select</option>
 <option>Milk</option>
 <option>Eggs</option>
 <option>Orange Juice</option>
 <option>Newspaper</option>
</select>
<span class="postselect">  </span>
```

Then set the select element to disappear:

```
select {
 display: none;
}
```

Next, set the span element to display as a block to enable the width and height properties. With those width and height properties set, the bottom border can be placed to match the rest of the form elements:

```
.postselect {
 display: block;
 width: 300pt;
 height: 1em;
 border: none;
 border-bottom: 1px solid #000;
}
```

As browsers implement attribute selectors from the CSS specification, styling forms for print becomes easier. Currently, the only browsers that support attribute selectors are Netscape Navigator 6+ and Opera 5+. When you use attribute selectors, it's easier to distinguish which form elements should be stylized than it is when you insert class attributes and their respective values in the markup.

In the following code, the first CSS rule applies only to input elements for text, while the second rule hides the Submit button and the Select drop box:

```
input[type="text"] {
  color: black;
  border-width: 0;
  border: 1px solid #000;
}
input[type="submit"], select {
  display: none;
}
```

Once your form is ready to be printed, be sure to include instructions on how users should handle the printed form. For example, if you want users to mail the form, add a mailing address to the page on which the form is printed.

See Also

Attribute selector documentation in the W3C specification at *http://www.w3.org/TR/CSS21/selector.html#attribute-selectors;* HTML 4.01 specification about the label tag at *http://www.w3.org/TR/html401/interact/forms.html#edef-LABEL.*

8.3   Inserting URLs After Links

Problem

You need to display URLs of links in an article when a web page is printed.

Solution

Instruct the browser to print the URLs of links in a paragraph by using the :after pseudo-element:

```
p a:after {
  content: " <" attr(href) "> " ;
}
```

Discussion

Selector constructs such as :after are known as pseudo-elements. The browser interprets the selector as though additional elements were used to mark up the web document.

For example, by using the following CSS, you can make the first letter of a paragraph two-em units in size:

```
p:first-letter {
  font-size: 2em;
}
```

You use the :after selector (or the :before selector) to insert generated content after (or before) an element. In this Recipe, the value of the href attribute, which contains the URL information, is placed after every anchor element in a p element.

To have brackets appear around the URL, place the quotes around the brackets. To add a buffer of space between the anchor element and the next inline content, put one space in front of the left bracket and one after the right bracket, then insert the URL using the attr(x) function. Whatever attribute is replaced for x, CSS finds the attribute in the element, returning its value as a string.

Another example of the power of this pseudo-element involves returning the value of abbreviations and acronyms in a buzzword-laden document. To accomplish this, first put the expanded form of the word or phrase in the title attribute for abbr or acronym:

```
<p>The <acronym title="World Wide Web Consortium">W3C</a>
makes  wonderful things like <abbr title="Cascading Style
Sheets">CSS</abbr>!</p>
```

Then, in the CSS rules, tell the browser to return the value for the title attribute:

```
abbr:after, acronym:after {
  content: " (" attr(title) ") ";
}
```

Currently, generating content through pseudo-elements works only in Netscape 6+, Mozilla, and Safari browsers.

See Also

Recipe 1.2 for more on setting type in a web document; the CSS 2.1 specification about generated content at *http://www.w3.org/TR/REC-CSS2/generate.html#content*.

8.4   Sample Design: A Printer-Friendly Page with CSS

In this sample design, you will transform an existing web document (as shown in Figure 8-3) to make it more suitable for print. Although CSS has changed the way we design for the Web, it also has allowed developers to change the way they provide printer-friendly versions of their documents. Instead of having to create separate pages or write scripts, you can use CSS to create a printer-friendly document as soon as the user hits the Print button. The HTML for the page isn't in the book because the miracle of CSS lets us change the presentation without having to change the HTML.

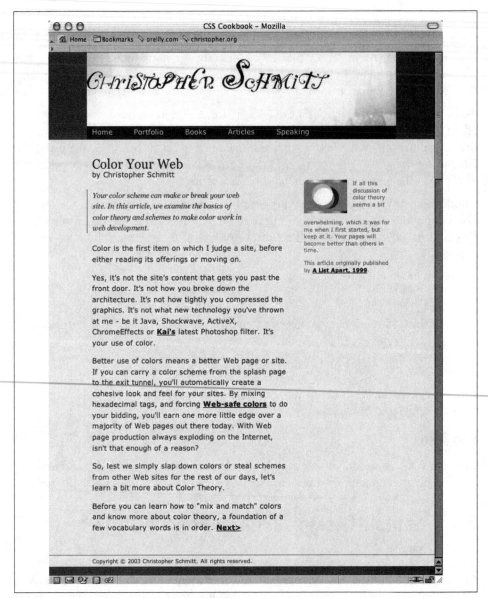

Figure 8-3. Web page stylized for screen delivery

When creating a style sheet for print, you actually use a web browser. This enables you to see quickly how the CSS rules affect the display of the document (just like for media delivery), but it's also easier on the environment and you save money by not wasting ink in the printer. So, comment out the style sheet used for the screen in order to create new CSS rules:

```
<!-- Hide screen media CSS while working on print CSS -->
<!-- link href="adv.css" type="text/css" rel="stylesheet"
media="screen" -->
<style type="text/css">
/* Print CSS rules go here */
</style>
```

Setting the Page for Black-and-White Printing

Apply the first CSS rule to the body element. In this rule, set the background color to white and set the type to black:

```
body {
  background-color: white;
  color: black;
}
```

Next, set the typeface for the page to a serif font. Reading text online in sans-serif is easier on the eyes, but in print media the serif font is still the choice for reading passages of text. For a later fallback choice, you might want to go with the Times typeface for print documents since it's installed on most (if not all) computers, and it's a workhorse of a font. In case your users don't have Times installed, supply alternatives as well:

```
body {
  background-color: white;
  color: black;
  font-family: Garamond, Times, "Times New Roman", serif;
}
```

Now you want to get rid of navigation-related links and other page elements you don't want to see in the final printout. This includes the main navigation bar below the main header, as well as internal anchors in the page itself. If you have a page with ad banners, it might be a good idea to hide those as well (see Figure 8-4):

```
#navigation, hr, body>div>a, #blipvert {
  display: none;
}
```

Designing the Main Heading

Because you are dealing with black and gray type on a white page, you have few options when it comes to designing how the main heading for the page should look. However, using what you have at your disposal, it's nonetheless easy to create a masthead that calls attention to itself.

First, set the background to black and the text to white:

```
#header h1 {
  color: white;
```

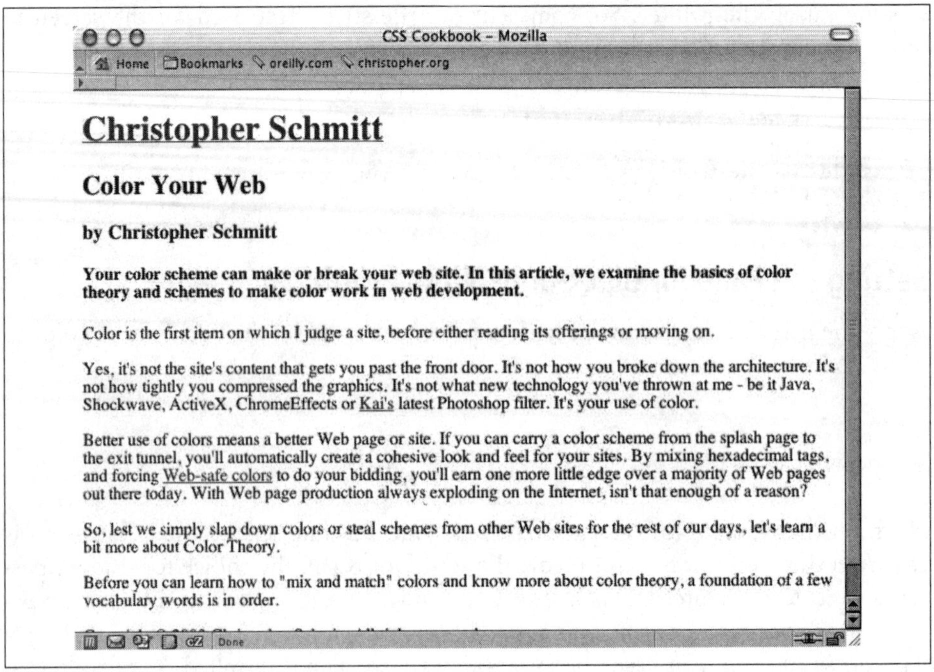

Figure 8-4. Hiding the navigation bar and other elements

```
    background-color: black;
}
```

Because you want people to actually read the header, you want the text to be white to create enough contrast. In this instance, the main header also acts as a homing device—it is a link to the home page. Therefore, the color of the heading is dictated by the style rules set for the links. To remedy this situation, add a separate rule:

```
#header h1 {
  background-color: black;
}
#header h1 a {
  color: white;
}
```

Now that the text is visible, stylize it a bit so that it stands out. Your goal is to center the text, increase the size of the text, and make all the letters uppercase:

```
#header h1 {
  background-color: black;
  font-size: 24pt;
  text-align: center;
  text-transform: uppercase;
}
```

Although this looks good, you can improve it by changing the typeface to sans-serif (so that it sticks out from the rest of the text in the document) and by adding some padding around the top and bottom of the heading (see Figure 8-5):

```
#header h1 {
  background-color: black;
  font-size: 24pt;
  text-align: center;
  font-family: Helvetica, Verdana, Arial, sans-serif;
  padding: 7pt;
  text-transform: uppercase;
}
```

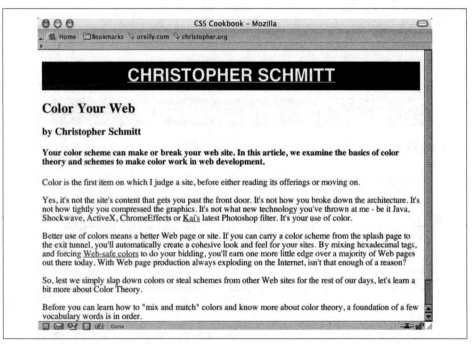

Figure 8-5. Stylizing the main header

Styling the Article Header and Byline

For the article title and byline, create a more dramatic approach by zeroing out the margins and padding of both the h2 and h3 elements:

```
#content h2 {
  padding: 0;
  margin: 0;
}
#content h3 {
  padding: 0;
  margin: 0 ;
}
```

Then increase the font size for the article title and create a thin hairline rule below it. Next, align the byline to the right and set the type style to italic (see Figure 8-6):

```
#content h2 {
  padding: 0;
  margin: 0;
  font-size: 20pt;
  border-bottom: 1px solid black;
}
#content h3 {
  padding: 0;
  margin: 0;
  text-align: right;
  font-style: italic;
}
```

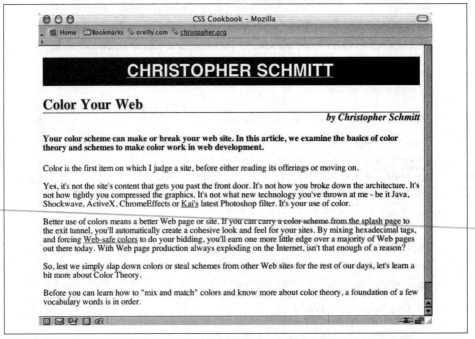

Figure 8-6. Designing the article header and byline

Gaining Attention Through the Teaser

Next up is the content in the h4 element. Because this content serves as a teaser for the article, it should be visually distinctive from the article text. To accomplish that, set the background to 30% black, change the typeface to sans-serif, and put in some padding (see Figure 8-7):

```
#content h4 {
  font-family: Helvetica, Verdana, Arial, sans-serif;
  border-top: 3pt solid black;
```

```
  background-color: #BCBECO;
  padding: 12pt;
  margin: 0;
}
```

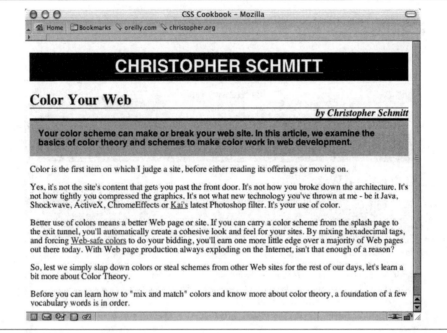

Figure 8-7. Setting up the article teaser

As for the content of the article, leave the text pretty much as it is except for two points of interest: leading, covered here, and links, covered in the next section.

Remember that in the body element, the font for the entire page is set with the serif typeface, and through inheritance that typeface style is picked up in the paragraph elements as well. However, you may want to space out the lines, or increase the leading, of the text in the paragraph. To do this, change the line-height property:

```
#content p {
  line-height: 18pt;
}
```

Displaying the URLs

Any links in the article become useless when printed. To make them beneficial to the reader when the page is printed, make sure all URLs from the links are displayed. To do that, set up a CSS rule to display the URLs after every link in the content division of the document. Also, for visual effect, remove the default underline of the links, make sure the font-weight is bold, and set the color to gray (see Figure 8-8):

```
#content a:after {
 content: " <" attr(href) "> ";
 font-family: courier, monospace;
 font-weight: normal;
}
a {
 text-decoration: none;
 font-weight: bold;
 color: #626466;
}
```

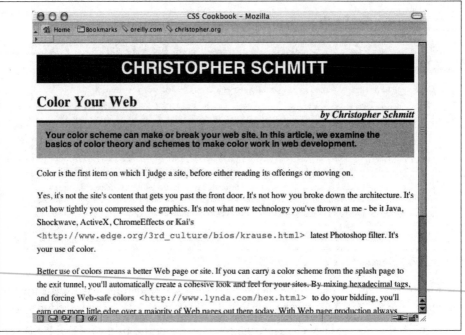

Figure 8-8. Adjusting the links and leading in the content

Finishing with the Footer

At this point you're ready to work your way down the page to the footer that contains the copyright notice. Because the main header is in a sans-serif typeface, balance the page by centering the copyright notice, create a line rule through the border-top property, and set the typeface to sans-serif as well (see Figure 8-9):

```
#footer {
 border-top: 1px solid #000;
 text-align: center;
 font-family: Helvetica, Verdana, Arial, sans-serif;
}
```

With the print CSS finished, copy the CSS rules and put them into an external style sheet called *print.css*. Then, uncomment out the CSS for screen media and associate the print CSS through the link element:

```
<link href="adv.css" type="text/css" rel="stylesheet"
media="screen" />
<link href="print.css" type="text/css" rel="stylesheet"
media="print" />
```

CHAPTER 9

Hacks and Workarounds

9.0   Introduction

When designing for the Web, developers historically have used hacks and workarounds to achieve certain effects. The mid-1990s saw a proliferation of such workarounds, among them single-pixel GIFs, font tags, and nested tables, to name just a few.

In this new millennium, CSS has allowed web designers to free themselves from these old workarounds. But although CSS 2 became a recommendation back in May 1998, only relatively recently have browser vendors fully implemented the standard in their products. To overcome the bugs in the browsers that have poor CSS support, web designers have once again resorted to using hacks and workarounds to achieve their designs.

There are many reasons why old browsers are still in use. Unlike web developers, most people don't automatically upgrade their browsers each time a new one is available. They tend to stick with the browser that's on their computer because it works fine and will get a new browser only when they purchase a new computer. Also, IT departments in many companies lock down the systems and prevent individuals from upgrading software applications on their own.

So even though problems might be solved by using newer versions of browsers, web developers still need to use hacks or workarounds to deliver the appropriate presentation to their audience that is unwilling or unable to upgrade.

This chapter covers techniques on how to deal with browsers that have spotty CSS support. Included in this chapter are methods to hide advanced style sheets from Netscape Navigator 4, deal with Internet Explorer 5.*x* for Window's unique interpretation of the box model, and more.

9.1   Hiding Certain Styles from Netscape Navigator 4.x

Problem

You want to keep Netscape Navigator 4.x from using certain CSS rules. For example, Navigator 4.x doesn't correctly inherit styles like font-family and color set for the body to elements like table, div, and p.

Solution

In a separate style sheet, place the CSS rules that you don't want the Netscape Navigator 4.x browser to use. Then use the @import method to associate the "advanced" CSS rules (making sure that the advanced style sheet comes after the basic to override styles from the basic style sheet):

```
<link rel="stylesheet" type="text/css" media="all" title="Basic CSS" href="/basic.
css" />
<style type="text/css" media="all">
 @import "/css/advanced.css";
</style>
```

Discussion

Netscape Navigator 4 was the first Netscape browser to contain support for CSS. Unfortunately, Netscape was developing the browser while CSS was being finalized. Also, Netscape was supporting its own proposal, JavaScript Style Sheets, known as JSSS, and was basing Navigator 4 on that technology. So, when the W3C went with CSS instead, the Netscape engineers had to do some quick jury-rigging to fix their implementation. This is why you can turn off CSS support in Navigator 4 just by turning off JavaScript in the program's preferences.

Because Navigator's CSS implementation was essentially a remapping to its JSSS engine, actual CSS support for the implementation of such things as the @import method of associated styles to a web page was woefully incomplete. And whatever CSS styles Navigator did include were implemented improperly. As newer browsers offered stronger and more robust support for CSS, a method for hiding certain CSS rules from Navigator 4 became a necessity if web developers were to embrace CSS-enabled designs.

Although the @import method works, you need to write the CSS rules in two separate files: one for Navigator 4 and another one for other browsers capable of handling the @import method. Another way of hiding styles from Navigator 4 and keeping the styles in a single style sheet is through a CSS comment workaround known as the Caio hack, named after the person who developed it, Caio Chassot.

In the following code example, styles are hidden from Navigator 4 through the hack:

```
.p1 {
 font-size: 200%;
 text-decoration: underline;
}
/*/*/
.p2 {
 font-size: 200%;
 text-decoration: underline;
}
/* */
.p3 {
 font-size: 200%;
 text-decoration: underline;
}
```

Here is the HTML code that is used in Figure 9-1:

```
<h2>Netscape Navigator 4 test</h2>
<p class="p1">This text is large and underlined.</p>
<p class="p2">This text is <em>neither</em> large nor underlined.</p>
<p class="p3">This text is large and underlined.</p>
```

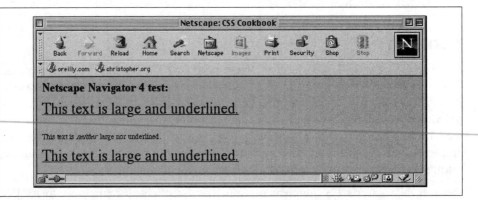

Figure 9-1. Netscape Navigator's comment parser problem used to hide certain styles

Navigator 4 interprets the comment snippet /*/*/ as an open comment, meaning that anything after it is hidden from the browser. Other browsers see the snippet as open and close comment tags. To close the hack to let Navigator 4 see the rest of the styles, add another pair of open and close comment tags, this time with a space between the asterisks:

```
/* */
```

You also can include the hack with inline styles:

```
<p style="/*/*/ color: font-size: 200%; text-decoration:
underline;">This inline-styled p is neither large nor underlined
in Navigator 4.</p>
```

Along with the comment parsing problem, Navigator 4 won't pull in style sheets when the media attribute equals all:

```
<link rel="stylesheet" type="text/css" href="/css/advanced.css"
media="all" >
<style type="text/css" media="all" >
.p2 {
 font-size: 200%;
 text-decoration: underline;
}
</style>
```

Navigator 4 won't interpret style sheets when there is more than one value for the media attribute. So, if you use a combination of values for the media attributes, Navigator 4 ignores the style sheet:

```
<link rel="stylesheet" type="text/css" href="/css/advanced.css"
media="screen, print" >
```

You also can hide styles from Navigator 4 by using descendant selectors—for instance, by placing the html element as a selector before the next selector (since Navigator 4 doesn't include the html element in the parsed document). In the following example, the text size and decoration won't appear in Navigator 4:

```
html .p2 {
 font-size: 200%;
 text-decoration: underline;
}
```

See Also

http://www.v2studio.com/k/css/n4hide/, Caio Chassot's web page about the workaround; Netscape's original proposal for JSSS at *http://www.w3.org/Submission/ 1996/1/WD-jsss-960822*; more issues about Navigator 4.x at *http://www.mako4css. com/Issues.htm*.

9.2 Delivering Alternative Values to Internet Explorer 5.x for Windows

Problem

You want to apply different CSS property values to the Internet Explorer 5.x for Windows browser, such as the value of the width property, to work around implementation of the Microsoft box model.

Solution

Put in the declaration you want Internet Explorer 5.*x* for Windows to handle, and then use what's called the box model hack to put in the corrected values you want other browsers to interpret:

```
div#content   {
 /* WinIE value first, then the desired value the next 2 times */
 background-color: red;
 voice-family: "\"}\"";
 voice-family: inherit;
 background-color: green;
}
html>div#content
 background-color: green;
 }
```

Discussion

Tantek Çelik, Microsoft's diplomat to the World Wide Web Consortium (W3C) CSS and HTML working groups, originally demonstrated how the box model hack could be used to fix Internet Explorer 5.*x* for Windows' approach to the box mode. This fix also applies to Internet Explorer 6 for Windows in quirks mode since it also uses the Microsoft box model.

CSS specifies that the width property defines the width of the content area of a box, and that any margin, border, or padding space should draw outside of that space. For example, in the following bit of code, the width of the element (as it is stated) is 500 pixels:

```
div#content {
 width: 500px;
 padding: 33px;
 margin: 50px;
 background-color: #666;
}
```

As seen in Figure 9-2, the box appears to be 566 pixels wide. The 66 "extra" pixels are from the padding being added outside the 500 pixels.

In Internet Explorer 5.*x* for Windows, the width isn't the stated value in the CSS. Instead, Microsoft's box model draws the box with the border and padding inside the specified width. To calculate the width of the content area for Internet Explorer 5.*x* for Windows, subtract the padding and borders from the stated width:

width property
− left border − left padding
− right padding − right border
= Microsoft's box model

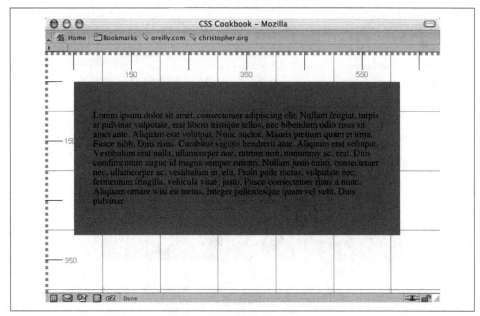

Figure 9-2. The box model correctly implemented in Mozilla

In the previous CSS example, the width determined by Internet Explorer 5.*x* for Windows is 434 pixels (see Figure 9-3):

500px − 33px − 33px = 434px

That's a difference of 66 pixels from the originally stated content area's width of 500 pixels for the block element. Because the box model is a fundamental aspect of design, it becomes paramount to fix any inconsistencies that can arise from this problem.

The box model hack uses a parsing bug to close the rule set prematurely, so anything after the two `voice-family` properties is ignored by Internet Explorer 5.*x* for Windows. However, because other browsers, such as Opera 5, can be vulnerable to this workaround, add this CSS rule:

```
html>div#content
  background-color: green;
}
```

This rule, affectionately referred to as the "Be Kind to Opera" rule, uses the child selector to reinforce the property for browsers like Opera that might get confused with the box model hack, but correctly implement child selectors.

See Also

http://www.w3.org/TR/CSS21/visudet.html#the-width-property for information on the `width` property as a part of the box model; *http://www.tantek.com/CSS/Examples/*

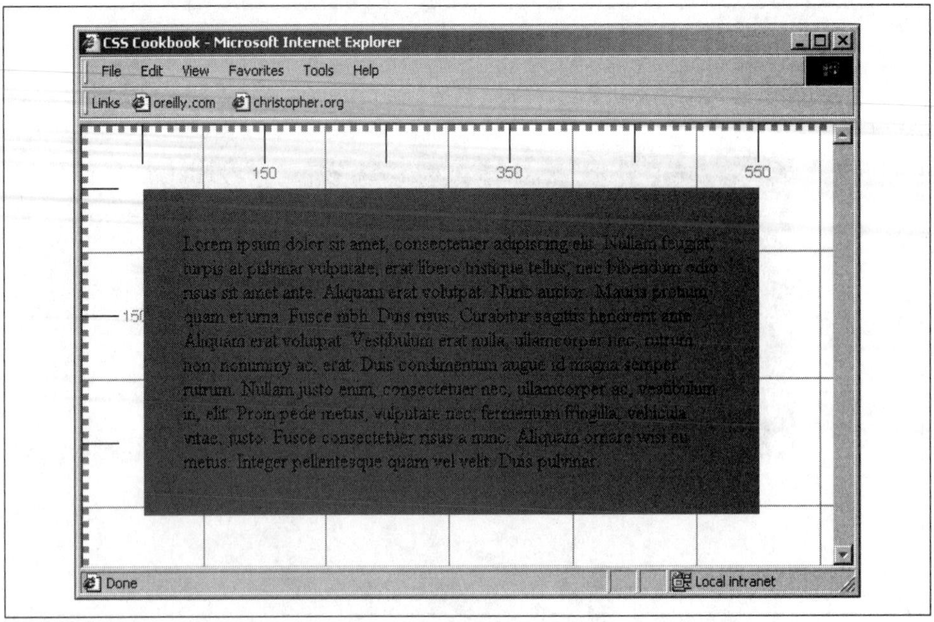

Figure 9-3. Internet Explorer 5.x for Windows' implementation of the box model

boxmodelhack.html for Tantek Çelik's explanation of the box model hack; *http://www.w3.org/TR/CSS21/aural.html#voice-char-props* for information about the voice-family property.

9.3   Removing Web Page Flicker in Internet Explorer 5.x for Windows

Problem

You want to remove the initial flicker, or flash, of unstyled content before Internet Explorer 5.x for Windows applies your CSS style sheet.

Solution

Add a link or script element as the child of the head element in your web document:

```
<head>
 <title>christopher.org</title>
 <link rel="stylesheet" type="text/css" media="print" href="print.css">
 <style type="text/css" media="screen">@import "advanced.css";</style>
</head>
```

Discussion

If a web page contains a style sheet associated by only the @import method, Internet Explorer 5.*x* for Windows' browsers first show the contents of the web page without any of the styles applied to the markup. After a split second, the browser redraws the web page with styles applied. Adding a link or script element in the head before the @import rule forces the browser to load the styles when it initially draws the page in the viewport.

This rendering phenomenon isn't a problem with the browser itself. The CSS specification doesn't specify whether this behavior is acceptable or not, so the browser is compliant with the specification. You or your audience might perceive this flicker as a bug or annoyance, though, so you should prevent it from occurring.

See Also

http://www.bluerobot.com/web/css/fouc.asp for an overview of the effect.

9.4   Keeping Background Images Stationary in Internet Explorer 6 for Windows

Problem

You want to have a fixed background image in Internet Explorer 6 for Windows.

Solution

Use the following JavaScript hack to force the effect. First copy the following code to call up the JavaScript code in your web page:

```
<head>
<script type="text/javascript" src="fixed.js"></script>
</head>
```

Then in the *fixed.js* file place the JavaScript code for the workaround, which can be found at this book's online sample archive *http://www.oreilly.com/catalog/cssckbk/* or from Andrew Clover's site at *http://doxdesk.com/software/js/fixed.html*.

Discussion

According to the CSS 2 specification, when a background image is fixed using the background-attachment property, it shouldn't move when the user scrolls the web page. In all versions of Internet Explorer for Windows, this property doesn't work at all.

However, this stunning JavaScript workaround developed by Andrew Clover fixes this problem by simply adding the JavaScript link to the web page. The JavaScript works by dynamically recalculating the position of the viewport as a user scrolls, and then it adjusts the background image accordingly.

See Also

Recipe 2.7 for more information about setting a fixed background image; the CSS specification for background-attachment at *http://www.w3.org/TR/CSS21/colors. html#propdef-background-attachment.*

9.5 Keeping CSS Rules from Internet Explorer 5 for Macintosh

Problem

You want to hide certain rules from Internet Explorer 5 for Macintosh.

Solution

To hide CSS rules from Internet Explorer 5 for Macintosh, insert a backslash in front of the closing comment with the characters */:

```
/* \*/
h1 {
  font-size: 200%;
  text-transform: uppercase;
  background-color: #666;
  }
```

After the rules pertaining to Internet Explorer 5 for Macintosh, insert another comment line:

```
/* */
p {
  text-transform: uppercase;
  }
```

Discussion

This method exploits a simple comment-parsing problem found in Internet Explorer 5 for Macintosh. The backslash before the closing comment causes the browser to think the comment actually has not closed; any valid CSS rules are hidden, allowing entire rule sets to be hidden from the browser until the next closing comment marker is hidden.

See Also

The specification about adding comments in CSS at *http://www.w3.org/TR/2004/CR-CSS21-20040225/syndata.html#comments.*

CHAPTER 10

Designing with CSS

10.0 Introduction

Although web builders often spend a lot of time working around browser bugs and reading about the latest tricks from the gurus, it's worth remembering that foremost, we're designers and CSS is simply a way to turn design ideas into reality.

CSS is the perfect technology for grabbing the attention of visitors to a web site. With CSS, instead of hacking HTML tables and slicing images to create eye-catching designs, you can go further with valid markup and still save on file sizes by ditching excess HTML and images. In short, you can do what any professional web designer should: create maximum impact with minimal resources.

At a basic level, a developer can learn all there is to know about CSS syntax and the technical limitations of the technology. But let's never forget that code merely implements the design. At its heart CSS is a *visual* language, and with that comes the need to understand, at least in some small way, how to use design principles with CSS.

With that in mind, this chapter explains how to design with CSS. Specifically, this chapter describes several methods for capturing attention through CSS-enabled techniques, including how to lead the eye with contrast, use excessively large text, create word balloons out of quotations, and use different image formats to create cohesive presentations.

10.1 Enlarging Text Excessively

Problem

You want to draw attention to a web page by enlarging some of the text as shown in Figure 10-1.

Figure 10-1. An example of excess type size

Solution

Increase the size of the heading so that it is out of proportion with the rest of the text. First use this HTML:

```
<h1>Hi.</h1>
```

Then use this CSS code:

```
h1 {
  font-size: 17em;
  margin: 0;
```

```
  padding: 0;
  text-align: center;
  font-family: Arial, Verdana, Helvetica, sans-serif;
}
```

Discussion

Obviously, any element that's larger than the other elements in the same environment stands out. So, when you want to call attention to an area of a web page, try using an excessive type size.

In this example, the size of the font in the word "Hi." has been set to 17em. In the font-size property, an em unit is equal to whatever the font-size of the container is. So, 17em units is equal to 17 times the default font size. There is no theoretical limit to how large you can size text, but in practice different browsers do max out at some point. Not everyone will have a monitor that's large enough to see type that is 1 mile (or 63,360 inches) tall:

```
h3 {
  font-size: 63360in;
}
```

See Also

Recipe 1-2 for specifying font measurements and sizes; "The Elements of Text and Message Design and Their Impact on Message Legibility: A Literature Review," from the Journal of Design Communication at *http://scholar.lib.vt.edu/ejournals/JDC/ Spring-2002/bix.html*; the CSS 2 specification for lengths (including em units) at *http://www.w3.org/TR/REC-CSS2/syndata.html#length-units*.

10.2 Creating Unexpected Incongruity

Problem

You need to grab the reader's attention by using two elements that don't seem to fit together.

Solution

Place one element visually inside the other. In the web page shown in Figure 10-2, which covers Earth's close call with an asteroid, an image of Earth from space was placed over an image of a game of pool.

The HTML for this page is simple:

```
<h2><span class="no">Earth News</span></h2>
<p>Earth escapes potential impact with killer asteroid;
will we escape the next one in 2014? <a href="more.html">Read
more</a></p>
```

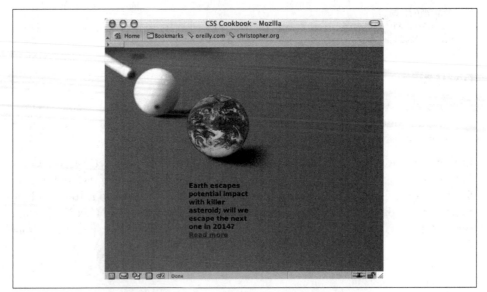

Figure 10-2. An image of Earth placed over an image depicting a game of pool

For the CSS, place the photo depicting the game of pool into the body element and position it in the upper left corner. Then use the image replacement technique discussed in Recipe 3-10 to place the photo of Earth for h2:

```
<style type="text/css">
body {
 background-color: #009E69;
 margin: 0;
 background-image: url(billiard.jpg);
 background-repeat: no-repeat;
}
h2 {
 background-image: url(earth.gif);
 position:absolute;
 width:126px;
 height:126px;
 z-index:1;
 left: 166px;
 top: 69px;
}
.no {
 display: none;
}
p {
 width: 120px;
 margin: 260px 100px 0 170px;
 font-family: Verdana, sans-serif;
 font-size: small;
 font-weight: bold;
```

```
    }
    </style>
```

Discussion

A great way to grab attention is to show something that is unexpected. Cleverly combining two different elements into one image can force viewers to pay attention to the image (as seen in Figure 10-3), or it can simply underscore the purpose of the content.

Figure 10-3. Photos of a child and man are combined

This example used two images—one of a pool cue and cue ball, and the other of Earth. The former image was placed as the background image for the body element. The image of Earth was placed in the background of h2 and was moved by setting the position to absolute. Then it was composited over the pool image.

See Also

Recipe 10.3 on combining unlike elements; Recipe 10.6 on combining different image formats.

10.3 Combining Unlike Elements to Create Contrast

Problem

You want to create contrast on a web page by integrating two different elements, like serif and sans-serif typefaces as shown in Figure 10-4.

Figure 10-4. Type elements juxtaposed in the same headline

Solution

Use different typefaces in the same headline. First adjust the markup to allow for changes in the font properties:

```
<h2>Cross<span>i</span>ng <span>Over</span></h2>
<h4>Sen. Jane Gordon (<span>I</span>-Utah) bolts GOP; <br />changes part<span>i</span></h4>
span>es to be <span>I</span>ndependent</h4>
```

Then manipulate the CSS for the span element to create a mixture of typefaces:

```
body {
 margin: 25% 10% 0 10%;
}
h2 {
 font-size: 2em;
 font-weight: bold;
 font-family: Arial, Verdana, Helvetica, sans-serif;
 text-transform: uppercase;
 text-align: center;
 padding: 0;
 margin: 0;
}
h2 span {
 font-family: Times, "Times New Roman", Georgia, serif;
 font-size: 1.1em;
 font-weight: normal;
```

```
  }
h4 {
 margin: 0;
 padding: 0;
 font-size: 1.25em;
 font-weight: bold;
 font-family: Arial, Verdana, Helvetica, sans-serif;
 text-transform: uppercase;
 text-align: center;
}
h4 span {
 font-family: Times, "Times New Roman", Georgia, serif;
 font-size: 1.1em;
 font-weight: normal;
}
```

Discussion

Combining unlike elements creates a visual contrast. In this example, different characteristics of the serif and sans-serif typefaces in the headline created the contrast. However, you can create contrast through imagery as well. For instance, in this example, you could have integrated Democratic and Republican political party symbols and placed them side by side. Or you could have gone for a more symbolic contrast by placing photos of two different types of parties side by side: one depicting a large social gathering at a club, and the other showing a girl blowing a noisemaker over a cupcake with a lit candle on top.

See Also

Recipe 8.6 on combining different image formats.

10.4   Leading the Eye with Contrast

Problem

You want to create a sense of depth or motion through text. On a page containing four paragraphs that are almost identical, it's hard to know which paragraph to look at first (see Figure 10-5). If you change font size across columns in a particular direction (e.g., decrease the size left-to-right) you lead the reader's eye (see Figure 10-6).

Solution

To lead the reader's eye, change the type size by adding a CSS rule like this:

```
/* Text size */
#layer4 {
 font-size: .7em;
 line-height: 20px;
}
#layer3 {
```

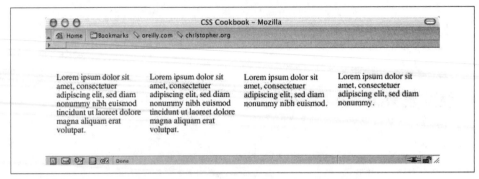

Figure 10-5. Four paragraphs that are almost identical

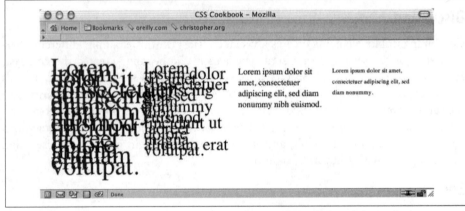

Figure 10-6. Changing the type size so that the reader's eye will scan from left to right

```
 font-size: 1em;
 line-height: 20px;
}
#layer2 {
 font-size: 2em;
 line-height: 10px;
}
#layer1 {
 font-size: 3em;
 line-height: 10px;
}
```

Discussion

Contrast occurs when there is an obvious difference between two elements. If there isn't any contrast on a page, the reader doesn't know what is important on the page. By manipulating an element's visual value, you can create contrast between two like elements. Some of those visual values include the following:

Size
Color
Shape
Position on a page
Direction
Density

Properly marked content has an inherent style because the browser uses its own style sheet to render the content when another style sheet isn't present. Headings, such as the h1 element, are stylized in a large, bold font and are separated from the paragraphs (see Figure 10-7). This different font provides the contrast to help readers make sense of the document.

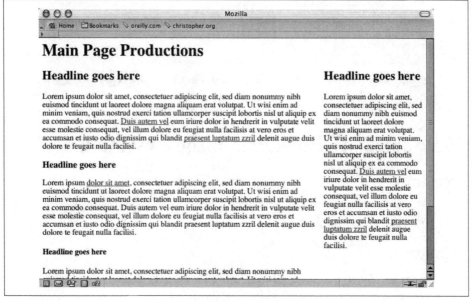

Figure 10-7. Drawing the eye toward the headings by setting them in a larger, bold font

Without the cues that can be provided through a style sheet, the reader's eye wanders throughout a document. The layout shown in Figure 10-8 creates a sense of confusion because it doesn't provide the reader with a clear sense of direction as to what to read first. The headings and copy all share the same values for font, type size, and type color.

See Also

http://www.lighthouse.org/color_contrast.htm for creating more effective contrast; *http://graphicdesign.about.com/library/weekly/aa012700a.htm* for more on the basics of designing with contrast.

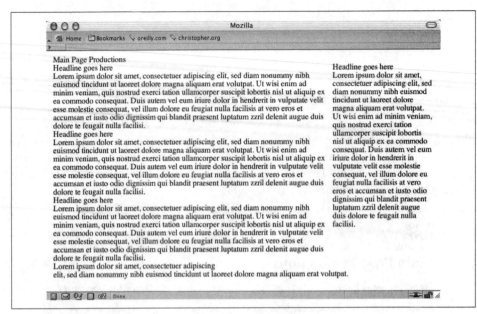

Figure 10-8. The page shown in Figure 10-7, but without contrast

10.5 Building a Panoramic Image Presentation

Problem

You want the width of an image to increase or decrease as a user resizes his browser window, as shown in Figure 10-9.

Solution

Place an image element that refers to a panoramic image into the background of a block-level element (see Figure 10-10):

```
<h1>Visit France City!</h1>
<div><img src="frenchtown.jpg" alt=" " /></div>
<h2>The quaint and charming little destination in France</h2>
```

Position the image element in the upper right corner of the block-level element and then hide the image by setting the display to none:

```
div {
  background-image: url(frenchtown.jpg);
  background-repeat: no-repeat;
  background-position: top right;
  height: 300px;
  border: 1px solid black;
  max-width: 714px;
}
div img {
```

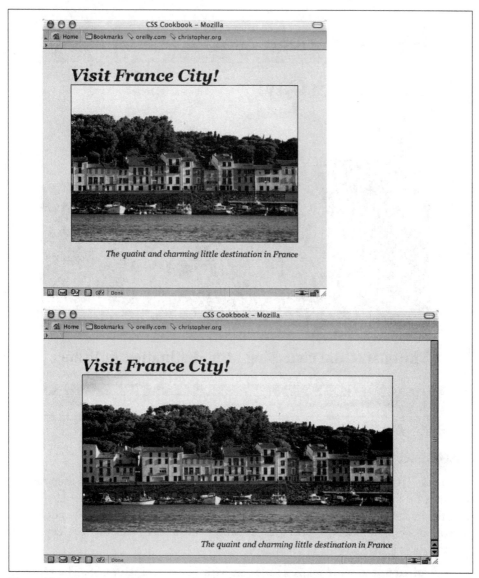

Figure 10-9. Browser window increased in size to show more of the panoramic image

```
    display: none;
}
```

When the image is placed as a background image, it will be resized based on the size of the browser window.

Figure 10-10. Panoramic photo placed on a web page

Discussion

To create a panoramic presentation, you need a wide photograph. You then need to position the image element in the upper right corner of the block-level element so that the image will grow or shrink depending on the size of the browser window. The use of max-width property constrains the width of the div element from expanding beyond the width of the image itself.

In this Solution, the same image is used in both the HTML and CSS. The rationale behind this approach is to make sure the image (or content) displays, even if the user agent rendering the page doesn't understand CSS.

See Also

http://www.creighton.edu/~jaypl/oldpage/panhow.html for more information on how to create panoramic pictures; the CSS 2.1 specification for max-width property at *http://www.w3.org/TR/CSS21/visudet.html#propdef-max-width*.

10.6   Combining Different Image Formats

Problem

You want to combine two different image formats into one presentation. For example, you want to combine GIF and JPEG images into one graphical presentation as shown in Figure 10-11.

Figure 10-11. Two different image formats combined into one

Solution

Place an image inside a block-level element such as a div or h2:

```
<h2><img src="headline_text.gif" alt="Headline image set in
GIF format" /></h2>
```

Using an image-editing program, separate the elements of the image into separate file formats (see Figure 10-12).

Figure 10-12. Two images that will be used to create one image

Name one of the images the same as the image referred to in the src attribute for the img element. Place the other image in the background of the block-level element to merge both images into one presentation.

```
h2 {
  background-image: url(headline_bkgd.jpg);
  background-repeat: none;
  width: 587px;
  height: 113px;
}
```

Discussion

The two prevailing image formats on the Web are GIF and JPEG. Both compress images in different ways. Typically, images with flat areas of color compress better in the GIF format, while JPEG images are better for photos or images that contain fine color gradations.

In the example shown in Figures 10-1 and 10-2, the file size of the two separate images added together is actually less than the file size of the final, combined image. This occurs because part of the image would work against the compression scheme of one file format. If you saved the presentation as one GIF, the photographic portions of the image would create an inflated file size. And if you saved the image as a JPEG, the areas of flat color would inflate the size. By splitting up the images into different formats that leverage their respective compression schemes, you reduce file sizes overall.

Although the method in this Solution uses background properties in CSS, you can accomplish the same effect by positioning block elements that contain inline images. For example, in Figure 10-13 you can see that the line art of the boat was overlaid on the photograph of the two children.

To make this method work, wrap the image elements in block-level div elements, as shown in the following HTML code:

```
<!DOCTYPE html PUBLIC "-//W3C//DTD XHTML 1.0 Transitional//EN"
    "http://www.w3.org/TR/xhtml1/DTD/xhtml1-transitional.dtd">
<html xmlns="http://www.w3.org/1999/xhtml">
 <head>
  <title>CSS Cookbook</title>
 </head>
 <body>
  <img src="kids.jpg" width="360" height="304"  alt="kids
playing" />
  <div id="boat"><img src="boat.gif" width="207" height="123"
   alt="boat" /></div>
  <div id="water"><img src="landscape.gif" width="315"
height="323"
   alt="landscape" /></div>
 </body>
</html>
```

Then, through CSS, set the position of the elements to absolute. By setting the position to absolute, you take the elements out of the normal flow of the web page,

Figure 10-13. Intricate combination of different image formats

and instead you assign values to the left, top, and z-index properties to determine their new placements:

```
#boat {
  position:absolute;
  width:207px;
  height:123px;
  z-index:2;
  left: 264px;
  top: 0;
}
#water {
  position:absolute;
  width:315px;
  height:323px;
  z-index:1;
  left: 359px;
  top: -20px;
}
```

The left and top properties indicate the placement of the images within their nearest positioned ancestor element or the initial containing block. In this case, it's the initial containing block to the div elements.

Furthermore, the body element's margin has a value of 0, meaning that the origin point is in the upper left corner of the browser's viewport.

```
body {
  margin: 0;
}
```

Even though this method works, if the web document is later modified, exact positioning becomes a design liability. For example, adding a simple headline above the images in the HTML results in the anomaly shown in Figure 10-14:

```
<h2>Kids Welcome New Boat!</h2>
 <img src="kids.jpg" width="360" height="304"  alt="kids
playing" />
 <div id="boat"><img src="boat.gif" width="207" height="123"
   alt="boat" /></div>
 <div id="water"><img src="landscape.gif" width="315" height="323"
alt="landscape" /></div>
```

Figure 10-14. Presentation breaks with addition of heading

Because the image of the children has not been positioned with absolute, it moves down the flow of the document. The other image stays in place because it has been positioned within the initial containing block and is still in the same place it was before the headline was added.

By using the background-positioning method within block-level elements, you can create a self-containing module. Then, when content is added to and removed from the web page, the presentation remains whole, as seen in Figure 10-15 and shown in the following code:

Figure 10-15. A different approach to combining images

```
<!DOCTYPE html PUBLIC "-//W3C//DTD XHTML 1.0 Transitional//EN"
    "http://www.w3.org/TR/xhtml1/DTD/xhtml1-transitional.dtd">
<html xmlns="http://www.w3.org/1999/xhtml">
 <head>
 <title>CSS Cookbook</title>
<style type="text/css">
body {
 margin: 5% 10% 0 10%;
}
#content {
 background-image: url(landscape.gif);
 background-repeat: no-repeat;
 background-position: bottom right;
 height: 400px;
 width: 674px;
}
h2 {
 margin: 0;
 padding: 0;
 background-image: url(kids.jpg);
 background-repeat: no-repeat;
 background-position: bottom left;
 height: 400px;
 width: 600px;
}
#boat {
 background-image: url(boat.gif);
 background-repeat: no-repeat;
```

```
     display: block;
     width: 207px;
     height: 123px;
     margin-left: 250px;
     margin-top: 75px;
   }
 </style>
 </head>
 <body>
  <div id="content">
    <h2>Kids Welcome New Boat!
     <span id="boat">
     </span>
    </h2>
  </div>
 </body>
 </html>
```

See Also

Recipe 10.2 on creating unexpected incongruity between two elements; Recipe 10.3 on combining unlike elements.

10.7   Making Word Balloons

Problem

You want to create a word-balloon effect as shown in Figure 10-16.

Figure 10-16. The word balloon

Solution

Mark up the content for a word balloon, and include both the text to appear in the word balloon as well as the name of the person cited as the source (see Figure 10-17):

```
<blockquote>
 <p>
```

```
<span>
 Be bold, baby!
 </span>
</p>
<cite>
 Christopher Schmitt
 </cite>
</blockquote>
```

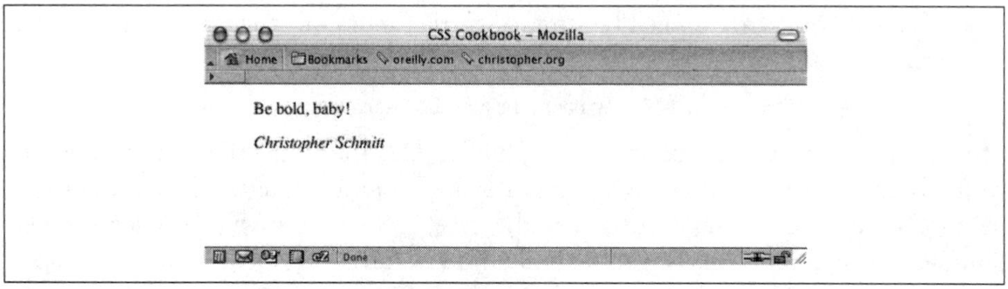

Figure 10-17. Structured content for a word balloon

Form the word balloon using the CSS border and background properties. Then align the cited text so that it falls underneath the balloon tail image:

```
blockquote {
 width: 250px;
}
blockquote p {
 background: url(balloontip.gif);
 background-repeat: no-repeat;
 background-position: bottom;
 padding-bottom: 28px;
}
blockquote p span {
 display: block;
 padding:  0.25em 0.25em 0.5em 0.5em;
 border: 1pt solid black;
 border-bottom-width: 0;
 font-size: 3em;
 font-family: "Comic Sans MS", Verdana, Helvetica, sans-serif;
 line-height: 0.9em;
}
cite {
 text-align: right;
 display: block;
 width: 250px;
}
```

Discussion

To create a word balloon you need at least one image, which includes a balloon tail and one border of the balloon (see Figure 10-18). The image is available for download at this book's site, mentioned in the Preface. You create the other three sides of the word balloon by setting the border in the span tag.

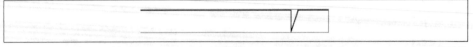

Figure 10-18. The word balloon tail

For a comic book look and feel, be sure to set the font family to `Comic Sans MS`, a free font from Microsoft:

```
font-family: "Comic Sans MS", Verdana, Helvetica, sans-serif;
```

If you have a computer running the Windows OS, the font might be installed on your computer already. Although this is a common font, some users might not have it installed on their systems. If that is the case, the browser will look for the next font, in the order listed in the value, until it finds a font available to render the page.

You can create a more whimsical presentation using the word-balloon technique by adjusting the markup and CSS slightly. First, place a span element with a class attribute set to `no` around the name in the `cite` element:

```
<blockquote>
 <p>
  <span>
  Be bold, baby!
  </span>
 </p>
 <cite>
  <span class="no">
  Christopher Schmitt
  </span>
 </cite>
</blockquote>
```

Next, in CSS, add the following rule, which keeps the text from being displayed in the browser:

```
.no {
 display: none;
}
```

Place a photograph in the `cite` element through the `background-position` property to finish the effect (see Figure 10-19):

```
cite {
 margin: 0;
 padding: 0;
 background-image: url(baby.jpg);
 background-position: 0 0;
 height: 386px;
 text-align: right;
```

```
    display: block;
    width: 250px;
}
```

Figure 10-19. Word balloon coming from an image

See Also

Background information about Comic Sans MS at *http://www.microsoft.com/typography/web/fonts/comicsns/default.htm*; propaganda on why not to use Comic Sans MS at *http://www.bancomicsans.com.*

10.8   Emphasizing a Quotation

Problem

You want to add emphasis to a quotation by large and bold quotation marks as shown in Figure 10-20.

Solution

First code the markup for the quotation (see Figure 10-21):

```
<blockquote>
<p>There is a tendency for things to right themselves.</p>
```

Figure 10-20. The stylized quotation

```
        <cite>Ralph Waldo Emerson</cite>
    </blockquote>
```

Figure 10-21. Quotation as it would normally appear

Then apply CSS rules to stylize the quote:

```css
blockquote {
  padding: 0;
  margin: 0;
  text-align: center;
}
p {
  font-size: 1em;
  padding-bottom: 3em;
  text-transform: lowercase;
  font-family: Georgia, Times, "Times New Roman", serif;
  margin: 0;
  padding: 0;
}
cite {
  display: block;
  text-align: center;
}
```

Finally, use pseudo-elements :before and :after to stylize the punctuation in the quotation as well as to place an em dash—a horizontal dash equal to the default size of the font—before the name of the cited source:

```css
blockquote p:before {
  content: "\201C";
  font-size: 1.2em;
  font-weight: bold;
```

```
  font-family: Georgia, Times, "Times New Roman", serif;
}
blockquote p:after {
 content: "\201D";
 font-size: 1.2em;
 font-weight: bold;
 font-family: Georgia, Times, "Times New Roman", serif;
}
cite:before {
 content: "\2014 ";
}
cite {
 display: block;
 text-align: center;
}
```

Discussion

Pseudo-elements are selector constructs that browsers use first to select portions and then to stylize a web page that can't be marked up through standard HTML. For instance, you can use pseudo-elements to stylize the first line of a paragraph or, in the case of this Recipe, to place generated content before and after an actual element.

In this Solution we insert smart quotes around the actual quotation. For the left double quotes, we use this declaration:

```
content: "\201C ";
```

Any text that you want displayed after an element needs to be marked off with double quotes. Because we are using double quotes to mark what should be displayed, we can't put another set of double quotes inside the first set. To put quotes around the quotation, we need to use the hexadecimal value for a quotation mark, which is 201C.

Because anything between the quotation marks automatically is generated as is, we need to escape the hexadecimal number that tells the browser to render the quotation marks by placing a forward slash in front of the double quotes.

The content property in the CSS 2.1 specification contains values for easily inserting quotation marks. For example, to re-create the left double quotes, use the following declaration:

```
content: open-quote;
```

However, note that open quote keyword value specification is implemented only in Mozilla and Opera. Also, note that the :before and :after pseudo-elements don't work in Internet Explorer 5+ for Windows and Internet Explorer for Macintosh.

See Also

Recipe 8.3 on how to include links in printouts of web pages using pseudo-elements; *http://homepages.luc.edu/~vbonill/Entities923-8472.html* for a list of HTML character entities; the CSS 2 specification for quotations for generated content at *http://www.w3.org/TR/REC-CSS2/generate.html#quotes.*

10.9 Placing a Drop Shadow Behind an Image

Problem

You want to place a drop shadow behind an image as shown in Figure 10-22.

Figure 10-22. A drop shadow is placed behind the image

Solution

Place the image element (as shown in Figure 10-23) inside a div element with the class attribute set to imgholder:

```
<div class="imgholder">
<img src="dadsaranick2.jpg" alt="Photo of Dad, Sara, Nick" />
</div>
```

To the div element, set the image alignment to the left so that text wraps around the image. Next set the background image of the drop shadow in two background properties. In the first background property use an image with an alpha transparency like PNG:

Figure 10-23. The image placed above the content

```css
div.imgholder {
 float:left;
 background: url(dropshadow.png) no-repeat bottom
  right !important;
 background: url(dropshadow.gif) no-repeat bottom right;
 margin: 10px 7px 0 10px !important;
 margin: 10px 0 0 5px;
}
```

As for the image itself, set the margin-right and margin-bottom properties to define how much of the shadow drop shadow image shows through. Also set a border property as well as padding to create a more dramatic effect:

```css
div.imgholder img {
 display: block;
 position: relative;
 background-color: #fff;
 border: 1px solid #666;
 margin: -3px 5px 5px -3px;
 padding: 2px;
}
```

Discussion

The first step is to create a drop shadow image in your image-editing program like Adobe Photoshop. It's best to create a background image sized 600 pixels by 600 pixels or larger. With the image that large, this technique can accommodate almost any image used in a web page.

The first image background property uses the !important rule to display the PNG file as the drop shadow. By using the PNG, the background color or image of the web document can be changed without affecting the drop shadow. For the other browsers that don't support this rule, like Internet Explorer for Windows,) go to the next background property and use the GIF image as the drop shadow instead.

The margin-left and margin-bottom property in the image element control the distance the drop shadow image appears out from the image. If your drop shadow distance on the right or left side is larger than five pixels (like the one used in this Solution), change the value accordingly.

See Also

The A List Apart article on creating CSS Drop Shadows at *http://www.alistapart.com/articles/cssdropshadows/*.

Resources

This appendix contains some of the top references, discussion groups, and tools on the Internet and is provided to help you when working with CSS.

When working with CSS, keep these two tips in mind: simplify and verify. Simplify by using only the selectors and properties you believe you need; any extras could cause some confusion down the road. Then verify the (X)HTML and CSS with the help of validators (two good validators are listed under the "Tools" section in this appendix).

Those two steps solve most problems developers encounter when working with CSS. However, if you still run into trouble, don't hesitate to ask for help from the web development communities listed in the "Discussion Groups" section of this appendix.

Discussion Groups

Babble List

http://www.babblelist.com/

Moderated by Christopher Schmitt and Andrew Porter Glendinning (*http://www. cerebellion.com/*), this web design and development mailing list targets advanced web design issues. The site offers a lively exchange of information, resources, theories, and practices of designers and developers.

css-discuss

http://www.css-discuss.org/

This mailing list, chaperoned by CSS expert Eric A. Meyer, who is the author of O'Reilly's *Cascading Style Sheets: The Definitive Guide*, aims to provide practical discussion about the application of CSS.

Usenet Stylesheets Newsgroup

news:comp.infosystems.www.authoring.stylesheets

Founded in 1997, this unmoderated newsgroup covers the theory and application of CSS. Topics for the group can include practical applications, questions about the specification, the benefits of CSS, implementation bugs in browsers, and more. You can find the FAQ document for the group at *http://css.nu/faq/ciwas-mFAQ.html*.

www-style (W3C Style Mailing List)

http://lists.w3.org/Archives/Public/www-style/

Maintained by the World Wide Web Consortium (W3C), this mailing list provides a venue for discussing the theories and future of CSS. Questions about the specification or about CSS proposals are welcomed; however, discussions revolving around practical applications of the technology are discouraged.

References

Meyer's CSS Support Charts

http://devedge.netscape.com/library/xref/2003/css-support/

If you run into problems developing with CSS, check the CSS Support Charts to determine if there is a problem with the browser(s) you are using. The CSS Support Charts comprise three charts: Mastergrid, Historical CSS1 Support, and CSS2 Selectors. The Mastergrid chart looks at current generation support for CSS1 properties, while the Historical CSS1 Support chart covers the browsers that support CSS but were launched before 2000. The CSS2 Selectors chart covers the level of support in browsers for CSS2 selectors.

W3C CSS Page

http://www.w3.org/Style/CSS/

This is the official site for CSS. At this site you can learn about the history of CSS, investigate learning resources and authoring tools, and read current CSS news.

CSS 2.1 Specification

http://www.w3.org/TR/CSS21/

Browser implementations of the CSS specification are sometimes a confusing mess. When tracking down how to achieve a certain look or an implementation bug, check the specification (as well as the CSS Support Charts).

HTML 4.01 Specification

http://www.w3.org/TR/html4/

To make the most out of using CSS for web design, you need to create your web documents with structured markup instead of using workarounds and hacks. Furthermore, you need to mark up your documents with elements to imply an inherent presentational meaning. For example, you need to highlight important words using the em element and not the b element. If you need to change your production methods, dig into the HTML specification and get to know the elements all over again.

XHTML 1.0 Specification

http://www.w3.org/TR/xhtml1/

Extensible HyperText Markup Language (XHTML) is a restructuring of HTML 4 in XML 1.0. Although XHTML markup is stricter than that of HTML 4, the benefits are simple: more logical markup, increased interoperability, and enhanced accessibility.

Tools

SelectORacle

http://gallery.theopalgroup.com/selectoracle/

A free service designed to help people learn more about complex CSS selectors by translating their meaning into plain English. CSS selectors can be submitted in one of two ways. The first method is to copy and paste a CSS selector into the form. The other method is to enter either a URL of a web page with an embedded style sheet or a URL to an external style sheet. The service then renders the CSS selector into easy to understand language.

W3C CSS Validator

http://jigsaw.w3.org/css-validator/

This free service, provided on the W3C server, checks CSS for proper structure. You can test your markup by uploading files, entering a web address in the form, and then copying and pasting the CSS into a form field. And if you are so inclined, you can download and install the validator on your own server.

W3C HTML Validator

http://validator.w3.org/

The W3C HTML validator is another free service from the W3C. Similar to the CSS validator, the HTML validator checks to see if your markup conforms to web standards.

Design Resources

Glish.com CSS Layout Techniques

http://www.glish.com/css/

One of the first collections of multi-column layouts created in CSS without the use of HTML tables.

BlueRobot.com Layout Reservoir

http://www.bluerobot.com/web/layouts/

This small but valuable resource covers two- and three-column layouts.

Real World Style

http://www.realworldstyle.com/

A design resource managed by Mark Newhouse, the goal of this site is to promote CSS-enabled designs, not only for modern, popular browsers that run on Macintosh and Windows OS, but also for browsers that run on Unix machines.

A List Apart: CSS Topics

http://www.alistapart.com/topics/css/

At A List Apart most of the articles published on the topic of CSS come in from web designers sharing their thoughts and breakthroughs with CSS-enabled design. A great resource to catch up on the latest CSS techniques.

Index

We'd like to hear your suggestions for improving our indexes. Send email to *index@oreilly.com.*

Document Type Definition (DTD), 145
Dreamweaver (Macromedia), 187
drop shadows, placing behind
        images, 236–238
drop-down menus and print-ready
        forms, 192
DTD (Document Type Definition), 145
dynamic visual menus, designing, 92–95

E

em element, highlighting text with, 35
em units, setting type size in, 6
embossed media type, 189
emphasizing quotations, 233–236
escaping hexadecimal values in CSS, 103
event links, adding to cells in calendars, 152

F

Fahrner, Todd, 9, 90
fantasy font family value, 2
FIR (Fahrner Image Replacement)
        method, 90
first line of paragraphs
    images in, 33
    indenting, 27
    setting style for, 32
:first-letter pseudo-element, 10
:first-line pseudo-element, 34
flicker in web pages, removing, 210
float property, 24
    three-column layout
        with fixed-width columns, 176–179
        with flexible columns, 173–176
    two-column layouts, creating, 166,
        168–170
:focus pseudo-class, 114, 116
folder tab navigation menus, creating, 92–95
font shorthand property, 16
font-family property, 2–5
fonts, 2–5
    different elements in same headline, 218
    leading the eye with contrast, 219–222
    main headings on web pages,
        designing, 199
    setting web pages for black-and-white
        printing, 197
    sizes of
        keywords for, 7–9
        overriding, 9
        specifying, 5–9

font-size property, 5–9, 12, 215
font-weight property, 71
footers on web pages, designing, 202
format of lists, changing, 100
forms, 111–138
    buttons for, 119–122
    login form example, 125–130
    onsubmit events and, 122
    print-ready, creating, 191–194
    registration form example, 129–138
    without tables, 123–125
full-bleed effect, creating, 39

G

getElementbyId(), 80
GIF and JPEG images, combining, 225
Glendinning, Andrew Porter, 239
glish.com layout techniques, 242

H

hacks and workarounds, 204–212
handheld media type, 189
hanging indents in lists, 107
Hansel and Gretel, 87
header cells in tables
    applying styles to, 133–135
    setting styles for, 146–148
headings on web pages
    borders and stylized text in, 17–19
    creating with stylized text, 15–17
    designing, 197–199
    images and stylized text in, 19–21
height property, 48, 60, 90
highlighting text, 35
Historical CSS1 Support chart, 240
horizontal menus, building, 80–84
horizontal rules, customizing, 58–61
:hover pseudo-class, 73
HTML 4.01 specification, 241
HTML tables
    border models for, 142
    hybrid layouts with CSS and, 159–163
    page layouts using, 158
    vs. CSS, 148
    (see also tables)
HTML text, creating pull quotes with, 21
HTML validator tool (W3C), 242
hybrid page layouts, using HTML tables and
    CSS, 159–163

About the Author

Christopher Schmitt is the president/CEO of Heatvision.com, Inc., a new media publishing and design firm, and is based in Tallahassee, FL.

An award-winning web designer who has been working with the Web since 1993, Christopher interned for both David Siegel and Lynda Weinman in the mid-'90s while he was an undergraduate at Florida State University working on a fine arts degree with an emphasis on graphic design.

He is the author of *Designing CSS Web Pages* (New Riders). He is also the co-author of *Photoshop CS in 10 Steps or Less* (Wiley) and *Dreamweaver MX Design Projects* (glasshaus) and contributed four chapters to *XML, HTML, and XHTML Magic* (New Riders). Christopher has also written for *New Architect Magazine, A List Apart, Digital Web*, and *Web Reference*.

In 2000, he led a team to victory in the Cool Site in a Day competition, where he and five other talented developers built a fully functional, well-designed web site for a nonprofit organization in eight hours.

At conferences such as The Other Dreamweaver Conference and SXSW, Christopher has given talks demonstrating the use and benefits of practical CSS-enabled designs. He is the list mom for Babble (*http://www.babblelist.com*), a mailing list community devoted to advanced web design and development topics.

On his personal web site, *http://www.christopher.org*, Christopher shows his true colors and most recent activities. He is 67 and doesn't play professional basketball but wouldn't mind a good game of chess.

Colophon

Our look is the result of reader comments, our own experimentation, and feedback from distribution channels. Distinctive covers complement our distinctive approach to technical topics, breathing personality and life into potentially dry subjects.

The animal on the cover of *CSS Cookbook* is a grizzly bear (*Ursus arctos horribilis*). The grizzly's distinctive features include humped shoulders, a long snout, and long curved claws. The coat color ranges from shades of blond, brown, black, or a combination of these; the long outer guard hairs are often tipped with white or silver, giving the bear a "grizzled" appearance. The grizzly can weigh anywhere from 350 to 800 pounds and reach a shoulder height of 4.5 feet when on all fours. Standing on its hind legs, a grizzly can reach up to 8 feet. Despite its large size, the grizzly can reach speeds of 35 to 40 miles per hour.

Some of the grizzly's favorite foods include nuts, berries, insects, salmon, carrion, and small mammals. The diet of a grizzly varies depending on the season and habitat. Grizzlies in parts of Alaska eat primarily salmon, while grizzlies in high mountain areas eat mostly berries and insects.

Grizzlies are solitary, and prefer rugged mountains and forests. They can be found in the Canadian provinces of British Columbia, Alberta, Yukon, and the Northwest Territories, and the U.S. states of Alaska, Idaho, Wyoming, Washington, and Montana.

The grizzly is considered a threatened species: only about 850 bears exist in the lower 48 states. Before the West was settled, the grizzly bear population was estimated to be between 50,000 and 100,000. Threats to the survival of the grizzly bear include habitat destruction caused by logging, mining, and human development, as well as illegal poaching.

Mary Anne Weeks Mayo was the production editor and Audrey Doyle was the copyeditor for *CSS Cookbook*. Jane Ellin proofread the book, and Mary Brady and Emily Quill provided quality control. Mary Agner provided production assistance. Judy Hoer wrote the index.

Ellie Volckhausen designed the cover of this book, based on a series design by Edie Freedman. The cover image is a 19th-century engraving from the Dover Pictorial Archive. Emma Colby produced the cover layout with QuarkXPress 4.1 using Adobe's ITC Garamond font.

David Futato designed the interior layout. This book was converted by Julie Hawks to FrameMaker 5.5.6 with a format conversion tool created by Erik Ray, Jason McIntosh, Neil Walls, and Mike Sierra that uses Perl and XML technologies. The text font is Linotype Birka; the heading font is Adobe Myriad Condensed; and the code font is LucasFont's TheSans Mono Condensed. The illustrations that appear in the book were produced by Robert Romano and Jessamyn Read using Macromedia FreeHand 9 and Adobe Photoshop 6. The tip and warning icons were drawn by Christopher Bing. This colophon was compiled by Mary Anne Weeks Mayo.

Related Titles Available from O'Reilly

Web Programming

ActionScript Cookbook

ActionScript for Flash MX Pocket Reference

ActionScript for Flash MX: The Definitive Guide, *2nd Edition*

Creating Applications with Mozilla

Dynamic HTML: The Definitive Reference, *2nd Edition*

Flash Remoting: The Definitive Guide

Google Hacks

Google Pocket Guide

HTTP: The Definitive Guide

JavaScript & DHTML Cookbook

JavaScript Pocket Reference, *2nd Edition*

JavaScript: The Definitive Guide, *4th Edition*

PHP 5 Essentials

PHP Cookbook

PHP Pocket Reference, *2nd Edition*

Programming ColdFusion MX, *2nd Edition*

Programming PHP

Web Database Applications with PHP and MySQL, *2nd Edition*

Webmaster in a Nutshell, *3rd Edition*

Web Authoring and Design

Cascading Style Sheets: The Definitive Guide, *2nd Edition*

CSS Pocket Reference

Dreamweaver MX 2004: The Missing Manual

HTML & XHTML: The Definitive Guide, *5th Edition*

HTML Pocket Reference, *2nd Edition*

Information Architecture for the World Wide Web, *2nd Edition*

Learning Web Design, *2nd Edition*

Web Design in a Nutshell, *2nd Edition*

Web Administration

Apache Cookbook

Apache Pocket Reference

Apache: The Definitive Guide, *3rd Edition*

Essential Blogging

Perl for Web Site Management

Squid: The Definitive Guide

Web Performance Tuning, *2nd Edition*

O'REILLY®

Our books are available at most retail and online bookstores.
To order direct: 1-800-998-9938 • *order@oreilly.com* • *www.oreilly.com*
Online editions of most O'Reilly titles are available by subscription at *safari.oreilly.com*

Keep in touch with O'Reilly

1. Download examples from our books

To find example files for a book, go to:

www.oreilly.com/catalog

select the book, and follow the "Examples" link.

2. Register your O'Reilly books

Register your book at *register.oreilly.com*

Why register your books?
Once you've registered your O'Reilly books you can:

*   Win O'Reilly books, T-shirts or discount coupons in our monthly drawing.

*   Get special offers available only to registered O'Reilly customers.

*   Get catalogs announcing new books (US and UK only).

*   Get email notification of new editions of the O'Reilly books you own.

3. Join our email lists

Sign up to get topic-specific email announcements of new books and conferences, special offers, and O'Reilly Network technology newsletters at:

elists.oreilly.com

It's easy to customize your free elists subscription so you'll get exactly the O'Reilly news you want.

4. Get the latest news, tips, and tools

www.oreilly.com

*   "Top 100 Sites on the Web"—PC Magazine
*   CIO Magazine's Web Business 50 Awards

Our web site contains a library of comprehensive product information (including book excerpts and tables of contents), downloadable software, background articles, interviews with technology leaders, links to relevant sites, book cover art, and more.

5. Work for O'Reilly

Check out our web site for current employment opportunities:

jobs.oreilly.com

6. Contact us

O'Reilly & Associates
1005 Gravenstein Hwy North
Sebastopol, CA 95472 USA

TEL: 707-827-7000 or 800-998-9938
       (6am to 5pm PST)

FAX: 707-829-0104

order@oreilly.com
For answers to problems regarding your order or our products. To place a book order online, visit:

www.oreilly.com/order_new

catalog@oreilly.com
To request a copy of our latest catalog.

booktech@oreilly.com
For book content technical questions or corrections.

corporate@oreilly.com
For educational, library, government, and corporate sales.

proposals@oreilly.com
To submit new book proposals to our editors and product managers.

international@oreilly.com
For information about our international distributors or translation queries. For a list of our distributors outside of North America check out:

international.oreilly.com/distributors.html

adoption@oreilly.com
For information about academic use of O'Reilly books, visit:

academic.oreilly.com

O'REILLY®

Our books are available at most retail and online bookstores.
To order direct: 1-800-998-9938 • *order@oreilly.com* • *www.oreilly.com*
Online editions of most O'Reilly titles are available by subscription at *safari.oreilly.com*